Bitcoin Guidebook

Digital Currency and Decentralized Finance

Contents

Introduction

In recent years, Bitcoin and cryptocurrencies have emerged as revolutionary forces in the world of finance and technology. As the first decentralized digital currency, Bitcoin has captured the attention of investors, technologists, regulators, and scholars alike. The Bitcoin blockchain serves as the backbone for this digital currency, providing a secure and transparent public ledger that records all transactions. This introduction aims to provide a comprehensive overview of Bitcoin, its underlying technology, its significance, and the various aspects that contribute to its ecosystem.

Bitcoin was introduced in 2008 by an enigmatic individual or group known as Satoshi Nakamoto. The release of the Bitcoin whitepaper laid the foundation for a peer-to-peer electronic cash system that promised to be independent of traditional financial institutions. The appeal of Bitcoin lies in its decentralized nature, which ensures that no single entity controls the network. This decentralization is achieved through a distributed ledger technology known as blockchain, which records all transactions in a transparent and immutable manner.

As a digital asset, Bitcoin differs significantly from traditional fiat currencies. It operates on a deflationary economic model, with a capped supply of 21 million bitcoins, which are gradually released through the process of mining. This controlled supply introduces unique economic dynamics, including the phenomenon of halving, where the rewards for mining new bitcoins are periodically reduced by half. Bitcoin's scarcity and the difficulty-adjusted mining process contribute to its value proposition as digital gold.

Understanding the mechanics of Bitcoin requires an appreciation of various technical concepts. The blockchain is composed of blocks that contain transaction data, each linked cryptographically to the previous block, forming an unbroken chain. Transactions are validated through a consensus mechanism known as Proof of Work, which necessitates computational effort to solve complex cryptographic puzzles. Miners, who perform this computational work, are rewarded with newly minted bitcoins and transaction fees.

Security and privacy are core tenets of Bitcoin. The use of public and private keys ensures that only the rightful owners can authorize transactions. While the public key is used to generate a Bitcoin address for receiving funds, the private key is a confidential piece of data used to sign transactions. The cryptographic principles underlying Bitcoin ensure that it is resistant to counterfeiting and double-spending.

Bitcoin's role extends beyond being a digital currency. It has sparked the development of an entire ecosystem of decentralized applications and financial services, collectively known as Decentralized Finance (DeFi). These applications leverage the transparency and security of blockchain to offer services such as lending, borrowing, and trading without intermediaries.

However, the rise of Bitcoin and cryptocurrencies has also prompted regulatory scrutiny and legal challenges. Governments and financial institutions are exploring ways to regulate this burgeoning sector to prevent illicit activities while fostering innovation. Taxation, compliance, and consumer protection are critical areas of focus in the regulatory discourse.

Investing in Bitcoin requires a thorough understanding of its market dynamics, risk factors, and regulatory environment. The volatility of cryptocurrency markets presents both opportunities and risks for investors. Various strategies, ranging from long-term holding to active trading, can be employed to navigate this market.

The future of Bitcoin and cryptocurrencies is a subject of ongoing debate and speculation. Technological advancements, such as the development of the Lightning Network for improved scalability, are poised to enhance Bitcoin's utility. The increasing interest from institutional investors and mainstream adoption suggests that Bitcoin is gradually becoming an integral part of the global financial system. However, challenges such as regulatory uncertainties, technological vulnerabilities, and market volatility continue to pose risks.

This book aims to provide a comprehensive guide to Bitcoin and Decentralized Finance, encompassing foundational concepts, technical details, economic implications, regulatory aspects, and future prospects. Each chapter is designed to impart a deep understanding of specific topics, enabling readers to appreciate the full spectrum of Bitcoin's impact on finance and technology. Whether you are a beginner seeking to learn the basics or an experienced individual looking to deepen your knowledge, this book offers valuable insights into the transformative world of Bitcoin and decentralized finance.

Chapter 1

Introduction to Bitcoin

Understanding Bitcoin involves appreciating its technical foundations, security mechanisms, and broader implications in decentralized finance and global economics. This chapter explores these aspects in detail, laying the groundwork for a comprehensive understanding of Bitcoin.

1.1 The Origin of Bitcoin

The advent of Bitcoin can be traced back to the wake of the 2008 financial crisis, a time plagued with deep mistrust in traditional financial systems. On November 1, 2008, an individual or group operating under the pseudonym Satoshi Nakamoto published a white paper titled *Bitcoin: A Peer-to-Peer Electronic Cash System*. This seminal document outlined the concept of Bitcoin, a decentralized digital currency designed to mitigate reliance on financial institutions and intermediaries.

Bitcoin was introduced as a solution to the double-spending problem inherent in digital cash systems. Traditional digital transactions require a trusted third party to verify and prevent double-spending, where a single digital token could be spent more than once. Nakamoto proposed a peer-to-peer network that timestamps transactions by hashing them into an ongoing chain of hash-based proof-of-work, forming a record that cannot be altered without redoing the proof-of-work.

```
#include <iostream>
#include <string>
```

```
#include <sstream>
#include <iomanip>
#include <openssl/sha.h>

std::string sha256(const std::string str) {
    unsigned char hash[SHA256_DIGEST_LENGTH];
    SHA256_CTX sha256;
    SHA256_Init(&sha256);
    SHA256_Update(&sha256, str.c_str(), str.size());
    SHA256_Final(hash, &sha256);
    std::stringstream ss;
    for(int i = 0; i < SHA256_DIGEST_LENGTH; ++i) {
        ss << std::hex << std::setw(2) << std::setfill('0') << (int)hash[i];
    }
    return ss.str();
}

int main() {
    std::string data = "example data";
    std::string hash = sha256(data);
    std::cout << "SHA-256 hash: " << hash << std::endl;
    return 0;
}
```

On January 3, 2009, Nakamoto mined the first block of the Bitcoin blockchain, known as the Genesis Block or Block 0. Embedded within the coinbase parameter of this block was the text: *The Times 03/Jan/2009 Chancellor on brink of second bailout for banks*. This message not only served as a timestamp but also as a critique of the incumbent financial system, reflecting the motivations behind Bitcoin's creation.

The primary innovation introduced by Bitcoin was the decentralized ledger system, commonly referred to as the blockchain. The blockchain ensures that all transactions are recorded in a transparent, immutable manner, validating each transaction through a consensus mechanism known as proof-of-work (PoW).

```
SHA-256 hash: a1f1a1c65a1f1ad991b1e574a2f1ab54aba1cd65a45f78ed5ea546c45a1b1f5e
```

Bitcoin's economic principles were also groundbreaking. Satoshi Nakamoto designed Bitcoin to have a finite supply, with a maximum of 21 million coins to be mined. This deflationary model contrasts sharply with fiat currencies, which can be printed ad infinitum by central banks, potentially leading to inflation. Nakamoto's model integrates meticulous mathematical algorithms to control the issuance rate of new bitcoins, halving the reward approximately every four years in an event known as the *halving*.

The adoption and subsequent growth of Bitcoin were catalyzed by early adopters who recognized its potential to disrupt centralized finance. On

May 22, 2010, a landmark exchange occurred when Laszlo Hanyecz, a Florida-based programmer, indirectly spent 10,000 bitcoins to purchase two pizzas, an event fondly commemorated as Bitcoin Pizza Day. This transaction demonstrated Bitcoin's practical utility as a medium of exchange and fueled further interest and investment in the nascent digital currency.

As Bitcoin's network expanded, it faced numerous challenges, including technical vulnerabilities, regulatory scrutiny, and skepticism from traditional financial entities. Despite these obstacles, Bitcoin continued to thrive, largely due to its robust protocol design and the proactive efforts of its community.

Satoshi Nakamoto's correspondence and contributions to Bitcoin ceased by the end of 2010, and their identity remains a mystery. Nevertheless, Nakamoto's departure did not impede Bitcoin's progress. The open-source nature of Bitcoin's code allowed developers worldwide to collaborate and enhance the protocol, ensuring its resiliency and evolution.

The origin of Bitcoin is a testament to the transformative potential of cryptography, distributed networks, and innovative economic models. It set the stage for the burgeoning field of decentralized finance (DeFi) and inspired a proliferation of alternative cryptocurrencies, each seeking to build upon or offer new solutions within the blockchain paradigm.

1.2 What is Bitcoin?

Bitcoin is a decentralized digital currency, created in 2008 by an unknown person or group of people using the pseudonym Satoshi Nakamoto. It allows peer-to-peer transactions to be executed without the need for a central authority, such as a bank or government. Bitcoin transactions are verified by network nodes through cryptography and recorded in a public distributed ledger called a blockchain.

The defining characteristic of Bitcoin is its decentralization. Unlike traditional currencies issued by central banks, Bitcoin is not governed by any single entity. Instead, it relies on a distributed consensus achieved through a network of computers, known as nodes. Each node maintains a copy of the blockchain and validates new transactions. This decentralization ensures that no single point of failure exists, enhancing Bitcoin's security and resilience against censorship and fraud.

Bitcoin's supply is capped at 21 million coins, a distinctive feature that introduces scarcity and a potential hedge against inflation. This supply cap is enforced by the Bitcoin protocol, which dictates that the rate of new coin creation decreases over time. This process, known as "halving," occurs approximately every four years, reducing the reward miners receive for adding a new block to the blockchain by 50%.

To understand Bitcoin's functioning, it is essential to comprehend the role of transactions. A Bitcoin transaction typically involves three components: inputs, outputs, and amounts. Inputs are references to previous transactions where the sender received Bitcoin. Outputs specify the recipient's address and the amount to be sent. Each transaction must be signed using the sender's private key, ensuring authenticity and preventing unauthorized spending.

```
transaction = {
    'inputs': [{
        'previous_tx': '<previous_transaction_hash>',
        'index': 0,
        'scriptSig': '<signature>'
    }],
    'outputs': [{
        'address': '<recipient_address>',
        'amount': 0.5
    }]
}
```

Upon broadcasting a transaction to the network, miners validate it by solving complex cryptographic puzzles. This process, known as Proof of Work (PoW), involves finding a nonce—a number that, when hashed along with the block's data, produces a hash with a specific set of leading zeros. The difficulty of this puzzle adjusts approximately every two weeks to ensure a consistent block generation time of about 10 minutes.

Once a miner successfully solves the puzzle, the block, containing the new transactions, is added to the blockchain. The miner is rewarded with newly created Bitcoin and transaction fees from the included transactions. This mechanism aligns miners' incentives with the security and maintenance of the network.

Bitcoin's architecture employs public and private keys to manage ownership. A public key, derived from a private key through elliptic curve cryptography, acts as an address to receive Bitcoin. The private key, kept secret by the owner, is used to sign transactions, proving ownership without revealing the key itself. Losing the private key results in the irreversible loss of access to the associated Bitcoin, highlighting the importance of secure key management.

Algorithm 1 Proof of Work (PoW) Algorithm

1: $block \leftarrow$ new block with transactions
2: $nonce \leftarrow 0$
3: **repeat**
4: $hash \leftarrow$ SHA-256$(block \| nonce)$
5: $nonce \leftarrow nonce + 1$
6: **until** $hash$ starts with leading zeros
7: Broadcast block to network
8: Receive block reward and transaction fees

```
from ecdsa import SigningKey, SECP256k1

# Generate a new private key
private_key = SigningKey.generate(curve=SECP256k1)

# Derive the public key from the private key
public_key = private_key.get_verifying_key()

print("Private Key:", private_key.to_string().hex())
print("Public Key:", public_key.to_string().hex())
```

The innovation of Bitcoin isn't limited to the digital currency itself but extends to its underlying technology, the blockchain. A blockchain is a sequential chain of blocks, each containing a list of transactions. Each block is linked to the previous one via a cryptographic hash of its header, creating a tamper-evident record. This structure ensures immutability, as altering any block would require re-mining all subsequent blocks, an infeasible task given the computational power required.

Bitcoin's design solves the double-spending problem, a significant challenge in digital currencies where the same unit could be spent multiple times. By ensuring transparency through public ledger access and relying on consensus mechanisms, Bitcoin prevents double-spending and assures participants of the integrity of transactions.

The Bitcoin network and its associated technologies represent a paradigm shift in how digital transactions can be securely and transparently conducted, independent of any central control. The implications extend beyond currency, influencing fields such as decentralized finance (DeFi), smart contracts, and other blockchain applications. A comprehensive understanding of Bitcoin entails appreciating its technical intricacies, economic principles, and potential impacts on global finance.

1.3 How Bitcoin Works

Bitcoin operates on a decentralized network, primarily relying on blockchain technology and cryptographic principles. Understanding its operation requires comprehension of these essential components, their interactions, and the mechanisms underpinning Bitcoin transactions.

A fundamental aspect of Bitcoin is the blockchain, a distributed ledger maintaining a continuous record of all transactions. Each block in the chain encapsulates transaction data and a unique identifier known as a hash. To preserve chronological order and integrity, every block contains the hash of the preceding block, forming a chain of connected records from the genesis block to the latest.

```
import hashlib

def calculate_hash(data, previous_hash):
    return hashlib.sha256((data + previous_hash).encode()).hexdigest()

# Example data and previous hash
data = "Transaction data"
previous_hash = "previous_block_hash"
current_hash = calculate_hash(data, previous_hash)
print(current_hash)
```

```
Example Output:
3ac225168df54212a25d69580a3057efb3b8ba39eb907a512b2b76a3f464b434
```

Transactions in the Bitcoin network commence when a user initiates the transfer of Bitcoin to another user. This process involves public and private keys. The public key functions as an address to which Bitcoin can be sent, while the private key enables the signing and authorization of transactions. The transaction details include the amount, sender, recipient, and a digital signature validating the sender's authorization.

Here is a conceptual flow of a Bitcoin transaction:

1. A Bitcoin user decides to send Bitcoin to another user. The sender creates a transaction specifying the recipient's address (public key), the amount, and their digital signature.

2. This transaction is broadcast to the Bitcoin network, composed of numerous nodes (computers) that validate and propagate the transaction.

3. The transaction remains unconfirmed until it is included in a block by a miner.

4. Miners, using computational power, compete to solve a complex mathematical problem, referred to as the Proof-of-Work. The first miner to solve the problem adds the new block containing the transaction to the blockchain.

5. The added block is propagated across the network, updating the distributed ledger.

The Proof-of-Work mechanism is central to Bitcoin mining and block validation. It ensures security and prevents malicious activities like double-spending. Miners must resolve a computationally intensive puzzle, typically involving finding a nonce that, when hashed, produces a hash with a predefined number of leading zeros.

```
import hashlib
import time

def proof_of_work(block_data, difficulty):
    nonce = 0
    start_time = time.time()
    target = "0" * difficulty
    while True:
        block_hash = hashlib.sha256((block_data + str(nonce)).encode()).hexdigest()
        if block_hash[:difficulty] == target:
            break
        nonce += 1
    end_time = time.time()
    return nonce, block_hash, end_time - start_time

# Example block data and difficulty level
block_data = "Sample block transaction data"
difficulty = 4 # Number of leading zeros required
nonce, block_hash, time_taken = proof_of_work(block_data, difficulty)
print(f"Nonce: {nonce}, Hash: {block_hash}, Time taken: {time_taken} seconds")
```

```
Example Output:
Nonce: 53134, Hash: 0000c1e68fe23e119d13880cb79e8d20c74a6d764269b4a1f2e98992ffd33727
Time taken: 3.89 seconds
```

The difficulty of the Proof-of-Work problem is dynamically adjusted approximately every two weeks to maintain an average block creation time of 10 minutes. This ensures the network's stability and predictability.

Upon successful mining, the new block containing the confirmed transactions is appended to the blockchain. All nodes then validate the block, ensuring it follows the network's consensus rules and updating their copy of the blockchain.

Bitcoin transactions are pseudonymous, meaning the public addresses do not inherently reveal the users' real identities. However, all transaction data on the blockchain is transparent and publicly accessible, allowing sophisticated analysis to infer possible identities and connections.

Bitcoin's decentralized consensus model mitigates a single point of failure, enhancing security and resilience. By distributing the network across numerous nodes, it prevents centralized attacks and manipulation, fostering trust among participants without necessitating a central authority.

Understanding the intricacies of Bitcoin's operation and technology elucidates its fundamental innovation in digital currency and decentralized systems. Proficiency in these concepts is crucial for advancing one's knowledge in blockchain technology and its applications.

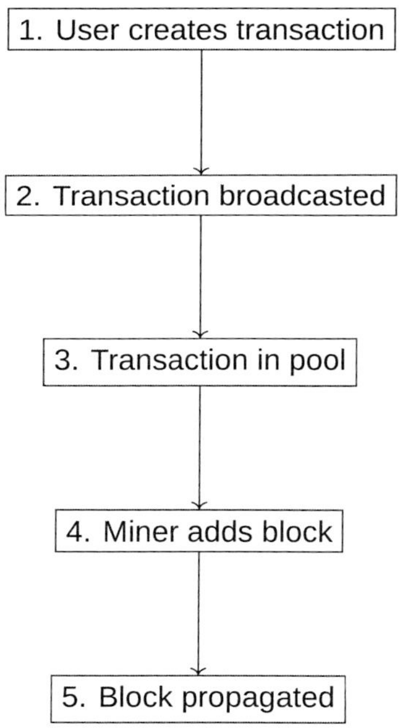

1.4 Bitcoin vs. Traditional Currency

The fundamental differences between Bitcoin and traditional currency stem from their origins, structure, and methods of transaction. Traditional currencies, also known as fiat currencies, such as the US Dollar (USD), Euro (EUR), or Japanese Yen (JPY), are issued and regulated by centralized authorities, usually national governments and central banks. Bitcoin, on the other hand, is a decentralized digital currency created in 2008 by an anonymous individual or group known as Satoshi Nakamoto. The underlying technologies and principles driving these currencies lead to stark contrasts in their management, operation, and perceived value.

Traditional currencies are typically issued in a controlled manner by central banks through monetary policies. Central banks have the authority to control the money supply, set interest rates, and implement measures to stabilize or stimulate the economy. This centralized control allows for monetary policy adjustments to respond to economic changes such as inflation, recession, or other financial crises. Fiat currencies are backed by the trust and authority of the government and derive their value from the stability and economic strength of the issuing nation.

In contrast, Bitcoin operates on a decentralized blockchain network without a central authority. It relies on a peer-to-peer network and cryptographic proof instead of trust in a central party. Bitcoin transactions are verified by network nodes through cryptography and recorded in a public ledger known as the blockchain. The issuance of new Bitcoins occurs through a process called mining, which involves network participants, known as miners, solving complex mathematical problems to validate transactions and add new blocks to the blockchain. This process is predetermined and follows a fixed supply schedule, ultimately capping the total number of bitcoins at 21 million.

One crucial distinction lies in the transaction mechanisms. Fiat currency transactions typically involve financial intermediaries such as banks, payment processors, or clearinghouses. These intermediaries facilitate the transfer of money between parties, ensuring security, compliance with regulatory standards, and resolution of disputes. However, the involvement of these intermediaries can introduce delays, additional costs such as transaction fees, and potential points of failure or security vulnerabilities.

Bitcoin transactions, however, occur directly between users without intermediaries, a feature enabled by the underlying blockchain technology. When a user initiates a Bitcoin transaction, it is broadcast to the network, verified by miners, and subsequently recorded on the blockchain. This process can reduce the transaction time and cost as there are no intermediaries involved. Nonetheless, transaction times and fees can fluctuate based on network congestion and the optional transaction fees set by users, which prioritize their transactions.

Another aspect where Bitcoin differs significantly from traditional currencies is in transparency and privacy. Fiat currencies offer varying degrees of privacy, but most transactions can be tracked and monitored by financial institutions and government authorities. This level of transparency is often necessary for regulatory compliance, anti-money laundering (AML) measures, and fraud prevention.

Bitcoin provides a different privacy model. Each Bitcoin wallet is associated with a public key, visible in the blockchain, and transactions are pseudonymous. This means while the transaction details are publicly accessible, the identities of the wallet owners are not directly linked to the public keys. Nonetheless, with sophisticated analysis techniques, it may be possible to infer user identities, linking transactions to real-world identities. As a result, Bitcoin can offer increased privacy compared to traditional banking systems but is not entirely anonymous.

Regarding the supply control, traditional currencies face inflation risks if a central bank decides to increase the money supply significantly. This was evident in historical hyperinflation cases, such as Zimbabwe, where excessive printing of money led to a dramatic loss of currency value. Central banks strive to balance monetary supply to promote economic stability but have the authority to alter it as deemed necessary.

Bitcoin's design inherently accounts for deflationary control. The total supply is capped at 21 million bitcoins, making it a finite resource. This algorithmic scarcity model results in what is often considered a deflationary currency, potentially increasing in value over time as demand grows while supply remains limited. Furthermore, the predictable issuance schedule of Bitcoins, halving the rewards for miners approximately every four years, introduces an additional layer of scarcity. This transparency in supply control has positioned Bitcoin as "digital gold" amongst some proponents, contrasting with the potentially inflationary nature of fiat currencies.

The value perception of Bitcoin versus traditional currencies also varies notably. Fiat currencies' value is influenced by economic policies, geopolitical stability, inflation rates, and trade balances. In contrast, Bitcoin's value derives from market demand, its utility as a medium of exchange, its perceived scarcity, and speculative investments. The volatility in Bitcoin's market price is significantly higher than that of traditional currencies, reflecting its relatively nascent status and the speculative nature of the cryptocurrency market.

Notably, the acceptance and legal status of Bitcoin and fiat currencies present stark contrasts. Fiat currencies are legally recognized as legal tender within their respective jurisdictions, meaning they must be accepted as a form of payment for all debts, public and private. Bitcoin, however, does not have universal legal tender status. Regulatory acceptance varies globally, with some countries embracing it as a legitimate form of payment and asset, while others impose stringent restrictions or outright bans. Consequently, this disparity impacts Bitcoin's utility and acceptance across different regions.

Fiat currencies benefit from established infrastructure, regulatory frameworks, and consumer protections that have been developed over centuries. Conversely, Bitcoin operates within newly emerging regulatory landscapes with ongoing developments in legal, technological, and security aspects. As this ecosystem evolves, so too does the comparative analysis between the inherent properties, advantages, and limitations of Bitcoin versus traditional fiat currencies.

1.5 Key Features of Bitcoin

Bitcoin possesses distinctive characteristics that differentiate it from traditional fiat currencies. These features allow Bitcoin to operate as a decentralized digital currency, thriving as a revolutionary financial instrument.

Bitcoin relies on **decentralization**. Unlike conventional currencies issued by central banks, Bitcoin is maintained by a network of nodes distributed globally. Each node contains a copy of the blockchain, an immutable ledger that records all transactions. Decentralization ensures there is no single point of failure and mitigates the risks of censorship or control by any single entity. This attribute renders Bitcoin resistant to manipulation or interference by central authorities.

At the core of Bitcoin's operation is the **blockchain technology**. The blockchain is an append-only, public ledger where transactions are grouped into blocks. Each block is linked to the preceding one through a cryptographic hash, forming a chain. The blockchain's security stems from the cryptographic principles utilized in its structure, ensuring that altering any information in a block would require altering all subsequent blocks, a computationally infeasible task.

Bitcoin implements a **proof-of-work (PoW)** consensus mechanism. To add a new block to the blockchain, miners compete to solve a complex mathematical problem; the first to solve it broadcasts the solution to the network. Other nodes verify the solution's correctness, and once consensus is reached, the block is appended to the blockchain. This process, known as mining, also serves the dual purpose of issuing new bitcoins and securing the network against fraudulent transactions.

The **fixed supply** of Bitcoin is another pivotal feature. Unlike fiat currencies, which can be printed at will by central banks, Bitcoin's supply is capped at 21 million coins. This scarcity is programmed into the protocol and predictable through the mining reward halving events, occurring approximately every four years. This deflationary nature can potentially preserve value over time, akin to commodities like gold.

Bitcoin's **pseudonymity** provides a level of user privacy. Transactions are conducted using alphanumeric addresses rather than personally identifiable information. While the transaction details are transparent and traceable on the blockchain, linking a Bitcoin address to an individual requires additional information, thus protecting user identities.

The **irreversibility of transactions** in Bitcoin further adds to its distinctive features. Once confirmed, transactions cannot be reverted, providing a finality absent in many traditional payment systems where chargebacks are possible. This attribute enhances security by eliminating risks associated with fraudulent reversals.

Bitcoin is also notable for its **divisibility**. Each bitcoin is divisible into 100 million smaller units called satoshis, named after its creator. This high degree of divisibility allows for microtransactions, enabling transactions of any scale and facilitating broader adoption in various economic contexts.

The **open-source nature** of Bitcoin promotes transparency and trust. Bitcoin's source code is publicly available, allowing any developer to review or contribute to its improvement. This open approach invites innovation, ensuring continuous enhancements to the protocol and its ecosystem.

Bitcoin's **portability** stands out due to its digital form. Transferring bitcoins across borders is as simple as initiating an online transaction, differing starkly from the limitations and costs associated with traditional banking and physical money transfers.

Lastly, Bitcoin benefits from a **robust security model**. The combination of cryptographic hashing, decentralized consensus, and proof-of-work provides a multi-faceted security approach, safeguarding the network from various attack vectors such as double-spending and Sybil attacks.

These features collectively enable Bitcoin to function as a decentralized digital currency, presenting a unique value proposition unmatched by traditional financial instruments.

1.6 Satoshi Nakamoto: The Mysterious Founder

Satoshi Nakamoto's identity remains one of the most intriguing mysteries in the world of digital currency. The name Satoshi Nakamoto is a pseudonym used by the person or group of people who developed Bitcoin and authored the Bitcoin whitepaper titled "Bitcoin: A Peer-to-Peer Electronic Cash System," published in 2008. Nakamoto's involvement with Bitcoin lasted until sometime in 2010 when they handed over control of the source code repository and network alert key to Gavin Andresen and other key members of the Bitcoin community, before disappearing from public view.

The pseudonymous creator communicated through forums and email, meticulously detailing the design and implementation of Bitcoin. Their use of anonymizing techniques preserved their true identity, ensuring that even a detailed analysis of writing style and communication patterns has not led to definitive identification.

```
"A purely peer-to-peer version of electronic cash would allow online
payments to be sent directly from one party to another without going
through a financial institution. Digital signatures provide part of
the solution, but the main benefits are lost if a trusted third
party is still required to prevent double-spending..."
```

Nakamoto's contributions extend beyond the original whitepaper. They also mined the first blocks of the Bitcoin blockchain, including the "genesis block" or block 0, which contains a hidden message. This message, embedded in the transaction data, reads: "The Times 03/Jan/2009 Chancellor on brink of second bailout for banks." This text is a reference to a headline in The Times newspaper, signaling Nakamoto's apparent motivation behind Bitcoin—to create a currency free from government interference and poorly managed centralized institutions.

```
"The Times 03/Jan/2009 Chancellor on brink of second bailout for banks"
```

Various attempts have been made to uncover Nakamoto's true identity, leading to speculation involving numerous individuals and entities. These include well-known cryptographers, academics, and even large organizations. Analysts have examined linguistic patterns in Nakamoto's writings, time zone activity patterns, and coding style, but no consensus has been reached.

Several individuals have either been suspected of being Nakamoto or have claimed to be the creator of Bitcoin. Some of these claims have gained significant media attention:

- Dorian Nakamoto: A Japanese-American man identified by a journalist, though he has consistently denied any connection to Bitcoin.
- Hal Finney: A well-known cryptographer and early Bitcoin contributor who corresponded with Nakamoto and received the first Bitcoin transaction.
- Nick Szabo: A computer scientist and cryptographer known for his work on digital contracts, whose writing style and interests closely align with the principles of Bitcoin.
- Craig Wright: An Australian computer scientist who has repeatedly claimed to be Nakamoto, though his assertions remain contentious and widely disputed in the community.

Nakamoto's anonymity plays a significant role in the nature of Bitcoin. Unlike traditional currencies managed by identifiable groups or institutions, Bitcoin's development and early operations were driven by an anonymous entity, aligning with the decentralized philosophy of the currency. This anonymity protects Nakamoto from legal repercussions and government regulations, which might arise from the creation and promotion of a disruptive financial system.

Nakamoto is estimated to possess approximately one million Bitcoins, attributed to early mining activities. This significant amount of Bitcoin, worth billions of dollars, has never been moved, contributing to the intrigue and speculation around Nakamoto's identity. If these Bitcoins were ever moved or sold, they could drastically impact the cryptocurrency market, highlighting Nakamoto's influence on Bitcoin's value and stability.

The legacy of Satoshi Nakamoto extends beyond Bitcoin. The creation of Bitcoin has spurred the development of numerous cryptocurrencies and decentralized technologies, fostering a broader movement towards decentralization in various sectors, including finance, supply chain management, and data storage.

In their final known correspondence, Nakamoto stated, "I've moved on to other things." This statement signifies the intended autonomy of the Bitcoin network, designed to operate independently of its creator. Nakamoto's departure underscores the strength and resilience of the decentralized model, allowing Bitcoin to thrive within a global ecosystem of contributors and stakeholders without reliance on a central figure.

Thus, while the true identity of Satoshi Nakamoto remains unresolved, their impact on the world is undeniable, secured through the continued existence and evolution of Bitcoin and the decentralized technologies it inspired.

1.7 Public and Private Keys

Bitcoin relies heavily on cryptographic principles, particularly the use of public and private keys, to ensure secure and verifiable transactions without requiring central authority. A public key and a private key form a cryptographic key pair, each playing a vital role in the Bitcoin network's security and functionality. Understanding these keys is fundamental to grasping how Bitcoin transactions are conducted securely.

Public keys are derived from private keys using elliptic curve cryptography (ECC). Specifically, Bitcoin employs the secp256k1 curve, a standard curve defined by specific mathematical constants. A 256-bit random number serves as the private key, which is then utilized to compute the corresponding public key through elliptic curve multiplication. This multiplication is a one-way function, which means that it is computationally infeasible to reverse the process and derive the private key from the public key.

```
import ecdsa
import hashlib

# Generate a private key
private_key = ecdsa.SigningKey.generate(curve=ecdsa.SECP256k1)

# Compute the public key
public_key = private_key.get_verifying_key()

# Convert keys to hexadecimal format
private_key_hex = private_key.to_string().hex()
public_key_hex = public_key.to_string().hex()

print("Private Key:", private_key_hex)
print("Public Key:", public_key_hex)
```

As shown in the example above, the private key is a random number generated within the bounds of the secp256k1 curve. The public key is derived from this private key and can be easily shared without compromising security. This derivation preserves the security of the private key while allowing the public key to be used as a Bitcoin address where others can send Bitcoin.

The primary utility of the public key in the Bitcoin network is to serve as an address that users can share with others to receive Bitcoin. However, due to the length of the public key, these keys are often hashed to create a more user-friendly Bitcoin address. The hashing process involves applying the SHA-256 algorithm followed by the RIPEMD-160 algorithm to the public key.

```
import base58

# Compute the SHA-256 hash of the public key
sha256_hash = hashlib.sha256(public_key.to_string()).digest()

# Compute the RIPEMD-160 hash of the SHA-256 hash
ripemd160 = hashlib.new('ripemd160')
ripemd160.update(sha256_hash)
hashed_public_key = ripemd160.digest()

# Add version byte (0x00 for Main Network)
versioned_payload = b'\x00' + hashed_public_key

# Compute the checksum
checksum = hashlib.sha256(hashlib.sha256(versioned_payload).digest()).digest()[:4]

# Append the checksum to the versioned payload
binary_address = versioned_payload + checksum

# Encode the binary address using Base58
bitcoin_address = base58.b58encode(binary_address)

print("Bitcoin Address:", bitcoin_address)
```

Through these processing steps, the lengthy public key is transformed into a Bitcoin address that is shorter and easier to manage. Notably, the Base58 encoding is used to ensure Bitcoin addresses are compact and minimize the risk of typographical errors, as it skips ambiguous characters.

The private key, essentially acting as a password, is used to sign transactions, ensuring that the funds can only be spent by the rightful owner who possesses the private key. When a user wishes to send Bitcoin, their wallet software utilizes the private key to create a digital signature that proves the user's ownership of the Bitcoin being spent. This signature is then verified by other nodes on the network using the corresponding public key.

```
# Some data to sign (typically the transaction data)
data_to_sign = b'Transaction Data'

# Generate the digital signature
signature = private_key.sign(data_to_sign)

print("Digital Signature:", signature.hex())
```

This digital signature is crucial because it provides three key assurances:

- Authentication: Verifies that the transaction was created by the holder of the private key.
- Integrity: Ensures that the transaction data has not been altered.
- Non-repudiation: Prevents the sender from denying the validity of the transaction.

Upon receiving a transaction, Bitcoin nodes use the digital signature to verify its authenticity and integrity before including it in a block on the blockchain. This verification is accomplished using the sender's public key.

```
# Verify the signature using the public key
is_valid_signature = public_key.verify(signature, data_to_sign)

print("Signature Valid:", is_valid_signature)
```

The security of Bitcoin transactions thus fundamentally hinges on the secure generation and storage of private keys by users. Loss or theft of the private key means losing access to the Bitcoin controlled by that key. Consequently, users are advised to employ secure methods, such as hardware wallets, to manage their private keys.

Given this robust cryptographic framework, public and private keys in Bitcoin serve as the foundational elements that enable secure, decentralized financial transactions. Through the intricate relationship between these keys, Bitcoin ensures that ownership and transfer of value can occur in a trustless, transparent manner.

1.8 The Role of Cryptography in Bitcoin

Bitcoin utilizes cryptographic principles to ensure secure transactions, maintain the integrity of the blockchain, and provide pseudonymity for its users. Cryptography, the science of encoding and decoding information, underpins the essential operations and security features of Bitcoin's decentralized system.

At the core of Bitcoin are two primary cryptographic mechanisms: hashing and public-key cryptography.

Hashing, a process that takes an input and produces a fixed-size string of bytes, typically appears as a hexadecimal number. Bitcoin employs the SHA-256 (Secure Hash Algorithm 256-bit) hashing function to secure the blockchain. SHA-256 is designed to be a one-way function, meaning that it is computationally infeasible to reverse the process—i.e., to derive the original input from the output hash. This property is crucial for ensuring the integrity of the blockchain, as any alteration in the data would result in a drastically different hash, clearly signaling tampering.

For example, consider the SHA-256 hashes of two similar inputs:

```
Input: "Bitcoin Guidebook"
SHA-256 Hash: cbb2f1972df59c0ad61d25da3564b0639bf39859f6a8423b9f0d2d42e9204984
```

```
Input: "Bitcoin Guidebook!"
SHA-256 Hash: 2
      f80beb65bcdcd18809d2d7a1c60bd1b156062ac5a298168a435e8c702876eb3
```

Even though the inputs differ only by an exclamation mark, their output hashes are significantly different, illustrating the sensitivity of the hash function to input changes.

In the Bitcoin blockchain, each block contains a reference to the previous block's hash, creating a chain of blocks (hence the term "blockchain"). This linkage ensures that altering any block in the chain would require recalculating the hashes of all subsequent blocks, a computationally impractical task, thereby securing the blockchain against tampering.

Public-Key Cryptography is another cornerstone of Bitcoin's security. This asymmetric cryptography involves a pair of keys: a public key and a private key. The public key is derived from the private key through a one-way function and can be shared with the world, whereas the private key remains confidential to the owner. In Bitcoin, these keys serve multiple purposes, including the creation of digital signatures and the formation of Bitcoin addresses.

Users sign transactions with their private key, producing a digital signature that can be verified by anyone using the corresponding public key. This verification process ensures that the transaction was indeed authorized by the owner of the private key without revealing the key itself.

Consider a simplified example of a Bitcoin transaction process:

```
1. User A wants to send 1 Bitcoin to User B.
2. User A signs the transaction with their private key:
   Signature = Sign(PrivateKey_A, TransactionData)
3. User A broadcasts the transaction, including the signature, to the Bitcoin network.
4. Nodes on the network use User A's public key to verify the signature:
   isValid = Verify(PublicKey_A, Signature, TransactionData)
```

The strength of public-key cryptography lies in its reliance on the computational difficulty of problems such as the discrete logarithm problem, ensuring that deriving the private key from the public key is practically impossible with current computational capabilities.

Elliptic Curve Digital Signature Algorithm (ECDSA) is the specific public-key cryptographic system used by Bitcoin. ECDSA is favored for its efficiency and security, offering strong cryptographic security with smaller key sizes. Bitcoin employs the secp256k1 elliptic curve, which is specifically chosen for its cryptographic properties that enhance both security and efficiency.

Bitcoin addresses are derived from public keys through a process involving both hashing and encoding:

```
1. Generate a public key from the private key using the elliptic curve function.
2. Obtain the SHA-256 hash of the public key.
3. Obtain the RIPEMD-160 hash of the SHA-256 hash.
4. Add a version byte to the beginning of the RIPEMD-160 hash.
5. Perform SHA-256 hashing twice on this extended RIPEMD-160 hash.
6. Take the first four bytes of the second SHA-256 hash; this is the checksum.
7. Append the checksum to the extended RIPEMD-160 hash.
8. Convert the resulting 25-byte array into a Base58 string; this is the Bitcoin address.
```

This comprehensive process ensures that Bitcoin addresses are not only secure but also error-resistant. Any slight change in an address during transmission would result in an invalid checksum, safeguarding against typos or other forms of corruption.

The combination of hashing and public-key cryptography culminates in a system that provides integrity, authenticity, and confidentiality within the Bitcoin network. These cryptographic principles are fundamental to maintaining the trust-less, decentralized nature of Bitcoin, allowing users to transact securely without relying on central authorities.

1.9 Bitcoin's Decentralized Nature

Bitcoin's decentralized nature is one of its most fundamental and distinguishing characteristics. Unlike traditional financial systems that rely on centralized authorities, such as banks or government entities, Bitcoin operates on a peer-to-peer network without a central point of control. This decentralization is rooted in the architecture of its underlying technology, the blockchain, combined with the consensus mechanisms and cryptographic techniques that govern its operations.

At the core of Bitcoin's decentralized nature is the blockchain, a distributed ledger that records all transactions across a vast network of nodes. Each node maintains a copy of the blockchain, ensuring redundancy and resilience against failures or attacks. Transactions are grouped into blocks, which are sequentially linked and cryptographically secured, forming an immutable chain. This structure prevents any single entity from altering past transactions, as altering one block would require altering all subsequent blocks, an endeavor computationally infeasible due to the required proof-of-work.

The proof-of-work consensus algorithm plays a pivotal role in maintaining decentralization. When a new block of transactions is proposed, miners (participants in the network who perform computational work) compete to solve a cryptographic puzzle. The first miner to solve this puzzle broadcasts the solution to the network, and after verification by other nodes, the new block is appended to the blockchain. This process makes it difficult for any single miner or group of miners to dominate the network, as the computational difficulty adjusts dynamically to ensure a consistent block production rate.

Another crucial aspect of Bitcoin's decentralization is the distributed nature of its ledger. Every node in the network has equal privileges and access to the ledger, promoting transparency and reducing the risk of manipulation. The consensus mechanism ensures that all nodes agree on the current state of the ledger, and any attempt to introduce a fraudulent transaction would be rejected by honest nodes.

Bitcoin's protocol also incorporates economic incentives to support its decentralized framework. Miners are rewarded with a fixed number of newly minted bitcoins and transaction fees for their computational efforts in securing the network. This not only incentivizes honest participation but also introduces new bitcoins into circulation, adhering to the principles of Bitcoin's deflationary economic model. The halving events, which reduce the block reward approximately every four years, contribute to Bitcoin's scarcity and value proposition.

Furthermore, Bitcoin's decentralized nature extends to user sovereignty over digital assets. Users control their bitcoins through cryptographic keys; specifically, a combination of a public key, which serves as an address for receiving funds, and a private key, which is used to authorize transactions. Control over the private key equates to control over the bitcoins associated with it, eliminating the need for intermediaries and empowering users to fully manage their funds.

Bitcoin's open-source nature and community-driven development also reinforce decentralization. The Bitcoin protocol is maintained by a diverse group of developers who collaborate on improvements and propose changes. These proposed changes undergo rigorous peer review and testing in testnet environments. Significant updates, like Segregated Witness (SegWit) or the Taproot upgrade, emerged through community consensus and thorough deliberation, ensuring that the network evolves without central direction.

A technical illustration of Bitcoin's decentralized nature can be observed in the way transaction validation is handled. The pseudocode for a simplified transaction validation mechanism is as follows:

```
def validate_transaction(transaction):
    inputs_value = 0
    for input in transaction.inputs:
        referenced_utxo = get_utxo(input.previous_output)
        if not verify_signature(input.signature, referenced_utxo.public_key):
            return False
        inputs_value += referenced_utxo.value

    outputs_value = 0
    for output in transaction.outputs:
        outputs_value += output.value

    if inputs_value < outputs_value:
        return False

    # Additional checks can include double-spending, and dust rules
    return True
```

The output for validation success can look as follows:

```
Transaction is valid.
```

Conversely, if validation fails due to signature mismatch or input-output value discrepancy, the output will be:

```
Transaction validation failed.
```

Decentralization ensures that no single participant can arbitrarily validate or invalidate transactions, thereby upholding integrity and trust in the system. Every node independently verifies transactions against the global ledger state, contributing to the consensus without centralized oversight.

Bitcoin's decentralized nature fundamentally alters traditional conceptions of trust and governance in financial systems. It empowers individuals, reduces dependency on centralized entities, and fosters a transparent, secure, and inclusive financial ecosystem.

1.10 Use Cases of Bitcoin

Bitcoin, as a decentralized digital currency, finds use cases that transcend traditional financial systems. Understanding these applications provides insights into its potential to transform various sectors. This section explores the prominent use cases, emphasizing Bitcoin's role in transactions, investment, remittances, charitable donations, and as a hedge against inflation.

Peer-to-Peer Transactions: One of the primary use cases of Bitcoin is facilitating peer-to-peer (P2P) transactions. Bitcoin enables direct transfer of value between parties without any intermediary such as a bank. This is advantageous because it can significantly reduce transaction fees, expedite the transfer process, and mitigate the risk of third-party interference or censorship. The convenience and security features inherent to the Bitcoin network make it an attractive option for individuals and businesses. This is particularly notable in regions with unstable banking infrastructures.

```
# Example of sending Bitcoin using a Python script and the Bitcoin library
from bitcoin import *

# Generate a new private key
my_private_key = random_key()

# Generate the corresponding public key
my_public_key = privtopub(my_private_key)

# Create a Bitcoin address
my_address = pubtoaddr(my_public_key)

# Display the Bitcoin address
print(f"Bitcoin Address: {my_address}")

# Transaction parameters
amount_to_send = 0.001 # in BTC
destination_address = '1A1zP1eP5QGefi2DMPTfTL5SLmv7DivfNa'

# Create the raw transaction
tx = mktx(prev_tx, prev_index, target_address, amount_to_send)
```

```
# Sign the transaction
signed_tx = sign(tx, 0, my_private_key)

# Broadcast the transaction to the network
broadcast_tx(signed_tx)
```

Investment and Speculation: Bitcoin has emerged as a significant asset class for investment and speculation. Since its inception, Bitcoin's value has shown substantial growth, thereby attracting investors keen on capital appreciation. Its volatile price movements provide opportunities for traders and investors to potentially earn high returns. Bitcoin is also considered by some as "digital gold" due to its deflationary nature and capped supply, which makes it a candidate for long-term value retention.

```
Output from executing investment analysis:
Initial Investment: $1,000
Yearly Return: 150%
Investment Value after 5 years: $11,390.625
```

Remittances: Bitcoin offers an efficient alternative for remittances, especially across borders. Traditionally, sending money internationally can be costly and slow due to intermediary banks and varying exchange rates. Bitcoin transactions can circumvent these issues by providing a low-cost, swift method for transferring funds globally, thus benefitting recipients by minimizing fees and expediting access to the funds.

Charitable Donations: Charitable organizations have started accepting Bitcoin as donations. This method offers a level of transparency and traceability through the blockchain, ensuring donors that their contributions reach the intended recipients. Bitcoin's P2P nature also means reduced transaction costs, maximizing the value of donations.

Hedge Against Inflation: Another notable use case for Bitcoin is as a hedge against inflation. Unlike fiat currencies which can be subject to inflationary pressures due to government monetary policies, Bitcoin's fixed supply of 21 million coins provides a deflationary characteristic. This limited supply potentially makes it a store of value in times of economic instability, where fiat currency values might depreciate.

These use cases highlight Bitcoin's versatility in addressing various financial needs beyond conventional methods, positioning it as a transformative force in the global financial landscape.

Chapter 2

Understanding Blockchain Technology

Blockchain technology, the underlying foundation of Bitcoin, is a decentralized and immutable ledger system that records transactions in a series of linked blocks. Each block contains a list of transactions and is cryptographically linked to the previous block, ensuring data integrity and security. The decentralized nature of blockchain eliminates the need for intermediaries and relies on consensus mechanisms like Proof of Work and Proof of Stake to validate transactions. This chapter delves into the structure, mechanisms, and various types of blockchain networks, along with their applications beyond cryptocurrencies, providing a detailed understanding of this transformative technology.

2.1 Introduction to Blockchain

Blockchain technology, a cornerstone of Bitcoin and other digital currencies, represents a novel approach to data management and transactions. At its core, a blockchain is a decentralized and immutable ledger, meaning it operates without a central authority and is resistant to modification of its data. The integrity and chronological order of transactions are maintained through cryptographic linking of consecutive blocks, forming an unalterable chain.

In a blockchain, each block contains a set of transactions, a timestamp, and a reference to the previous block via a cryptographic hash. This hash function takes an input and produces a fixed-size string of characters, which appears random and unique to each input. The link between blocks is akin to creating a sequence of data points that depend crucially on the data in the preceding blocks, ensuring any attempted alteration would require altering all subsequent blocks. This characteristic forms the underlying basis for blockchain's security and data integrity.

The decentralized nature of blockchain manifests through its distributed ledger system, where a network of nodes—computers participating in the blockchain network—maintain a copy of the entire blockchain. Transactions are validated and added to the blockchain through a consensus mechanism agreed upon by the network participants. In Bitcoin's case, this mechanism is known as Proof of Work (PoW), where nodes, also referred to as miners, compete to solve complex mathematical problems to validate transactions and create new blocks.

The creation of a new block follows a systematic process:

```
def create_block(transactions, previous_hash):
    block = {
        'index': len(blockchain) + 1,
        'timestamp': time.time(),
        'transactions': transactions,
        'previous_hash': previous_hash,
        'nonce': 0
    }
    block['hash'] = hash_block(block)
    return block

def hash_block(block):
    encoded_block = json.dumps(block, sort_keys=True).encode()
    return hashlib.sha256(encoded_block).hexdigest()
```

In the provided pseudocode, the create_block function outlines the structure of a block by including an index, timestamp, transactions, previous block's hash, and a nonce. The block's hash is computed using the SHA-256 hashing algorithm, guaranteeing a fixed-size hash string. The hash_block function converts the block into a JSON string, encodes it, and computes the hash value.

Once a block is created, the miners in the network begin a process known as mining, where they attempt to find a nonce value that, when combined with the block's data, produces a hash meeting the network's difficulty target—a condition often involving a specific number of leading zeros in the hash string. This process can be computationally intensive and time-consuming, ensuring that the creation of new blocks maintains a consistent interval, approximately every 10 minutes in Bitcoin's network.

The validation of a block and the transactions it contains are confirmed through consensus. In PoW, the first miner to solve the cryptographic puzzle announces their solution to the network, and other nodes verify the correctness of the proposed solution. If validated, the new block is added to their copy of the blockchain, commonly referred to as the longest chain rule, ensuring the chain's accuracy and immutability.

Example output of a block hash:
0000000000000000000c1b9e6f83cfe6a5e6aa7f31452c8d9b79d8d2c3d9c924

Blockchain's use cases extend beyond cryptocurrency applications. Beyond facilitating digital currency transactions, blockchain technology finds utility in various domains such as supply chain management, healthcare, and finance. Its features of transparency, traceability, and security allow for robust applications where trust and data integrity are vital.

The integration of smart contracts, self-executing contracts with the terms of the agreement directly written into code, further enhances blockchain's capabilities. Smart contracts streamline and automate complex processes, ensuring transactions and agreements are executed without the need for intermediaries, reducing costs, and increasing efficiency.

As we delve deeper into the functionalities and implications of blockchain technology, we understand that its potential to revolutionize data management and transactional trust extends far beyond Bitcoin and into broader societal and technological realms.

2.2 The Structure of a Block

A block in a blockchain serves as a container for transactional data, maintaining the integrity and immutability of the ledger. Each block comprises several key components that ensure its functionality and security: the block header, the block body, and metadata. Understanding these components is crucial for grasping how blockchain technology works at a granular level.

The block header is a critical part of each block, containing metadata that enables linking with preceding blocks, hence forming a chain. The block header itself consists of the following fields:

- **Previous Block Hash:** This field contains the cryptographic hash of the previous block's header. This linkage ensures the immutability of the blockchain, as any change in a previous block's data would necessitate changes in all subsequent block headers.

- **Merkle Root:** The Merkle root is a single hash representing all transactions within the block. Transactions are organized in a binary Merkle tree structure, and the root hash of this tree is stored in the block header. This structure allows quick and efficient verification of the integrity and existence of transactions within the block.

- **Timestamp:** This field records the precise time at which the block was created, typically in Unix epoch format. The timestamp helps maintain chronological order and is instrumental in the validation process.

- **Nonce:** A nonce is a random value that miners adjust to vary the hash output of the block header. This value is pivotal in the Proof of Work consensus mechanism, as it ensures that finding a valid hash meets the difficulty criteria set by the network.

- **Difficulty Target:** This field represents the difficulty level of the hash puzzle that miners must solve to add the block to the blockchain. It is periodically adjusted by the network to maintain a consistent block generation time, regardless of changes in mining power.

- **Version Number:** This indicates the version of blockchain protocol rules being followed, allowing upgrades and modifications without disrupting the blockchain's continuity.

The block body contains the bulk of data in a block: the transactions. Each transaction in the block body is a transfer of value between participants and includes several fields:

- **Sender Address:** The origin address of the transaction, typically represented as a public key.

- **Receiver Address:** The destination address of the transaction.

- **Amount:** The value being transferred from the sender to the receiver.

- **Transaction Fee:** Optional fee paid to incentivize miners for including the transaction in a block.
- **Signature:** Cryptographic proof that the sender authorized the transaction. It is generated using the sender's private key.
- **Transaction ID:** A unique identifier for the transaction, often derived from hashing the transaction data.

The process of collecting transactions into a block involves several steps. Transactions are first validated individually for correctness, such as ensuring the sender has sufficient funds and the signature is valid. Once validated, transactions are organized in a binary Merkle tree to generate the Merkle root.

Below is a simplified Python code snippet demonstrating the creation of a Merkle root from a list of transactions:

```
import hashlib

def hash_pair(a, b):
    return hashlib.sha256((a + b).encode('utf-8')).hexdigest()

def merkle_root(transactions):
    if len(transactions) == 1:
        return transactions[0]
    new_level = []
    for i in range(0, len(transactions)-1, 2):
        new_level.append(hash_pair(transactions[i], transactions[i+1]))
    if len(transactions) % 2 == 1:
        new_level.append(hash_pair(transactions[-1], transactions[-1])) # Duplicate
            last hash if odd number
    return merkle_root(new_level)

transactions = [
    "tx1", "tx2", "tx3", "tx4",
    "tx5"
]

print("Merkle Root:", merkle_root(transactions))
```

The output of this program would be:

```
Merkle Root: 71657e98d04211c5397735c968db904f5ec5f079ed60c0e529cd68c448b2b021
```

With transactions organized into a Merkle tree and the Merkle root calculated, the block header is then constructed. The block, composed of its header and body, is propagated across the network. Miners work to find a valid nonce by hashing the block header repeatedly until the resulting hash meets the network's difficulty target.

Upon successfully finding a valid nonce, the block is broadcasted to the network, where others verify its validity. Verification includes checking the correctness of the previous block hash, the integrity of the Merkle root, and the satisfaction of the difficulty target, among other criteria.

By examining the structure of a block and its components, it becomes apparent how blockchain technology achieves its goals of decentralization, security, and immutability. The meticulous organization within each block, supported by cryptographic principles, is fundamental to the robustness of blockchain systems.

2.3 How Blocks are Linked: The Blockchain

In a blockchain, blocks are linked together in a linear, chronological order, forming a chain of blocks. This linkage is crucial for maintaining the integrity and security of the blockchain. Each block contains a unique identifier called a hash, which is derived from the data within the block. The hash of each block is a fixed-size, alphanumeric string that serves as a digital fingerprint for the block's contents.

The process begins with the creation of the first block, known as the genesis block. This block does not reference any previous block. The subsequent blocks, however, each include a reference to the hash of the previous block. This creates a chain, as shown below:

Block 0		Block 1		Block 2
Hash:...		Hash:...		Hash:...
Prev: Null	←+	Prev:...	←+	Prev:...

Block 3		Block 4		Block 5
Hash:...		Hash:...		Hash:...
Prev:...	←+	Prev:...	←+	Prev:...

In this linked structure, if a block is altered, its hash will change. Since each block references the hash of the previous block, a change in one block will invalidate all subsequent blocks. This interdependence ensures the immutability of the blockchain. Any attempt to change a block requires recalculating the hash for that block and all subsequent blocks, making it computationally infeasible to alter historical data.

To further understand how blocks are linked, let us delve into the specifics of what a hash function is and how it fits into the blockchain. A hash function takes an input and returns a fixed-size string of bytes. The output appears random, but it is determined by the input. This means that the same input will always produce the same output, but even the smallest change to the input will produce a significantly different output. One of the most commonly used hash functions in the blockchain is SHA-256.

```
import hashlib

message = "Hello, Blockchain!"
hash_object = hashlib.sha256(message.encode())
hex_dig = hash_object.hexdigest()
print(hex_dig)
```

```
2a3f8e0e38f66e36315c0c658d2f8fb1cc182e31775154f39e2d20fb0c6c188c
```

The above code demonstrates how a given input message is converted into a SHA-256 hash. This hash, represented as a hexadecimal string, serves as a digital signature for the message. In the context of blockchain, every block's hash includes the hash of the previous block, thus linking the blocks together.

The integrity of the blockchain is further reinforced through consensus mechanisms, which ensure that all participants (nodes) in the network agree on the validity of transactions and the order of blocks. The most common consensus mechanisms are Proof of Work (PoW) and Proof of Stake (PoS), which work to deter malicious activities and achieve distributed consensus.

Consider a scenario where an attacker attempts to insert a fraudulent transaction into block 2. This would alter block 2's hash, breaking the linkage with block 3 since block 3 contains the original hash of block 2. The adversary would then need to re-mine (recalculate the hash for) block 2 and all subsequent blocks to restore the validity of the blockchain. Given the computational power required for this task—especially in large blockchains—such an attack is practically unfeasible, thereby ensuring the blockchain's robustness.

Furthermore, the blockchain employs cryptographic principles to link and secure the blocks. Each block header contains, among other fields, the Merkle root—a hash of all the transactions in the block. The Merkle tree structure allows efficient and secure verification of the transactions. Any change in a single transaction would alter the Merkle root, which in turn would change the block's hash, thus disrupting the continuity of the blockchain.

Merkle trees enable a compact and efficient way to verify the integrity and consistency of transactions within a block. They allow for quick verification of the data integrity by storing hashes of the transactions in a manner that a single hash alteration impacts the parent hashes, and ultimately, the Merkle root. This hierarchical hashing provides a mechanism to efficiently ascertain the integrity of large sets of data.

Understanding how blocks are linked in a blockchain is fundamental to appreciating the inherent security and immutability of the technology. The cryptographic linking of blocks through hash functions, combined with consensus mechanisms and Merkle trees, forms the backbone of blockchain's architecture, maintaining an unalterable ledger of transactions in a decentralized manner.

2.4 Decentralization and Consensus Mechanisms

Decentralization and consensus mechanisms are fundamental concepts underpinning the architecture and functionality of blockchain technology. The decentralization paradigm shifts control from a single centralized entity to a distributed network of nodes, enhancing security, transparency, and trust within the system. Consensus mechanisms are protocols that enable distributed nodes in a blockchain network to agree on the state of the ledger and ensure that all copies are synchronized correctly.

Decentralization

Decentralization in blockchain technology refers to the distribution of both data and control across multiple nodes in a network. Unlike traditional centralized systems where a single point of control exists, blockchain networks distribute the authority to manage and validate transactions to all participants. This decentralization has several implications:

- **Enhanced Security**: Decentralization diminishes the risk of a single point of failure. Since the data is not kept in just one location, it reduces vulnerability to hacking, fraud, or accidental loss.
- **Transparency**: All participants in the network have access to the same data. Transactions recorded on the blockchain are visible to all nodes, making the system inherently transparent and reducing the possibility of data manipulation.
- **Trustlessness**: In decentralized systems, trust is achieved not through relying on a central authority but through cryptographic

proofs and consensus protocols. Participants do not need to trust each other but can trust the system as a whole.

To understand decentralization, consider the following simplified code snippet indicating a peer-to-peer communication model:

```
class Node:
    def __init__(self, node_id, peers):
        self.id = node_id
        self.peers = peers
        self.ledger = []

    def broadcast_transaction(self, transaction):
        for peer in self.peers:
            peer.receive_transaction(transaction)

    def receive_transaction(self, transaction):
        self.ledger.append(transaction)
        print(f'Node {self.id} received transaction: {transaction}')

# Initialization and transaction broadcasting
node_A = Node(node_id='A', peers=[])
node_B = Node(node_id='B', peers=[node_A])
node_C = Node(node_id='C', peers=[node_A, node_B])

node_C.broadcast_transaction('Tx1')
```

The code illustrates nodes within a decentralized network broadcasting transactions to their peers. In this model, if a single node fails, the network remains operational since other nodes maintain the data.

Consensus Mechanisms

Consensus mechanisms form the crux of how decentralized blockchain networks make collective decisions. They ensure that all nodes agree on the current state of the blockchain, thereby maintaining the integrity and security of the system. Two of the most prominent consensus mechanisms are Proof of Work (PoW) and Proof of Stake (PoS).

Proof of Work (PoW)

Proof of Work is a consensus algorithm originally used in Bitcoin. It requires participants (miners) to solve complex cryptographic puzzles to validate transactions and create new blocks. The primary principles of PoW include:

- **Difficulty and Puzzles**: The puzzles must be challenging enough to ensure that finding solutions is computationally intensive and time-consuming.
- **Energy Consumption**: Due to the computational power required,

PoW consumes significant energy, raising concerns about environmental impact.

- **Security**: PoW is secure because altering a block would require redoing the proof of work for that block and all subsequent blocks, which is computationally impractical for large networks.

The process for PoW is typically depicted in the following algorithmic structure:

Algorithm 2 Proof of Work Algorithm

```
Input: Block data, target difficulty
Output: Valid block with nonce
Initialize nonce to 0
while true do
    hash ← SHA-256(block_data, nonce)
    if hash < target_difficulty then
        return block_data, nonce
    else
        Increment nonce
    end if
end while
```

This algorithm iterates over nonce values until the hash satisfies the target difficulty, thereby validating the block.

Proof of Stake (PoS)

Proof of Stake is an alternative consensus mechanism that reduces the energy consumption associated with PoW. In PoS, validators are chosen to create new blocks based on the number of coins they hold and are willing to "stake" as collateral. Key points include:

- **Deterministic Selection**: Validators are chosen based on their stake and other factors such as coin age or randomization, making the process more efficient.
- **Reduced Energy Usage**: Unlike PoW, PoS does not require solving complex puzzles, thereby significantly reducing energy consumption.
- **Security and Penalties**: Validators are incentivized to act honestly, as malicious behavior can lead to the loss of their staked coins.

The selection process in PoS can be represented using the pseudocode below:

```
def select_validator(validators):
    total_stake = sum(validator.stake for validator in validators)
    pick = random.uniform(0, total_stake)
    current = 0
    for validator in validators:
        current += validator.stake
        if current > pick:
            return validator
```

This function selects a validator based on the proportion of their stake relative to the total stake in the network, ensuring fairness in the selection process.

Decentralization and consensus mechanisms collectively establish the foundation for blockchain technology, ensuring that it remains secure, transparent, and trustless. Through consensus, decentralized networks maintain coherency and integrity, allowing blockchain to function as a reliable and robust distributed ledger system.

2.5 Proof of Work vs. Proof of Stake

Bitcoin's consensus mechanism, the method by which the network confirms and validates transactions, is one of the most critical aspects of its blockchain technology. Two primary consensus mechanisms dominate the blockchain landscape: Proof of Work (PoW) and Proof of Stake (PoS). Understanding these mechanisms is pivotal for comprehending how blockchain networks function and maintain integrity.

Proof of Work (PoW) was the original consensus algorithm in blockchain technology, famously employed by Bitcoin. PoW requires network participants, known as miners, to solve complex mathematical problems to add a new block to the blockchain. The difficulty of these mathematical puzzles is dynamically adjusted to ensure the steady production of blocks, typically averaging one block every ten minutes for Bitcoin. The mathematical problem that miners must solve is essentially finding a nonce (an arbitrary number used once) that, when hashed with the block's data, produces a hash output with a specific number of leading zeros.

```
def proof_of_work(block, target_difficulty):
    block_nonce = 0
    while True:
        hash_result = sha256(str(block) + str(block_nonce))
        if hash_result < target_difficulty:
```

```
            return block_nonce
        block_nonce += 1
```

In the pseudocode above, the proof_of_work function attempts various nonces until the hash result meets the difficulty criteria. The computational effort required to perform this task ensures that altering any block would require redoing the work for that block, making it computationally impractical to alter the blockchain.

One significant critique of PoW is its energy consumption. The need for constant computational effort translates to high electricity usage, raising environmental and economic concerns. Bitcoin's entire network, for example, has been estimated to consume more electricity than some countries. This intrinsic energy demand is a barrier to scalability and sustainability.

Proof of Stake (PoS) offers a contrasting approach to reaching consensus in a blockchain network. Instead of relying on computational power to validate transactions and secure the network, PoS requires validators to hold and lock up a certain amount of cryptocurrency as a stake. In this mechanism, the probability of being chosen to validate a block or confirm transactions and receive rewards is proportional to the amount of cryptocurrency held.

```
def proof_of_stake(validators, total_stake):
    total_weight = sum(validator.stake for validator in validators)
    selection = random.uniform(0, total_weight)
    running_total = 0
    for validator in validators:
        running_total += validator.stake
        if running_total >= selection:
            return validator
```

In the pseudocode above, the proof_of_stake function selects a validator based on the proportion of their stake relative to the total stake. Validators are chosen to forge or validate the next block based on their stakes, which aligns their incentives directly with the health and success of the network.

PoS has several advantages over PoW. Firstly, it significantly reduces energy consumption since it does not require extensive computational work to validate transactions. This makes PoS a more eco-friendly and sustainable option. Secondly, PoS encourages token holders to maintain their stake, thus reducing the liquidity of the token and potentially stabilizing its value. Thirdly, it improves the scalability of the network, allowing for a higher transaction throughput.

However, PoS is not without challenges. One major concern is the so-called "Nothing at Stake" problem, where validators might validate multiple competing chains because there is little cost to do so. To address this, many PoS systems impose penalties and design mechanisms to ensure validators are economically penalized for acting against the interests of network consensus. Another critique is the risk of centralization, where a small number of validators with large stakes could dominate the network.

Hybrid approaches and variations of PoS, such as Delegated Proof of Stake (DPoS) and other models, have been developed to balance the trade-offs between security, decentralization, and efficiency, continually refining blockchain's consensus mechanisms to better suit diverse applications and networks.

```
Output of PoS Validator Selection Simulation:
Validator ID: 4, Stake: 500 selected.
Validator ID: 2, Stake: 300 selected.
Validator ID: 1, Stake: 150 selected.
```

Both PoW and PoS provide unique advantages and challenges. PoW's energy-intensive nature ensures high security and immutability, while PoS offers more scalability and environmental sustainability. Understanding these mechanisms exposes the intrinsic and extrinsic incentives shaped by the design of blockchain networks and their impact on the broader framework of digital currency and decentralized finance.

2.6 Blockchain Networks: Public, Private, and Consortium

Blockchain networks can be broadly classified into three categories: public, private, and consortium. Each type of blockchain network offers specific advantages and disadvantages, depending on the use case, required level of decentralization, privacy, and trust among participants.

Public blockchains are open and fully decentralized networks. Anyone can join the network, participate in the consensus process, and perform transactions. A well-known example of a public blockchain is Bitcoin. Public blockchains are characterized by their transparency and security, as transactions and data are visible to all participants. The consensus mechanisms, such as Proof of Work (PoW) and Proof of Stake (PoS), ensure that no single entity can control the network, thereby making it more resistant to attacks. However, the openness and transparency of public blockchains can lead to scalability issues and slower transaction times due to the extensive computational work required to achieve consensus.

Private blockchains, in contrast, operate in a closed environment where only selected participants are granted access. These blockchains are typically managed by a single organization or entity, which means the level of centralization is higher compared to public blockchains. Access controls and permissions are strictly enforced, ensuring that only authorized participants can validate transactions and access the ledger. Private blockchains are often used in enterprise settings where privacy and speed are paramount. They offer higher transaction speeds and efficiency due to the reduced number of participants and the lack of need for extensive consensus mechanisms. Despite these advantages, private blockchains can lack transparency and are more vulnerable to insider threats, given the centralized control.

Consortium blockchains, or federated blockchains, represent a hybrid approach combining elements of both public and private blockchains. In these networks, the consensus process is controlled by a pre-selected group of nodes, often representing multiple organizations. This structure aims to combine the decentralized nature of public blockchains with the privacy and efficiency of private blockchains. Consortium blockchains are particularly useful in scenarios where multiple organizations need to collaborate and share data but do not necessarily trust each other. A prime example is supply chain management, where different entities benefit from the shared control of the ledger. The consensus mechanisms in consortium blockchains can vary but are generally designed to be efficient and secure, leveraging different approaches to validate transactions without the extensive computational effort required in public blockchains.

To provide a deeper understanding of these blockchain network types, consider the following differentiating factors in more detail:

- **Network Participation:** Public blockchains allow anyone to participate, while private blockchains restrict access based on permissions set by the managing entity. Consortium blockchains grant access to nodes pre-selected by participating organizations.

- **Consensus Mechanisms:** Public blockchains typically use resource-intensive consensus mechanisms like PoW and PoS, which involve solving complex cryptographic puzzles or holding a stake in the network. These mechanisms ensure high security but can result in slower transaction processing.

Private blockchains, due to their controlled nature, often use more lightweight consensus protocols, such as Raft or Practical Byzantine Fault Tolerance (PBFT), which provide faster transaction times and lower overhead. Consortium blockchains may use varieties of consensus mechanisms tailored to balance security, efficiency, and the trust levels agreed upon by the member organizations.

- **Transparency and Privacy:** In public blockchains, all transactions and data are visible to every participant, thus providing the highest level of transparency. Private blockchains offer minimal transparency, as the data is accessible only to authorized entities, ensuring a higher degree of privacy. Consortium blockchains strike a balance, with data being accessible to all authorized members but not to the general public, thus providing controlled transparency and privacy.

- **Performance and Scalability:** Public blockchains often face challenges with scalability and performance due to the need for extensive consensus processes and the large number of participants. Private blockchains can achieve higher performance levels and better scalability as they manage fewer and more controlled access points. Consortium blockchains can also offer good scalability and performance by limiting the number of block-signing nodes while still providing decentralized control.

Finally, it is crucial to understand the application domain when choosing the type of blockchain network. Public blockchains are ideal for cryptocurrencies, applications requiring high decentralization, and open-source projects. Private blockchains suit corporate applications where control over access and data privacy is crucial. Consortium blockchains are advantageous in inter-organizational cooperation scenarios, such as financial transactions involving multiple banks, joint ventures creating shared platforms, and industry collaborations.

Each blockchain type serves distinct purposes, and selecting the appropriate one hinges on balancing decentralization, privacy, efficiency, and trust requirements for the specific application or industry need.

2.7 Nodes and Mining in Blockchain

In the blockchain ecosystem, nodes are fundamental components that facilitate the operation of the network. A node in blockchain terminology is any device that maintains a copy of the blockchain and participates in the network's validation and consensus process. Nodes can vary in their roles and functions, and understanding these distinctions is crucial for comprehending how blockchain networks achieve distributed consensus and maintain immutability.

- **Full Nodes:** A full node is a device that hosts a complete copy of the blockchain. Full nodes validate all transactions and blocks against predefined consensus rules, ensuring the integrity and security of the blockchain. They download and store the entirety of blockchain data, which can be a considerable amount of storage, especially for well-established blockchains like Bitcoin. Full nodes play a critical role in maintaining the decentralized nature of the network by independently verifying the authenticity of each transaction and block.

- **Lightweight Nodes:** Also known as Simplified Payment Verification (SPV) nodes, lightweight nodes do not store a complete copy of the blockchain. Instead, they only download block headers and rely on full nodes for transaction validation and querying. Lightweight nodes offer a balance between resource efficiency and network participation, allowing devices with limited storage and computational power, such as mobile devices, to engage with the blockchain.

- **Mining Nodes:** Mining nodes, also known as miners, are specialized full nodes that participate in the process of block creation. Mining involves solving complex cryptographic puzzles to propose new blocks to the blockchain. The process of mining is synonymous with the consensus mechanism of Proof of Work (PoW) and, to a lesser extent, Proof of Stake (PoS) when it involves validation tasks. Mining nodes expend computational resources to compete for the opportunity to add the next block to the blockchain. The successful miner is rewarded with cryptocurrency incentives, known as block rewards, and transaction fees.

```
# A simplified example of a mining algorithm in Python for educational purposes

import hashlib
```

```
import time

max_nonce = 2**32 # 4 billion
target = 2**240 # Arbitrary target for demonstration purposes

def proof_of_work(block, target):
    for nonce in range(max_nonce):
        hash_result = hashlib.sha256(f"{block}{nonce}".encode()).hexdigest()
        if int(hash_result, 16) < target:
            return hash_result, nonce
    return None

block = "block data"
start_time = time.time()
hash_result, nonce = proof_of_work(block, target)
end_time = time.time()

print(f"Block mined: {hash_result} with nonce: {nonce} in {end_time - start_time}
    seconds")
```

The above Python script demonstrates a simplified proof-of-work algorithm. In a real-world scenario, the mining process involves far more complexity, including the incorporation of previous block references (hashes), Merkle roots, and network difficulty adjustment mechanisms.

- **Mining Pools:** Due to the computational intensity and variance in reward distribution, individual miners often combine resources into mining pools. A mining pool is a collective of miners who share their computational power to increase the probability of solving the cryptographic puzzle and earning the block reward. Mining pools then distribute the reward proportionally, based on the work contributed by each miner.

The role of mining in blockchain encompasses both the validation and the immutability of the blockchain data. Mining ensures that new transactions are added in a manner that is compliant with the protocol rules and provides economic incentives for participants to engage in the network honestly. Moreover, the mining process establishes a temporal sequence of transactions, securing the blockchain from potential tampering or double-spending attacks.

- **Node Communication:** For the blockchain to function as a decentralized network, nodes must communicate. This communication happens through peer-to-peer (P2P) protocols, where nodes share data such as block information, transaction data, and network status updates. Nodes utilize various algorithms to enhance data propagation efficiency and reduce network latency, ensuring the swift dissemination of critical information across the network.

```
Output:
Block mined: 000000000000000000004b4b4bccaf3e9078a12d91f90202e1c3cae9b48a5b4bb with nonce: 123456 in 0.67 seconds
```

Overall, the diverse types of nodes, from full nodes to mining nodes, constitute a robust and interconnected framework that supports blockchain technology. Each node type has specific responsibilities and capabilities, contributing collectively to the stability, security, and decentralization of the blockchain network. Nodes and mining activities are integral to the blockchain's operation, promoting trustless validation and consensus across distributed ledger systems.

2.8 Smart Contracts: The Basics

Smart contracts are self-executing contracts with the terms of the agreement directly written into lines of code. These contracts automatically enforce and execute the contractual clauses when pre-defined conditions are met, thereby facilitating, verifying, or enforcing the negotiation or performance of a contract without the need for a trusted third party.

Smart contracts were first proposed by Nick Szabo in 1994, who described them as a set of promises, specified in digital form, including protocols within which the parties perform on these promises. However, the idea gained significant traction with the advent of blockchain technology, most notably through the Ethereum blockchain, which provides a decentralized platform for running smart contracts.

```
pragma solidity ^0.8.0;

contract SimpleContract {
    uint public value;

    function setValue(uint _value) public {
        value = _value;
    }

    function getValue() public view returns (uint) {
        return value;
    }
}
```

Smart contracts are stored on a blockchain and are immutable, ensuring that once deployed, the code cannot be altered. They feature deterministic behavior, meaning given the same inputs, a smart contract will always produce the same outputs. This ensures reliability and trustworthiness in contract execution.

- **Deterministic Execution**: A smart contract's code deterministically ensures the precise execution of contract terms and conditions as programmed, without any deviations.

- **Immutability**: Once deployed on the blockchain, the smart contract's code is immutable. This guarantees that the contract's terms cannot be tampered with, providing a high degree of security.
- **Transparency**: Smart contracts provide transparency to all parties involved. Any participant can verify the contract's logic and its execution, ensuring accountability and trust.
- **Automation**: Smart contracts automatically execute the terms of the contract based on predefined rules, eliminating the need for manual intervention. This can significantly reduce administrative costs and decrease the time required to enforce contracts.
- **Security**: By residing on the blockchain, smart contracts inherit the security features of the underlying blockchain technology. They use cryptographic principles to ensure that transactions are secure and that the contract's integrity is maintained.
- **Efficiency**: Automation of contract enforcement reduces the need for intermediaries, such as lawyers or escrow agents, streamlining processes and reducing associated expenses.
- **Reduced Chances of Fraud and Error**: The deterministic nature and immutability of smart contracts make them resistant to fraud and errors. This leads to more reliable and error-free contract execution.
- **Trustless Computation**: Parties to a smart contract do not need to trust each other, but can rely on the underlying technology to ensure the contract terms are fulfilled. This is particularly beneficial in trustless environments.
- **Financial Transactions**: Smart contracts are extensively used for financial transactions. They facilitate decentralized finance (DeFi) applications such as lending, borrowing, trading, and insurance without intermediaries.
- **Supply Chain Management**: Smart contracts can automate and enforce the terms of agreements between suppliers and buyers, providing transparency and streamlining logistics operations.

- **Digital Identity**: Smart contracts enable the creation of digital identities that are secure, verifiable, and self-sovereign, allowing individuals to control their own identity data without relying on centralized authorities.

- **Tokenization**: Through smart contracts, real-world assets can be tokenized, allowing fractional ownership and easy transferability on the blockchain. This includes tangible assets like real estate and intangible assets like intellectual property.

```
pragma solidity ^0.8.0;

import "@openzeppelin/contracts/token/ERC20/ERC20.sol";

contract RealEstateToken is ERC20 {
    constructor(uint256 initialSupply) ERC20("RealEstateToken", "RET") {
        _mint(msg.sender, initialSupply);
    }
}
```

- **Complexity**: Writing and understanding smart contracts can be complex, requiring specialized knowledge in programming and blockchain technology. Errors or bugs in the code can lead to unintended consequences.

- **Legal Status**: The legal status of smart contracts is still evolving. While they can execute code, their enforceability in traditional legal systems may be uncertain, which can impact their utility in binding legal agreements.

- **Scalability**: Blockchain networks face scalability challenges, and since smart contracts operate on these networks, they can suffer from latency and high transaction costs, especially during peak usage times.

- **Security Risks**: While smart contracts are secure, they are not immune to vulnerabilities. Code vulnerabilities can be exploited, leading to significant losses, as seen in events like The DAO hack in 2016.

Smart contracts represent a powerful evolution in contract negotiation and enforcement, leveraging blockchain technology to create secure, efficient, and transparent contractual agreements. However, it is important to address their limitations and continue developing robust frameworks to maximize their potential.

2.9 Applications of Blockchain Beyond Bitcoin

Blockchain technology, while initially developed as the foundation for the cryptocurrency Bitcoin, possesses numerous applications beyond digital currency. These applications leverage the fundamental properties of blockchain, such as decentralization, immutability, and transparency. In this section, we explore various sectors where blockchain has been effectively applied, yielding innovative solutions and efficiencies.

- **1. Supply Chain Management**

  Supply chain management benefits significantly from blockchain technology. By recording every transaction on a transparent ledger, blockchain enhances the traceability of products from the origin to the end consumer. Each stakeholder in the supply chain network can securely update the status of the goods, thereby reducing fraud and errors. This system ensures that all participants have access to real-time data, assisting in verifying the authenticity and provenance of products. For instance, IBM's Food Trust blockchain platform enables retailers and consumers to trace the journey of food products, ensuring quality and reducing contamination risks.

- **2. Healthcare**

  Blockchain technology addresses many challenges in the healthcare industry, including data integrity, security, and interoperability. By utilizing a blockchain-based system, healthcare providers can maintain accurate and up-to-date patient records, accessible only to authorized parties. This ensures patient privacy while enabling seamless data sharing among different healthcare entities.

  Blockchain can also be instrumental in pharmaceutical supply chains, where it helps to trace drugs from manufacturers to pharmacies, thereby combating counterfeit medications. A practical example is the MediLedger project, which employs blockchain to create a secure network for tracking pharmaceuticals.

- **3. Financial Services**

  Beyond cryptocurrencies, blockchain offers numerous applications in traditional financial services, promoting efficiency and reducing costs. Blockchain can streamline processes such as cross-border payments, clearing, and settlement, enhancing transaction speed and transparency. It also facilitates the creation and management of digital identities for anti-money laundering (AML) and know-your-customer (KYC) regulations.

Decentralized Finance (DeFi) platforms, built on blockchain, exemplify the disruption of traditional finance. These platforms offer services such as lending, borrowing, and trading without intermediaries. Smart contracts, self-executing contracts with predefined terms, further automate and secure these transactions.

- **4. Real Estate**

  Blockchain technology has transformative potential in the real estate sector by simplifying property transactions and enhancing transparency. The technology can facilitate secure and transparent record-keeping of property ownership, lease agreements, and land registrations. Smart contracts can automate the transfer of property ownership upon meeting predefined conditions, reducing the need for intermediaries, and thus cutting costs and reducing fraud.

  An example is Propy, a platform that uses blockchain to enable real estate transactions online. Propy's system ensures that all documents are securely stored on the blockchain, accessible to all parties involved in the transaction, thus streamlining the process.

- **5. Voting Systems**

  Blockchain offers a framework for creating secure, transparent, and tamper-proof voting systems. By recording votes on a decentralized ledger, the technology ensures that each vote is counted accurately and cannot be altered or deleted. This increases trust in electoral processes and reduces the risk of fraud.

  Countries and organizations are experimenting with blockchain-based voting systems to enhance democratic processes. For instance, the government of Sierra Leone conducted a blockchain-based pilot for its elections, which demonstrated the potential for secure and credible voting.

- **6. Intellectual Property and Royalties**

  Blockchain can be used to protect intellectual property (IP) rights and manage royalties efficiently. By timestamping creations on the blockchain, creators can establish proof of ownership, which can be leveraged in legal disputes. Additionally, blockchain can automate royalty payments through smart contracts.

The music industry has seen blockchain applications for ensuring artists receive fair payments when their music is streamed or downloaded. Services like Mycelia and MediaChain provide decentralized platforms for managing music rights and payments, ensuring transparency and fairness.

- **7. Government and Public Records**

  Blockchain has the potential to streamline government services and enhance the management of public records. By deploying blockchain-based systems, governments can maintain secure and immutable records for identity management, vehicle registrations, and property titles. These systems can reduce bureaucratic inefficiencies and improve public trust.

  The nation of Estonia has been a pioneer in this field, implementing blockchain technology in its e-residency program, enabling secure digital identities and efficient public service delivery.

- **8. Energy Sector**

  In the energy sector, blockchain can facilitate the creation of decentralized energy markets where consumers can trade energy directly with each other. This peer-to-peer model can increase the efficiency of energy distribution and reduce costs.

  ```
  Example: Power Ledger
  Power Ledger, an Australian company, uses blockchain to create a
  marketplace for renewable energy.
  Through its platform, users can buy and sell excess solar energy
   stored in battery units with
  their neighbors, promoting sustainable energy use.
  ```

- **9. Education**

  Blockchain technology can transform the education sector by providing a secure and transparent way to issue, verify, and share academic credentials and certificates. This system helps prevent fraud and simplifies the verification process for employers and other institutions.

  For instance, the Massachusetts Institute of Technology (MIT) has implemented a blockchain-based system for issuing digital diplomas, ensuring that the credentials are tamper-proof and easily verifiable by third parties.

- **10. Arts and Collectibles**

  Blockchain is revolutionizing the way artists and collectors buy, sell, and authenticate art and collectibles. Non-Fungible Tokens (NFTs) are unique digital assets stored on the blockchain that can represent ownership of digital or physical items. NFTs allow artists to tokenize their work, ensuring scarcity and enabling direct transactions with buyers.

  The platform OpenSea, for example, provides a marketplace for buying and selling NFTs, including art, music, and virtual items, ensuring that transactions are transparent and verifiable.

These diverse applications underscore blockchain technology's broad potential beyond its origins in cryptocurrency. By harnessing the inherent properties of blockchain, various industries can achieve greater efficiency, transparency, and security, driving innovation across multiple domains.

```
pragma solidity ^0.8.0;

contract RoyaltyContract {
    address public artist;
    uint public royaltyPercentage;

    constructor(address _artist, uint _royaltyPercentage) {
        artist = _artist;
        royaltyPercentage = _royaltyPercentage;
    }

    function payRoyalty() external payable {
        uint royalty = msg.value * royaltyPercentage / 100;
        payable(artist).transfer(royalty);
    }
}
```

2.10 Challenges and Limitations of Blockchain Technology

Despite the numerous advantages and transformative potential of blockchain technology, it is not without its challenges and limitations. Addressing these issues is critical for the widespread adoption and optimization of blockchain systems.

One of the foremost challenges facing blockchain technology is **scalability**. As the size of the blockchain grows, so does the computational complexity and the amount of storage required to maintain the full history of transactions. The Bitcoin blockchain, for instance, has grown significantly since its inception. This growth poses problems for both transaction throughput and data storage. The current transaction rate for Bitcoin is approximately seven transactions per second (TPS), which is vastly inferior compared to conventional payment systems such as Visa, which can process thousands of transactions per second.

Blockchain's **energy consumption** is another significant concern. Proof of Work (PoW) consensus, employed by many blockchains, requires miners to solve complex cryptographic puzzles, a process that is highly energy-intensive. The computational power necessary for these operations results in substantial electricity usage, contributing to environmental concerns. For example, the Bitcoin network's energy consumption has been compared to that of entire countries.

Latency is an associated issue, particularly within PoW-based blockchains. The process of solving cryptographic puzzles and confirming transactions is time-consuming, leading to delays in transaction finality. This can impact user experience, especially in applications requiring immediate confirmation.

```
const bitcoin = require('bitcoinjs-lib')
const network = bitcoin.networks.testnet

let keyPair = bitcoin.ECPair.makeRandom({ network: network })
let { address } = bitcoin.payments.p2pkh({ pubkey: keyPair.publicKey, network:
    network })
console.log("Bitcoin Address: " + address)
```

```
Bitcoin Address: n2eMqTT929pb1RDNuqEnxdaLau1rxy3efi
```

Another considerable challenge is **security**. While blockchain's immutable nature and cryptographic principles enhance security, they are not foolproof. Vulnerabilities can arise from poorly designed smart contracts, 51% attacks (where an entity controls the majority of mining power), and other exploits. Smart contracts, despite their potential, have been found susceptible to bugs and exploits, sometimes leading to significant financial losses.

Interoperability between different blockchain networks presents another formidable challenge. Each blockchain operates independently with its own protocols, making cross-chain communication difficult. The lack of standardized protocols hampers the integration of blockchain networks, impeding the broader adoption of the technology.

Privacy concerns also arise, especially in public blockchains. While blockchain transactions do not directly link to personal identities, the transaction history is transparent and traceable. Advanced methods such as blockchain analytics can potentially de-anonymize users, creating privacy risks. Although privacy-centric blockchains like Monero and Zcash address these issues to some extent, they also face scrutiny from regulatory bodies.

Regulatory and legal hurdles form part of the broader challenges. The decentralized nature of blockchain systems often clashes with existing regulatory frameworks that emphasize centralized oversight and control. Cryptocurrency regulations vary significantly across jurisdictions, creating uncertainty and complexity for blockchain projects. Legal recognition of blockchain records and smart contracts remains inconsistent, further complicating matters.

Furthermore, there are **governance issues**. Decentralization, while a strength, can also lead to conflicts regarding protocol upgrades, scaling solutions, and other crucial decisions. The infamous Bitcoin and Bitcoin Cash hard fork is a prime example, where disagreements within the community led to the creation of a separate blockchain.

Adoption barriers exist due to the lack of general understanding of the technology. The steep learning curve, technical intricacies, and the relative novelty of blockchain create resistance among potential adopters. User-friendly interfaces and educational resources are critical for overcoming these barriers.

Lastly, **development ecosystem** maturity is another concern. Although development tools and platforms for blockchain technology have advanced, they still lag behind more established software ecosystems. Improved development frameworks, robust testing tools, and better documentation are essential to support developers in creating reliable blockchain applications.

These challenges highlight the need for ongoing research, innovation, and cooperation among stakeholders to address the limitations and fully realize the potential of blockchain technology.

Chapter 3

Bitcoin Mining

Bitcoin mining is the process of validating and adding new transactions to the Bitcoin blockchain through complex cryptographic computations. Miners use specialized hardware to solve mathematical puzzles, ensuring network security and consensus. Successful miners are rewarded with newly minted bitcoins and transaction fees. This chapter explains the mining process, hardware involved, economic incentives, and challenges, including mining difficulty, environmental impact, and the future outlook for Bitcoin mining.

3.1 What is Bitcoin Mining?

Bitcoin mining is a foundational process within the Bitcoin network that involves contributing computational power to solve intricate cryptographic puzzles. These puzzles are essential for validating and securing transactions on the blockchain, the decentralized ledger that underpins Bitcoin. Through this validation process, miners enable the addition of new blocks to the blockchain, a critical mechanism for maintaining the integrity and continuity of the network.

At its core, Bitcoin mining serves two main purposes: securing the network and minting new bitcoins. The process is based on a consensus algorithm known as Proof of Work (PoW), where miners compete to solve a cryptographic challenge. The first miner to solve the challenge gets the right to add a new block of transactions to the blockchain. This miner is subsequently rewarded with newly generated bitcoins along with any transaction fees associated with the transactions included in the block. This symbiotic relationship between providing security and gaining rewards makes mining a self-sustained and incentivized activity.

Miners employ specialized hardware to perform these computations. This hardware is specifically designed to compute the hash function SHA-256 used in Bitcoin mining. The hash function takes an input and produces a fixed-size alphanumeric string. The uniqueness of SHA-256 is its predictability and collision resistance, making it near impossible to reverse-engineer the input from the output, or to find two distinct inputs that produce the same output hash.

The mining process begins with gathering a set of unconfirmed transactions from the memory pool (mempool). These transactions are then organized into a candidate block, which also includes a reference to the previous block header, the hash of the current candidate block, a nonce (a 32-bit arbitrary number miners vary to change the hash output), and other metadata. The objective for miners is to adjust the nonce such that the resulting hash of the block header is less than a specified target, known as the difficulty target. The target is adjusted periodically, approximately every two weeks, to ensure that blocks are mined at a consistent rate, roughly every ten minutes.

The cryptographic puzzle can be mathematically represented as finding a nonce n such that:

$$\text{SHA-256}(\text{SHA-256}(\text{block\_header})) \leq \text{difficulty\_target}$$

This extensive trial-and-error method consumes substantial computational power and energy. The difficulty level is dynamically adjusted by the Bitcoin protocol based on the network's total computational power, or hash rate, ensuring blocks continue to be mined at regular intervals despite increases or decreases in mining activity.

The addition of a mined block to the blockchain follows a verification process by the entire network. Nodes on the Bitcoin network validate the new block and its transactions based on predefined consensus rules. Upon validation, the block is appended to the longest chain of blocks that represents the canonical Bitcoin blockchain. The miner who successfully mined the block is rewarded, and the process restarts with miners attempting to solve the next puzzle for the subsequent block.

Bitcoin mining thus serves as the backbone of the Bitcoin network, facilitating transaction validation and security. The mechanisms of mining ensure decentralization, as no single entity can control the entire process. Instead, it leverages distributed consensus to uphold the integrity and trust in the Bitcoin cryptosystem.

3.2 The Mining Process Explained

Bitcoin mining is the act of adding new transactions to the Bitcoin blockchain by compiling them into blocks. This intricate task involves various computational steps, each playing a critical role in maintaining the decentralized and secure nature of the Bitcoin network. The mining process can be elucidated by breaking it down into the following essential components: transaction collection, block construction, proof of work, block validation, and network propagation.

First, miners begin by gathering unconfirmed transactions from the Bitcoin network's mempool, a database of all pending transactions. When a user initiates a transaction, it is broadcasted to the network and lands in this pool. Miners select a set of transactions from the mempool, often prioritizing those with higher transaction fees attached, since fees are part of their compensation.

Once a miner has a set of transactions, they proceed to construct a new block. Each block has a specific format consisting of a block header and the list of transactions. The block header contains crucial metadata such as the version number, the previous block's hash, the Merkle root, timestamp, difficulty target, and a nonce.

The Merkle root is a cryptographic summary of all transactions in the block. It is generated by hashing each transaction, then hashing pairs of transaction hashes together, recursively, until a single hash remains, known as the Merkle root. This structure efficiently validates the integrity and order of transactions within the block.

The core of the mining process involves solving the proof of work problem. Proof of work is a computational puzzle that miners must solve to add their block to the blockchain. This puzzle revolves around finding a nonce that, when combined with the block header and hashed using the SHA-256 algorithm, produces a hash value below a certain target difficulty. This target difficulty is adjusted approximately every 2016 blocks to ensure a new block is mined roughly every ten minutes, regardless of the total network hash rate.

```
block_header = previous_block_hash + Merkle_root + timestamp + difficulty_target
nonce = 0

while sha256(block_header + nonce) >= target_difficulty:
    nonce += 1

return nonce
```

The ‘nonce‘ is a variable that miners adjust to find a valid hash. Because SHA-256 produces a pseudorandom output, miners must perform numerous hash operations to find a sufficient solution, which demands substantial computational power.

Upon finding a valid nonce, the miner broadcasts the newly mined block to the network. Other nodes receive this block and validate it by checking the proof of work and ensuring all transactions within the block are legitimate and adhere to the protocol rules, such as correct signatures and double-spending prevention. Once validated, the new block is appended to the blockchain, making the included transactions officially confirmed.

Network propagation is the final step, wherein the validated block spreads to the entire network. This is crucial for maintaining consistency across the distributed ledger, as every node updates its local copy to reflect the latest block. If multiple blocks are found around the same time, a temporary fork occurs, and nodes may have different perspectives on the latest block. However, the blockchain protocol resolves such forks by eventually selecting the longest valid chain; this often results when subsequent blocks make one of the chains demonstrably longer.

The successful miner earns a dual incentive: a block reward, which includes newly minted bitcoins, and the aggregate of transaction fees from the included transactions. This reward mechanism incentivizes the contribution of computational resources, ensuring the network’s security and robustness against adversarial attacks.

Mining demands persistent updates and adaptations due to the rising difficulty level and technological advancements in mining hardware. Therefore, understanding the fundamental steps in the mining process reinforces the comprehension of Bitcoin’s security and operational dynamics.

3.3 Mining Hardware: ASICs and GPUs

Bitcoin mining hardware has evolved significantly since the inception of the cryptocurrency, transitioning through several phases marked by increasing computational power and energy efficiency. Early miners employed central processing units (CPUs), but the rapid escalation in mining difficulty necessitated a shift to more powerful technologies. Key among these advancements have been Graphics Processing Units (GPUs) and Application-Specific Integrated Circuits (ASICs), each with distinct characteristics, advantages, and limitations.

GPUs were the first major leap after CPUs in the evolution of Bitcoin mining hardware. Designed initially for rendering video graphics, GPUs are well-suited for the parallel processing needs of mining. The architecture of a GPU allows it to handle multiple operations simultaneously, making it more efficient at solving the complex mathematical problems required in Bitcoin's proof-of-work (PoW) algorithm.

```
from hashlib import sha256

def mine(block_number, transactions, previous_hash, nonce_start=0, difficulty=2):
    prefix_str = '0' * difficulty
    for nonce in range(nonce_start, int(1e9)):
        text = str(block_number) + transactions + previous_hash + str(nonce)
        hash_result = sha256(text.encode('utf-8')).hexdigest()
        if hash_result.startswith(prefix_str):
            return hash_result, nonce
    return None, None
```

While GPUs offered a significant improvement over CPUs, their general-purpose nature means they are not as optimized for Bitcoin mining as ASICs. ASICs represent the current state of the art in Bitcoin mining hardware. ASICs are custom-built chips designed specifically for performing the SHA-256 hashing operations used in Bitcoin's PoW.

The advantage of ASICs over GPUs and CPUs lies in their specialized design. An ASIC is tailored to execute a particular hashing function with maximum efficiency, reducing the energy consumption per hash significantly compared to GPUs. This specificity ensures that ASICs can achieve much higher hash rates — the number of hashes computed per second — while maintaining lower power usage. As a result, ASIC miners have become predominant in the Bitcoin mining ecosystem due to their superior performance and cost-efficiency.

The progression from GPUs to ASICs can be observed through several generations of ASIC hardware, each marked by incremental improvements in performance. For example, early ASIC miners like the Bitmain Antminer S1 could achieve hash rates of 180 GH/s while consuming 360 watts of power. In contrast, newer models like the Antminer S19 Pro can achieve hash rates of up to 110 TH/s with a power consumption of 3250 watts.

Model	Hash Rate	Power Consumption
Antminer S1	180 GH/s	360 Watts
Antminer S19 Pro	110 TH/s	3250 Watts

Table 3.1: Comparison of ASIC miners

Despite their advantages, ASICs are not without drawbacks. One significant issue is their lack of versatility; ASICs designed for Bitcoin mining cannot be repurposed for other computational tasks, rendering them obsolete if they fail to remain profitable or if the Bitcoin protocol changes. Moreover, the high initial cost of ASIC hardware can be a barrier to entry for new miners. The rapid pace of technological advancement in ASIC development also means that hardware can become outdated relatively quickly, compelling miners to continually invest in new equipment to remain competitive.

Another critical aspect of the ASIC versus GPU debate involves decentralization. The advent of ASICs has led to increased centralization within the Bitcoin network. ASIC miners, often consolidated in large-scale mining farms, can amass substantial hash power, potentially leading to dominance by a few large entities. This centralization poses risks to the security and decentralization principles foundational to Bitcoin.

To counteract these concerns, some alternate cryptocurrencies have adopted different proof-of-work algorithms designed to be ASIC-resistant, maintaining a more level playing field for GPU miners. However, for Bitcoin itself, the shift towards ASICs appears to be a permanent trajectory, driven by the unrelenting quest for efficiency and higher hash rates.

Understanding the characteristics and trade-offs of GPU and ASIC mining hardware is essential for anyone involved in Bitcoin mining. Investing in the right equipment, managing costs, and staying abreast of technological advancements are crucial components of maintaining profitability and contributing to the network's security.

3.4 Proof of Work: How it Secures the Network

Proof of Work (PoW) is a consensus algorithm fundamental to Bitcoin's security and integrity. PoW requires participants, referred to as miners, to solve complex mathematical puzzles to validate transactions and add them to the blockchain. This mechanism prevents malicious actors from easily manipulating the blockchain, ensuring a decentralized and trustless system.

At the core of PoW, the primary objective is to find a nonce, a value that, when hashed with specific transaction data, results in a hash that meets predefined criteria. These criteria involve the hash value beginning with a certain number of leading zeros. The relationship between the hash function and this criterion can be formalized as follows:

$$\text{SHA-256}(\text{Block Header} + \text{Nonce}) < \text{Target}$$

where SHA-256 represents the cryptographic hash function used by Bitcoin, and Target denotes the difficulty level.

The difficulty is dynamically adjusted approximately every two weeks (or every 2016 blocks) to ensure that the average time between block generations remains around 10 minutes. This adjustment is essential due to the changing hash rate, which is the cumulative computational power of the Bitcoin network.

```
import hashlib

def proof_of_work(header, difficulty_bits):
    target = 2 ** (256 - difficulty_bits)
    nonce = 0
    while True:
        hash_result = hashlib.sha256(str(header) + str(nonce)).hexdigest()
        if int(hash_result, 16) < target:
            return nonce, hash_result
        nonce += 1
```

In the above simplified Python code, the 'proof_of_work' function continually hashes the block header concatenated with a nonce until it finds a hash result that is lower than the target, which is derived from the difficulty level.

The requirement for compute-intensive puzzles ensures that legitimate miners expend significant computational resources. This expenditure, colloquially known as "work," secures the network by making it financially costly and time-consuming for any adversary to alter past blocks. Each block in the blockchain is linked to the previous one through its hash, creating an immutable sequence. Altering any block would necessitate recalculating the hash for that block and all subsequent blocks, a task that would require an infeasible amount of computational power.

$$\text{Block Hash} = \text{SHA-256}(\text{Previous Block Hash} + \text{Merkle Root} + \text{Timestamp} + \text{Nonce})$$

In the above formulation, each component (previous block hash, Merkle root, timestamp, and nonce) contributes to the overall security and integrity of the blockchain. The Merkle root represents a condensed cryptographic summary of all transactions within the block, ensuring that transaction data cannot be tampered with without affecting the block hash.

An illustrative output of a successful hash generation attempt might look like this:

```
Header: 0000000000000000000c6f8000e8e000000000000000000000000000000000000
Nonce: 2083236893
Hash: 0000000000000000000d4e800a907d000000000000000000000000000000000000
```

Here, the resulting hash begins with the leading zeros required by the difficulty target, and this information is appended to the blockchain.

The PoW mechanism effectively makes tampering infeasible by requiring considerable brute-force effort and providing a concrete economic incentive for honest participation in the network's security. The block reward and transaction fees compensate miners for their investments in hardware and electricity, motivating them to continue supporting the network's operations.

Overall, Proof of Work is vital in maintaining Bitcoin's robustness against attacks, ensuring that the network remains decentralized and resistant to efforts aimed at compromising its ledger of transactions.

3.5 Mining Difficulty and Hash Rate

Bitcoin mining difficulty and hash rate are integral components that directly affect the efficiency and feasibility of the mining process. Understanding these concepts involves delving into the mechanisms that regulate the production of new blocks and ensure the stability and security of the Bitcoin network.

The **difficulty** of Bitcoin mining is a measure of how hard it is to find a hash below a given target. This target is a 256-bit number that the header hash of a new block must be less than or equal to for the block to be added to the blockchain. The Bitcoin network adjusts this difficulty approximately every two weeks (or every 2016 blocks) to maintain an average block creation time of 10 minutes, regardless of the total mining power of the network. This self-correcting mechanism ensures that blocks are added to the blockchain at a steady and predictable rate.

Mathematically, the difficulty can be expressed as:

$$\text{Difficulty} = \frac{\text{Difficulty\_target}}{\text{Current\_target}}$$

where *Difficulty_target* is a constant value (2^{224} - 1 for Bitcoin's genesis block) and *Current_target* is the current hash target. The initial difficulty was set to 1. As more miners join and the overall hash rate—the total computational power—of the network increases, the current target adjusts downward, making it harder to find a valid hash and thus increasing the difficulty.

The term **hash rate** (or hashing power) denotes the total number of hash operations that the network can perform per second. It is usually measured in hashes per second (H/s). Higher hash rates indicate more computational power and generally correlate with greater mining difficulty, as more miners compete to solve the cryptographic puzzles. A rise in hash rate typically follows an increase in miner activity or technological advancements in mining hardware.

```
# Example calculation of hash rate
# Consider a miner performing 1 trillion (10^12) hashes per second
hash_rate = 10**12 # hashes per second
print(f"Hash Rate: {hash_rate} H/s")
```

The interplay between hash rate and difficulty ensures the robustness of the Bitcoin network. When the hash rate increases significantly—due to data center expansions or advancements in ASIC technology—the network automatically adjusts the difficulty to uphold the 10-minute block interval. Conversely, a drop in hash rate due to miner exits triggers a decrease in the mining difficulty, making it feasible for the remaining miners to continue validating and adding new blocks.

The difficulty adjustment mechanism can be illustrated through the following pseudo-code:

The dynamic nature of difficulty and hash rate provides resilience against sudden influxes of mining hardware or potential attacks that

Algorithm 3 Difficulty Adjustment Algorithm

```
procedure AdjustDifficulty
    expectedTime ← 2016 × 10 minutes
    actualTime ← time taken to mine last 2016 blocks
    if actualTime < expectedTime then
        newDifficulty ← currentDifficulty × expectedTime / actualTime
    else
        newDifficulty ← currentDifficulty × expectedTime / actualTime
    end if
    Update Mining Target with newDifficulty
end procedure
```

aim to alter the blockchain's integrity. For example, if a malicious entity or a mining pool gains significant hash power temporarily (a scenario known as the "51% attack"), the difficulty adjustment would ensure that over time, the increased difficulty curbs the undue influence.

The balance maintained by the difficulty adjustment serves not only as a protective measure but also influences miners' economic decisions. When the network difficulty rises too high, it can render small-scale mining operations unprofitable, leading to an exit of less efficient miners and concentration of mining power in large-scale operations or pools.

In practical mining operations, miners consistently monitor the hash rate and track the network difficulty to optimize their mining strategies. With the advent of advanced ASICs (Application-Specific Integrated Circuits) and the potentially lower cost per hash, mining farms have considerably contributed to the increase in global hash rate, prompting corresponding adjustments in difficulty.

Environmental considerations are increasingly relevant as higher hash rates correspond to substantial energy consumption. Estimations of the electrical usage of large-scale mining operations spotlight the necessity for sustainable energy practices within the industry. Mining entities are thus incentivized to leverage renewable energy sources to mitigate ecological impact while maintaining profitable hash rates.

Finally, observing trends in hash rate and mining difficulty helps predict future changes in block production and overall network security. As the Bitcoin mining landscape evolves, so too does the equilibrium maintained by these intertwined factors.

```
# Example calculation for difficulty adjustment
expected_time = 2016 * 10 * 60 # expected time in seconds
actual_time = 2000 * 10 * 60 # actual time taken
current_difficulty = 15.0 # example current difficulty

if actual_time < expected_time:
    new_difficulty = current_difficulty * (expected_time / actual_time)
else:
    new_difficulty = current_difficulty * (expected_time / actual_time)

print(f"New Difficulty: {new_difficulty}")
```

3.6 Mining Pools and Solo Mining

Bitcoin mining can be pursued through two primary methods: mining pools and solo mining. This section explores these methods in detail, highlighting their mechanisms, advantages, and disadvantages to provide a thorough understanding.

Mining pools consist of groups of miners who combine their computational resources to increase their chances of successfully mining a block. They share the rewards proportionally based on the amount of computational power each miner contributes. Pooling methods can prevent the high variance in income that individual miners often face. Several components and mechanisms are essential to understand how mining pools operate effectively.

When a miner joins a pool, they are provided with partial work. The pool coordinator assigns these partial works known as "shares." The miner works to solve these shares, and while these shares may not always result in a block solution, they serve as a record to the pool operator of the individual miner's contribution.

The share difficulty is a fraction of the actual Bitcoin network difficulty. Shares are easier to solve compared to the block itself, making it feasible to measure how much work each miner contributes. Pools use different structures and payout schemes. Among the common payout methods are:

- **Pay-Per-Share (PPS):** Miners receive a fixed amount for each valid share they submit. This method provides immediate payouts and lowers the risk to miners, but the pool operator assumes risk.
- **Proportional (PROP):** Rewards are distributed at the end of a

mining round. Miners get a proportion of the total rewards based on the number of shares they have contributed during that round.

- **Pay Per Last N Shares (PPLNS):** This method uses a more complicated formula, where rewards are distributed to miners based on the shares they submitted in the last N shares cycle. It helps to prevent pool hopping behavior.
- **Full Pay-Per-Share (FPPS):** In addition to the block reward, this method also distributes transaction fees among miners, providing them with a higher but steady payout.

Pools enhance the predictability and frequency of payouts. However, they also come with certain disadvantages, such as security concerns, reliance on pool operators, and potential centralization risks. Pool operators mandate fees, which could range from 1% to 3% or higher, reducing the miner's effective earnings. Pool hopping and other forms of gaming the system can also present issues if the pool's payout scheme is improperly designed.

On the other hand, solo mining, as the name suggests, involves miners working independently to solve hash computations and add new blocks to the blockchain. Miners retain the entirety of the block reward and transaction fees from successfully mined blocks. Solo mining requires a substantial amount of hash power and is typically feasible for those with significant computational resources.

The variance in solo mining is considerable, leading to long periods without any reward, followed by occasional large payouts. Due to the increased mining difficulty, solo mining has become less attractive for individual miners who cannot afford the high-performance hardware required to compete against large-scale mining operations.

Here is an example configuration of a solo mining setup using the Bitcoin Core client:

```
rpcuser=username
rpcpassword=password
rpcallowip=127.0.0.1
server=1
daemon=1
gen=1
genproclimit=-1
```

Upon setting this configuration in the bitcoin.conf file, start the Bitcoin client:

```
$ bitcoind -daemon
```

Solo mining entails having a complete copy of the blockchain, facilitating direct communication with the Bitcoin network. This independence offers an additional layer of security and control, eliminating reliance on pool operators.

Despite the potential rewards, the computational power and energy costs associated with solo mining can be prohibitive. As a result, pool mining remains the dominant choice among miners, balancing risk and reward through collective effort.

The decision between joining a mining pool or solo mining ultimately hinges on the miner's resources, risk tolerance, and long-term strategy. While mining pools offer consistent returns and require less individual hash power, solo mining grants full control and total reward per block mined but demands significant investment and patience.

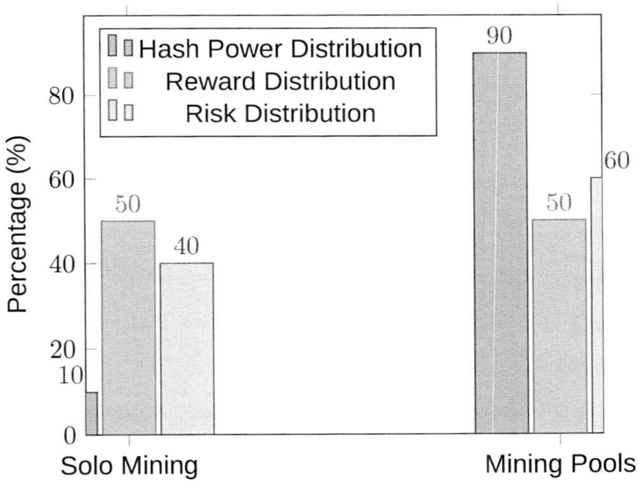

3.7 Economics of Bitcoin Mining

Bitcoin mining is a highly intricate process that intertwines advanced cryptography with economic incentives designed to ensure the functioning, security, and decentralization of the network. Understanding the economics of Bitcoin mining is crucial to appreciate how market dynamics, individual profitability, and network stability are sustained.

Capital Investment:

Bitcoin mining requires a substantial initial capital investment. Various components contribute to the overall cost, including hardware acquisition, infrastructure setup, and ancillary equipment. The most critical component is specialized mining hardware, primarily Application-Specific Integrated Circuits (ASICs), developed exclusively for Bitcoin mining. The rapid advancement in ASIC technology fosters a continuous cycle of obsolescence and upgrade, compelling miners to reinvest profits in next-generation equipment to remain competitive.

```
# Sample estimated cost of an ASIC miner
miner_cost = 12000 # USD
ancillary_equipment_cost = 3000 # USD
total_initial_cost = miner_cost + ancillary_equipment_cost
```

Operational Expenses:

Operational expenses in Bitcoin mining predominantly consist of electricity consumption, cooling infrastructure, maintenance, and occasional repairs. Since mining is energy-intensive, electricity is the most significant recurring expense. The profitability of mining operations is highly sensitive to changes in electricity costs. Miners often establish operations in locations with low electricity rates to maximize returns. For instance, mining farms are frequently located in regions with an abundance of hydroelectric power.

```
# Example of calculating monthly electricity cost
electricity_rate = 0.05 # USD per kWh
power_consumption = 1350 # kW
monthly_cost = electricity_rate * power_consumption * 24 * 30
print(f"Monthly electricity cost: {monthly_cost:.2f} USD")
```

Mining Revenue:

Bitcoin miners generate revenue through block rewards and transaction fees. Initially, the block reward was 50 BTC per block, but it undergoes halving approximately every four years. Currently, it stands at 6.25 BTC per block, as of the latest halving event in May 2020. Additionally, miners receive transaction fees from transactions included in the mined block. However, the relative contribution of transaction fees to the mining revenue has historically been lower compared to the block reward, yet it is expected to grow in significance as block rewards diminish.

```
Current Block Reward: 6.25 BTC
Total BTC Earned = Block Reward + Transaction Fees
```

Breakeven Analysis:

To determine the profitability of Bitcoin mining, a breakeven analysis is undertaken. This involves calculating the point at which total revenue equals total costs. Miners must consider the price of Bitcoin, hash rate, block reward, and electricity costs to determine the effective breakeven point. Factors such as mining difficulty and hardware efficiency directly affect profitability calculations.

$$\text{Breakeven Point} = \frac{\text{Total Costs}}{\text{Revenue per Mined Block}}$$

Market Dynamics:

The economics of Bitcoin mining are significantly influenced by market dynamics, including Bitcoin price volatility and global hash rate distribution. An increase in Bitcoin price generally leads to an influx of miners, raising the overall network hash rate and, subsequently, the mining difficulty. Conversely, a steep decline in Bitcoin price can render mining unprofitable for many, causing a reduction in the network hash rate.

Bitcoin Price	Mining Difficulty	Network Hash Rate
High	High	High
Low	Low	Low

Table 3.2: Impact of Bitcoin Price on Network Metrics

Pool and Solo Mining:

Economic considerations also inform the choice between pool and solo mining. In solo mining, the miner attempts to solve the cryptographic puzzle independently, which can result in higher variances in revenue. Pool mining, on the other hand, allows miners to pool their resources and collective hash power to solve blocks more frequently, providing a steady albeit shared stream of income. Pool operators typically charge a fee that is deducted from the overall rewards.

Pool Mining Fee: 1.25%
Effective Earnings = Total Rewards * (1 - Pool Fee)

Regulations and Legal Compliance:

Lastly, the regulatory environment significantly impacts the profitability and viability of mining operations. Regulations concerning energy usage, environmental impact, taxation, and digital currency legality vary by jurisdiction and can impose additional costs or barriers to entry. Miners must navigate these legal landscapes to ensure compliance and optimize operational efficiency.

The interplay between these economic factors shapes the landscape of Bitcoin mining, driving innovations and influencing strategic decisions within the ecosystem.

3.8 Environmental Impact of Bitcoin Mining

The environmental impact of Bitcoin mining is an increasingly important consideration as the cryptocurrency continues to grow in popularity and usage. The intensive energy consumption required for mining operations has prompted scrutiny from environmentalists and regulators alike. This section delves into the various aspects of the environmental footprint of Bitcoin mining, explaining the sources of energy consumption, the carbon footprint, and potential mitigation strategies.

Bitcoin mining operations require a significant amount of computational power to solve the cryptographic puzzles essential for adding new blocks to the blockchain. This computational power is provided by mining hardware such as Application-Specific Integrated Circuits (ASICs) and Graphics Processing Units (GPUs), which consume large amounts of electrical energy. The energy consumption can be quantified by the total network hash rate, which reflects the aggregate processing power of all miners in the Bitcoin network.

The majority of Bitcoin mining operations are concentrated in regions with access to cheap electricity. While this often includes areas with abundant renewable energy sources like hydroelectric power, it also includes regions heavily reliant on coal and other fossil fuels. Therefore, the environmental impact varies significantly based on the energy mix of the electricity sources used by miners.

One of the primary metrics to assess the environmental impact of Bitcoin mining is the carbon footprint. This is a measure of the amount of carbon dioxide (CO_2) emissions produced as a result of electricity consumption. The equation to calculate the carbon footprint is given by:

$$\text{Carbon Footprint} = \text{Electricity Consumption} \times \text{Emission Factor}$$

Where:

- *Electricity Consumption* is measured in kilowatt-hours (kWh) and represents the amount of electricity used by mining hardware.
- *Emission Factor* is the amount of CO_2 emissions per kWh of electricity consumed, typically measured in kg CO_2/kWh.

```
# Sample code to calculate the carbon footprint of Bitcoin mining

# Inputs
electricity_consumption_kwh = 1000000 # Example consumption in kWh
emission_factor_kg_per_kwh = 0.5 # Example emissions factor in kg CO2/kWh

# Calculation
carbon_footprint = electricity_consumption_kwh * emission_factor_kg_per_kwh

# Output
print(f"Carbon Footprint: {carbon_footprint} kg CO2")
```

```
Carbon Footprint: 500000.0 kg CO2
```

The carbon footprint varies depending on the location of mining operations. For instance, miners in Iceland and Quebec benefit from surplus hydroelectric power, resulting in a lower carbon footprint. Conversely, miners in countries with coal-dominated energy grids, such as China, contribute significantly higher CO_2 emissions.

Given the substantial environmental impact, several strategies have been proposed to mitigate the adverse effects:

- **Transition to Renewable Energy Sources:** Encouraging and incentivizing the use of renewable energy sources for mining operations can drastically reduce the carbon footprint. Wind, solar, and hydroelectric power are viable alternatives that offer clean and sustainable energy.
- **Energy Efficiency Improvements:** Advances in mining technology can improve the energy efficiency of mining hardware. ASIC manufacturers continuously strive to design chips that deliver higher performance per watt, thereby reducing overall energy consumption.
- **Regulatory Measures:** Governments and regulatory bodies can implement policies to limit the environmental impact of cryptocurrency mining. Such measures may include taxing carbon emissions, providing subsidies for renewable energy usage, and setting energy consumption standards for mining operations.
- **Geographical Diversification:** Distributing mining operations across various geographical regions with abundant renewable energy can help balance the environmental impact. This also reduces the reliance on regions with high carbon footprints.
- **Improved Grid Integration:** Enhanced integration of mining operations with the electricity grid can enable better energy man-

agement. Demand-side response techniques can be employed to balance the load on the grid, utilizing excess renewable energy during periods of low demand.

While these strategies present viable solutions, their implementation requires coordinated efforts from various stakeholders, including miners, hardware manufacturers, energy providers, and regulators. The transition to a more sustainable mining ecosystem is crucial for minimizing the environmental impact as Bitcoin continues to scale.

Additionally, ongoing research and innovation are pivotal in developing new technologies that can further mitigate the environmental footprint of Bitcoin mining. Future advancements may include the use of alternative consensus mechanisms, such as Proof of Stake, that inherently consume less energy compared to Proof of Work. These changes must be carefully evaluated to maintain the security and decentralization of the Bitcoin network.

3.9 Rewards and Incentives for Miners

Bitcoin mining serves to secure the Bitcoin network by contributing computational power to verify transactions and add them to the blockchain. Miners are incentivized to invest in often-expensive mining hardware and electricity through rewards, which come in two main forms: the block subsidy and transaction fees. In this section, we will examine these rewards in detail, the economic factors driving mining, and how blockchain protocol adjustments like halving events impact miner incentives.

At the core of the Bitcoin reward structure is the block subsidy, which is composed of newly minted bitcoins. When a miner successfully appends a new block to the blockchain, they are granted the block reward, initially set at 50 bitcoins per block when Bitcoin launched. The Bitcoin protocol includes a mechanism called the "halving event," where this reward is halved approximately every four years, or after every 210,000 blocks. As of the latest halving in May 2020, the block subsidy is reduced to 6.25 bitcoins per block. This halving process ensures that the total supply of bitcoins remains finite, capped at 21 million.

In addition to the block subsidy, miners earn transaction fees that users attach to their transactions. When the block subsidy decreases due to halving events, transaction fees become a more significant portion of the miner's revenue. Transaction fees are not fixed and can vary greatly based on how much users are willing to pay for their transactions to be included quickly in the blockchain. During periods of high network congestion, transaction fees rise as users compete to prioritize their transactions.


```
{
  "txid": "6b0c...f6b2",
  "size": 226,
  "vsize": 144,
  "weight": 576,
  "fee": 0.0001,
  "vin": [...],
  "vout": [...]
}
```


Economic viability for miners is determined by the cumulative value of block subsidies and transaction fees against the costs incurred from hardware investment, operational expenditures, and energy consumption. The mining hardware costs include the initial purchase price of ASICs (Application-Specific Integrated Circuits) or GPUs, regular maintenance, and cooling mechanisms to ensure optimal operation. Energy consumption is a significant cost, as mining rigs require substantial electrical power to perform continuous computations. Therefore, miners often seek regions with low electricity costs or utilize renewable energy sources to enhance profitability.

Table 3.3: Reward Breakdown (Block #630000, May 2020)

Category	Value
Block Subsidy	6.25 BTC
Transaction Fees	0.70 BTC
Total Reward	6.95 BTC

As part of their economic strategy, miners may join mining pools to stabilize their income. Mining pools aggregate the computational power of multiple miners to increase the probability of successfully mining a block. In these pools, rewards are distributed proportionally based on the contributed computational power.

```
Pool total hash rate = 1000 TH/s
Miner A's hash rate = 100 TH/s
Miner B's hash rate = 50 TH/s
Miner A's share of reward = 10%
Miner B's share of reward = 5%
```

The shifting emphasis from block subsidies to transaction fees as Bitcoin approaches its total supply limit implies a transition where network security dependence progressively relies on transaction fees. This transition represents a critical aspect of Bitcoin's long-term sustainability, requiring continuous demand for transaction throughput.

```
Year: 2140
Block Reward: 0 BTC
Transaction Fees per Block: Average 1.5 BTC
```

Miners' incentives are undeniably aligned with maintaining network security and processing transactions efficiently. This alignment, embedded in the Bitcoin protocol, ensures that as long as the economic rewards outweigh the associated costs, miners will continue to allocate resources to support and secure the network. This incentive structure is fundamental to the decentralized nature and operational integrity of Bitcoin.

3.10 Future of Bitcoin Mining

The future of Bitcoin mining presents numerous possibilities shaped by technological advancements, regulatory changes, and shifts in the economic landscape. Anticipating these changes is crucial for both current and prospective miners, as well as for stakeholders in the broader cryptocurrency ecosystem. This section explores the key factors likely to influence the future of Bitcoin mining, with an emphasis on technological innovation, regulatory developments, and economic trends.

Technological advancements will play a pivotal role in the evolution of Bitcoin mining. One significant area of development is the consistent improvement in mining hardware efficiency. Modern Application-Specific Integrated Circuits (ASICs) have already surpassed the capabilities of Graphic Processing Units (GPUs) in terms of hashing power and energy consumption. Future enhancements are expected to produce even more efficient ASICs, potentially utilizing new semiconductor materials and design architectures to further reduce power consumption and increase processing power. Cutting-edge advancements such as quantum computing, while not immediately applicable, could potentially revolutionize mining by enabling the rapid solving of cryptographic puzzles, although they may also necessitate fundamental changes to Bitcoin's consensus algorithm to maintain security.

The integration of renewable energy sources into mining operations is another emerging trend. With growing concerns about the environmental impact of Bitcoin mining, there is a concerted effort within the industry to harness sustainable energy. Solar, wind, and hydroelectric power are increasingly being used to operate mining facilities, reducing the carbon footprint associated with mining activities. Investments in renewable energy technologies and the development of more energy-efficient mining protocols are likely to continue, driven by both economic incentives and regulatory pressures to minimize environmental impact.

Regulatory developments around the world will significantly impact the future of Bitcoin mining. Governments are starting to recognize the importance of cryptocurrencies and are beginning to develop frameworks to regulate their use. These regulatory measures can have both positive and negative effects on mining. For example, clear regulations could provide legal certainty, encouraging investment and innovation. Conversely, restrictive regulations could hinder mining operations, particularly in regions with stringent energy usage policies or where cryptocurrency activities are not legally recognized. The global regulatory landscape is dynamic, and miners must stay informed about regional policies that could influence their operations.

Economic factors, including the price of Bitcoin, energy costs, and transaction fees, will also drive the future of Bitcoin mining. The price of Bitcoin directly affects the profitability of mining operations; higher prices typically incentivize increased mining activity, while lower prices may force less efficient miners out of the market. Energy costs, which constitute a significant portion of mining expenses, are subject to fluctuations and regional differences. Thus, miners constantly seek regions with low-cost electricity to maximize their profit margins. Additionally, transaction fees, which miners earn alongside block rewards, will become increasingly important. As the Bitcoin network evolves and the block subsidy decreases over time due to the halving event, transaction fees will need to sustain mining operations.

Emerging mining strategies, such as participating in mining pools or transitioning to pooled mining models, will influence the future dynamics of the industry. Joining mining pools allows individual miners to combine their computational resources, thus increasing their chances of earning rewards and achieving more consistent payout structures. This collective approach mitigates the risks associated with the high variance of solo mining. As mining difficulty continues to rise and the competition for block rewards intensifies, the role of mining pools is expected to grow, potentially leading to greater centralization within the network.

The constant evolution of mining software plays a crucial role in the future of Bitcoin mining. Software that optimizes the mining process, enhances security, and provides better management tools for mining operations will be essential. The development of distributed mining protocols may also emerge, allowing miners to contribute their hashing power more flexibly and efficiently without significant initial capital investments in hardware.

Research into alternative consensus mechanisms, while not directly related to Bitcoin mining, could influence broader trends in the cryptocurrency space. Although Bitcoin is committed to the Proof of Work (PoW) consensus algorithm, ongoing research into Proof of Stake (PoS) and other energy-efficient consensus methods might inspire changes in the protocol or emergent cryptocurrencies that compete with Bitcoin. While a shift from PoW to another consensus mechanism for Bitcoin is unlikely due to its decentralized nature and the need for broad consensus among stakeholders, such developments warrant consideration.

Continuous improvements in blockchain technology and protocols are crucial for scaling and enhancing the Bitcoin network. Innovations such as the Lightning Network aim to address scalability issues by enabling faster and cheaper off-chain transactions, potentially reducing the burden on the main blockchain and impacting the overall mining landscape. These technological improvements will ensure the sustainability and efficiency of the Bitcoin ecosystem.

Ongoing collaboration between miners, developers, and other stakeholders will be essential in navigating the future challenges and opportunities in Bitcoin mining. Engaging in community discussions, participating in protocol upgrades, and adhering to best practices will fortify the network's resilience and advancement.

```
import psutil

def get_power_usage():
    # Return system power usage in watts
    return psutil.sensors_battery().power_plugged

def optimize_mining():
    while True:
        power_usage = get_power_usage()
        if power_usage > threshold:
            reduce_hash_rate()
        else:
            maximize_hash_rate()

optimize_mining()
```

```
Output:
Power usage monitored. Adjusting hash rate accordingly.
```

Analyzing current trends, predicting technological breakthroughs, and understanding regulatory landscapes are fundamental to preparing for the future of Bitcoin mining. By adapting to advancements and remaining vigilant about policy changes, miners and stakeholders can navigate the complexities of the evolving mining ecosystem.

Chapter 4

Bitcoin Wallets and Security

Bitcoin wallets are essential tools that store cryptographic keys and facilitate secure transactions. They come in various forms including software, hardware, paper, and brain wallets, each offering different levels of security and convenience. This chapter explores the types of wallets, their setup, and best practices for securing them. It also covers the importance of backup and recovery, as well as strategies for dealing with lost or stolen bitcoins to ensure the safety of digital assets.

4.1 Introduction to Bitcoin Wallets

A Bitcoin wallet is a fundamental component in the use and management of Bitcoin and other cryptocurrencies. It functions as a tool that stores cryptographic keys and facilitates the sending and receiving of Bitcoin. It is important to understand that Bitcoin itself is not stored within the wallet; rather, the wallet contains the information, specifically the private and public keys, necessary to access and manage Bitcoin on the blockchain.

A private key in Bitcoin is a randomly generated 256-bit number that is used to sign transactions and provide proof of ownership. This key must be kept secure, as possession of the private key allows access to the associated Bitcoin funds. In contrast, a public key is derived from the private key and serves as an address to which Bitcoin can be sent. Public keys can be shared openly, while private keys must be protected.

```
Private Key:  E9873D79C6D87DC0FB6A5778633389AFO76F05FB133C2DAADB4C01E7AE69963F
Public Key:   04B0BD634234ABDC895AB250C605DA7DAE72B982BB421CFD6A55A7CA0D927B7B
```

Bitcoin wallets come in various forms, each offering different levels of security and convenience. These forms can be broadly classified into hot and cold wallets, with hot wallets being connected to the internet and cold wallets being offline. The choice of wallet type depends on factors such as the user's technical proficiency, the amount of Bitcoin being stored, and the preferred balance between accessibility and security.

Hot wallets include software wallets, which can be further categorized into desktop, mobile, and web wallets. These wallets are connected to the internet and provide a high degree of accessibility and ease of use. However, they are more susceptible to cybersecurity threats such as hacking or malware. Conversely, cold wallets are physical devices or printed media that store Bitcoin offline, thereby providing increased security at the cost of decreased convenience. Examples of cold wallets include hardware wallets, paper wallets, and brain wallets.

The process of setting up a Bitcoin wallet typically involves the generation of a new private-key/public-key pair, securing the private key, and creating backup mechanisms to prevent loss of access. Additionally, securing a Bitcoin wallet requires implementing best practices such as using strong passwords, enabling multi-signature security, and protecting backup phrases. Backup and recovery mechanisms are critical as they allow users to regain access to their Bitcoin in case of device loss or malfunction.

To illustrate the practicality and security considerations of Bitcoin wallets, let us examine the procedure for generating and securing a new wallet using command-line tools. Suppose we use a Python script with the bitcoinlib library to generate a new wallet.

```
from bitcoinlib.wallets import Wallet, create_key

# Create a new wallet
w = Wallet.create('MyNewWallet')
print(f"New wallet name: {w.name}")

# Generate a key pair
key = create_key()
print(f"Private Key: {key.key()}")
print(f"Public Key: {key.public_hex()}")
```

The output of this script demonstrates the basic structure of a wallet generation process, revealing both the private and public keys:

```
New wallet name: MyNewWallet
Private Key:     <Generated_Private_Key>
Public Key:      <Generated_Public_Key>
```

This private key must be stored securely, and multiple layers of security can be applied to protect it. For example, it is advisable to use hardware wallets, which store private keys in a secure chip, protecting them from online attacks.

Bitcoin wallets serve crucial roles beyond storage, including transaction facilitation and identity verification. When sending Bitcoin, users must sign the transaction with their private key to confirm their identity and willingness to transfer funds. The public key, included in the transaction, and blockchain mechanisms ensure that only the rightful owner can send Bitcoin.

These elements collectively underline the importance of Bitcoin wallets in the secure and efficient management of digital currencies.

4.2 Types of Bitcoin Wallets: Hot vs. Cold Wallets

Bitcoin wallets can be broadly categorized into two main types: hot wallets and cold wallets. Each type has distinct characteristics, usage scenarios, and security implications.

Hot wallets are Bitcoin wallets that are connected to the internet. They are convenient for everyday transactions but are inherently more vulnerable to hacks and malware. Conversely, cold wallets are not connected to the internet and are used for secure, long-term storage. They offer increased protection against unauthorized access and cyber threats but may be less convenient for frequent transactions.

Hot wallets include desktop wallets, mobile wallets, and web wallets. These wallets allow users to access their bitcoins quickly and easily, making them ideal for regular use and spending. However, they are susceptible to various online threats such as phishing attacks, keyloggers, and other malware that can compromise the private keys.

```
from bitcoin import *

# Generate private key
my_private_key = random_key()
```

```
# Generate public key from private key
my_public_key = privtopub(my_private_key)

# Generate Bitcoin address from public key
my_bitcoin_address = pubtoaddr(my_public_key)

print(my_bitcoin_address)
```

The output of this code execution may look like the following:

```
1A1zP1eP5QGefi2DMPTfTL5SLmv7DivfNa
```

Mobile wallets are applications that run on smartphones and tablets, allowing for the storage and transaction of bitcoin on-the-go. They are typically user-friendly and provide QR code scanning features for quick payments. Some popular mobile wallets include Electrum, Mycelium, and the Bitcoin Wallet app.

Desktop wallets are software applications that run on a personal computer. They offer a higher degree of security compared to mobile and web wallets as the private keys are stored on the user's computer. Examples of desktop wallets are Electrum, Bitcoin Core, and Armory.

Web wallets, also known as online wallets, can be accessed via any web browser. They are the least secure of the hot wallets since the private keys are often stored by the service provider. While they offer high convenience and accessibility, users must rely on the security practices of the third-party service provider. Coinbase and Blockchain.info are examples of web wallets.

Cold wallets include hardware wallets, paper wallets, and brain wallets. These wallets are designed for long-term storage and maximal security, keeping private keys offline.

Hardware wallets are physical devices that securely store the user's private keys. They often come with security features such as pin codes and two-factor authentication. Hardware wallets are highly resistant to malware and hacks since the private keys are stored in a specialized secure environment. Popular hardware wallets include Trezor, Ledger Nano S, and KeepKey.

To use a hardware wallet, the device must be connected to a computer or mobile device. Transactions are signed within the hardware wallet itself, ensuring that the private keys never leave the device. The following is an example schematic for a transaction using a hardware wallet:

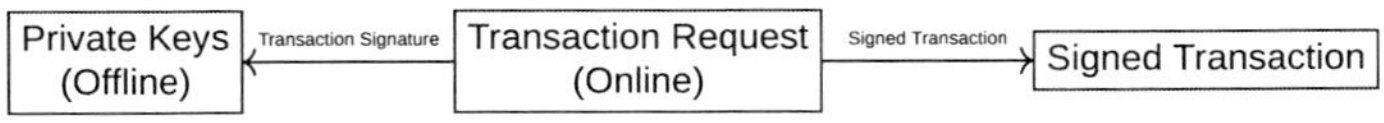

Paper wallets involve generating a Bitcoin address and private key, which are then printed on a piece of paper. This paper must be kept safe and secure, as anyone with access to it can spend the bitcoins. One can generate paper wallets using websites like bitaddress.org, but must ensure they are not connected to the internet while generating the keys for added security.

```
from bitcoin import *

# Generate private key
private_key = random_key()

# Generate Bitcoin address
public_key = privtopub(private_key)
bitcoin_address = pubtoaddr(public_key)

# Printing private key and Bitcoin address for paper wallet
print(”Private Key:”, private_key)
print(”Bitcoin Address:”, bitcoin_address)
```

Finally, brain wallets are created by memorizing a passphrase. This passphrase is converted into a private key using a hashing algorithm. These types of wallets are highly susceptible to brute-force attacks and are not recommended for significant amounts of bitcoin. Instead, they are better suited for small amounts and experimental purposes.

Understanding the differences between hot and cold wallets, as well as the specific characteristics of each, allows users to make informed decisions based on their individual security needs and usage habits. For everyday transactions and accessibility, hot wallets are preferable. For secure, long-term storage, cold wallets provide unparalleled security.

4.3 Software Wallets: Desktop, Mobile, and Web

Software wallets are applications that store and manage private keys necessary for facilitating Bitcoin transactions. These wallets operate in different environments and are generally categorized into three primary types: desktop wallets, mobile wallets, and web wallets. Each category offers distinct advantages and potential security concerns, catering to various user needs and preferences. A comprehensive understanding of these types helps in making informed decisions about securing digital assets.

Desktop wallets are installed directly on a personal computer, providing a blend of security and convenience. Because these wallets reside on the user's local storage, they minimize reliance on third parties, thereby enhancing privacy and control. However, security is highly contingent upon the integrity of the host machine. It is paramount to ensure that the computer is free from malware and up-to-date with the latest security patches. Firewalls, antivirus software, and secure passwords further bolster the defense against unauthorized access.

The process of initiating a transaction with a desktop wallet involves creating and securely storing private keys. Some commonly used desktop wallets include Bitcoin Core, Electrum, and Armory. Below is a basic outline of how to set up and use a desktop wallet using the Electrum wallet as an example:

```
# Download the Electrum installation file from the official website:
$ wget https://download.electrum.org/4.1.2/electrum-4.1.2-x86_64.AppImage

# Make the downloaded file executable:
$ chmod +x electrum-4.1.2-x86_64.AppImage

# Run the Electrum wallet:
$ ./electrum-4.1.2-x86_64.AppImage
```

After installation, the wallet will prompt the user to create a new wallet or restore an existing one. For a new wallet, the software generates a seed phrase that must be written down and stored securely, as it is essential for wallet recovery in case of software failure or device loss.

Mobile wallets, as the name implies, operate on smartphones, offering the advantage of portability and accessibility. These wallets are particularly beneficial for users requiring frequent, on-the-go transactions. Though convenient, mobile wallets demand rigorous security practices due to the higher risk associated with mobile environments. Measures such as biometric authentication, encryption, and regular updates are critical to maintaining the security of mobile wallets.

Popular mobile wallets include Mycelium, Trust Wallet, and Breadwallet (BRD). The setup is generally straightforward, similar to desktop wallets. Users download the wallet app from the official app store, follow the setup instructions, and back up the seed phrase. Below is an example of setting up a mobile wallet using Mycelium:

```
# Download the Mycelium app from Google Play Store or Apple App Store.
# Open the application and follow the on-screen instructions to create a new wallet.
# Write down the seed phrase presented by the app.
# Confirm the seed phrase by entering it back into the app.
```

```
# Set a secure password for accessing the wallet.
```

Web wallets operate within a web browser, offering a high level of accessibility from any internet-connected device. They are often provided by online service platforms, making them highly convenient but also potentially less secure than desktop or mobile wallets due to the reliance on third-party servers. Users must trust the service provider to maintain robust security protocols. It is advisable to use web wallets for small to moderate amounts of bitcoins and always enable two-factor authentication (2FA) to add an extra layer of security.

Prominent web wallets include Coinbase, Blockchain.info, and BitGo. Setting up these wallets usually involves signing up on the platform's website, securing the account with a strong, unique password, and activating 2FA. Here is an example of setting up a web wallet on Blockchain.info:

```
# Navigate to the official website: https://www.blockchain.com/
# Click on "Get started" to create a new wallet.
# Fill in the required information including a secure password.
# Verify your email address through the confirmation link sent by Blockchain.info.
# Enable two-factor authentication (2FA) for added security.
```

Each type of software wallet serves a different purpose based on user needs and security preferences. Desktop wallets are favored for their balance of control and security but are ideal for users whose transactions are primarily conducted from a single, secure location. Mobile wallets excel in providing convenience for frequent transactions but require robust security practices due to the nature of the mobile environment. Web wallets facilitate ease of access and are suitable for users needing to access their funds from various devices; however, they inherently depend on the trustworthiness and security diligence of the service provider.

Balancing convenience and security is critical when choosing a software wallet. Regular backups, encryption of private keys, and adherence to security best practices ensure the integrity and safety of Bitcoin assets across all wallet types.

4.4 Hardware Wallets: Physical Security

Hardware wallets represent a physical device designed specifically for securing and managing private keys used in cryptocurrency transactions. They offer a robust solution for mitigating risks associated with software-based wallets, particularly regarding the protection against malware and hacking attempts. The security mechanisms inherent in hardware wallets aim to safeguard users' digital assets through a combination of physical and digital defenses.

- **Design and Functionality**

  Hardware wallets, often resembling USB flash drives in form, integrate a secure hardware element capable of securely storing private keys. This element ensures that private keys never leave the device even when connected to a computer or mobile device, significantly reducing the risk of exposure to malicious software. The wallet typically includes a small display screen and buttons, which facilitate user interaction for transaction verification and authorization.

  A fundamental principle in the design of hardware wallets is that the private keys are stored in a secure chip isolated from the rest of the device. This chip is tamper-resistant and undergoes rigorous assessment to meet security standards such as Common Criteria or FIPS 140-2. The user interface elements, such as the screen and buttons, provide a means to verify transaction details (e.g., destination address and amount) before explicitly confirming the transaction on the secure device.

- **Initialization and Use**

  When a hardware wallet is first set up, it generates a new private key or allows the user to restore an existing wallet using a seed phrase. The seed phrase is typically a set of 12, 18, or 24 words that can be used to recover the wallet in case the hardware device is lost or damaged. It is crucial to write down this seed phrase and store it securely offline. Losing the seed phrase equates to losing access to the funds controlled by that wallet.

  Here is an example of initializing a hardware wallet:

```
# Step 1: Connect the hardware wallet to a computer via USB.
# Step 2: Follow the on-screen instructions to set up a new wallet.
# Step 3: Record the seed phrase securely.
# Step 4: Set a PIN or password for additional security.
```

  For everyday use, the hardware wallet needs to be connected to a computer or smartphone through USB or Bluetooth interfaces. Users interact through a companion application to initiate transactions. The hardware wallet remains the final authority to approve and sign the transaction securely.

```
# Step 1: Connect the hardware wallet to a computer or smartphone.
# Step 2: Open the companion wallet application.
# Step 3: Enter transaction details: recipient's address and amount.
# Step 4: Verify the details on the hardware wallet's screen.
# Step 5: Confirm and authorize the transaction using the device buttons.
# Step 6: The transaction is signed on the device and broadcast to the
    blockchain.
```

- **Security Features**
  - *PIN Protection*: The device is typically secured with a PIN code that must be entered upon each connection. Multiple incorrect attempts generally result in device lockout, adding a layer of protection against unauthorized access.
  - *Secure Elements*: The private keys are stored within a secure element that is resistant to tampering attempts. This ensures the integrity and confidentiality of the private keys.
  - *Transaction Verification*: Users must manually verify transaction details on the device's screen and approve them using physical buttons. This helps prevent fraud, as the transaction cannot be altered by malware on the connected computer.
  - *Backup and Recovery*: The seed phrase generated during the wallet's initial setup provides a means of recovery. It ensures that the user can restore their assets on a new device in case of hardware failure or loss.

- **Purchase Considerations**

  When selecting a hardware wallet, it's important to purchase directly from the manufacturer or authorized resellers to avoid risks of tampering. Verifying the authenticity of the device upon receipt is also crucial. Additionally, users should consider the device's compatibility with different cryptocurrencies and wallets to ensure it meets their specific needs.

```
# Step 1: Verify the holographic seal on the package.
# Step 2: Check the device for signs of tampering.
# Step 3: Confirm the firmware by installing the official companion
    application.
```

- **Usage Best Practices**

  Ensuring the physical security of the hardware wallet is as critical as securing the digital aspects. Users should store the wallet in a safe, preferably one that is fire and water-resistant, to protect against physical threats. Regularly checking for firmware updates and applying them as necessary helps maintain the security posture against newly identified vulnerabilities.

Users should always be cautious about phishing attempts and ensure that interactions with the wallet occur only through official and trusted applications. In the event of loss or theft, immediately moving funds using the seed phrase on a new hardware wallet is the recommended course of action.

Through a combination of advanced security features, ease of use, and best practices, hardware wallets offer a reliable and secure way to manage Bitcoin and other cryptocurrencies. They present an essential tool in the arsenal of any individual serious about safeguarding digital assets against the multifaceted risks present in the digital world.

4.5 Paper Wallets and Brain Wallets

Paper wallets and brain wallets are forms of cold storage that provide offline solutions for securing Bitcoin. These methods are utilized when the utmost security is desired, reducing exposure to online threats. This section delves into the mechanics of creating and using paper and brain wallets, their security implications, and best practices for their utilization.

A paper wallet is a physical document that contains a public address for receiving Bitcoin and a private key, which allows spending or transferring the Bitcoin stored at that address. Generating a paper wallet usually involves using an offline computer to avoid exposure to malware or other security risks. Common tools for generating paper wallets include websites like bitaddress.org, which can be downloaded and run offline.

1. **Generating a Paper Wallet**

To generate a paper wallet:

- Visit a reliable paper wallet generator website and download the HTML page.
- Disconnect your computer from the internet for security purposes.

- Open the downloaded HTML file in a web browser.
- Follow the on-screen instructions to generate a new Bitcoin address.
- Print the resulting page, which will display the public address and the private key.
- Store the printed paper wallet in a secure, offline location such as a safe or a safety deposit box.

Here is an example of a generated public address and private key using the bitaddress.org tool:

```
Public Address:
1A1zP1eP5QGefi2DMPTfTL5SLmv7DivfNa

Private Key:
5Kb8kLf9zgWQnogidDA76MzPL6TsZZY36hZWp8PPZZZZZZZZZBnir1rxDsFGd
```

The security of a paper wallet lies in its offline nature, making it immune to online hacks or malware. However, there are risks such as physical theft, damage, or loss. Therefore, it is recommended to create multiple copies and store them in separate, secure locations.

A brain wallet, in contrast, involves generating a private key and corresponding public address by using a passphrase that can be easily remembered. This passphrase undergoes transformation through a hashing algorithm to create the private key. One popular hashing algorithm for this purpose is SHA-256.

1. **Generating a Brain Wallet**

To generate a brain wallet, choose a strong, unique passphrase that is at least 12 words long and not easily guessable. Here is a step-by-step example using Python with the hashlib library to create a SHA-256 hash of a passphrase:

```
import hashlib

# Example passphrase
passphrase = "correct horse battery staple"

# Create SHA-256 hash of the passphrase
private_key = hashlib.sha256(passphrase.encode()).hexdigest()

print(f"Private Key: {private_key}")
```

Executing this Python code will produce an output similar to the following:

```
Private Key: e6024d7b5ab9a54ef9c775c63e1aa2b1679ea4d44e789d1209e02cdf27c1f9f6
```

The resulting private key can be converted into a public key using Bitcoin libraries such as bitcoinlib in Python. It is imperative to ensure the chosen passphrase is strong and unique. Weak or common passphrases can be susceptible to brute-force attacks, as attackers may use precomputed tables of common phrases to generate possible private keys.

Brain wallets are highly convenient as they eliminate the need for physical storage solutions. Nonetheless, the primary risk involves forgetting the passphrase. If the passphrase is forgotten, the Bitcoin stored at the corresponding address is irrecoverable.

Both paper wallets and brain wallets provide secure ways to store Bitcoin offline, catering to different user needs. Paper wallets are suitable for those who prefer physical backups, whereas brain wallets cater to individuals who trust their ability to remember complex passphrases. Adopting best practices such as generating wallets offline, using strong passphrases, and securely storing the details is critical for ensuring the security of these cold storage methods.

4.6 Setting Up a Bitcoin Wallet

Setting up a Bitcoin wallet involves steps that ensure secure management and accessibility of cryptocurrency assets. Here, we discuss the detailed process for each of the primary types of wallets: software, hardware, paper, and brain wallets.

To begin with, the user needs to understand the type of wallet suitable for their requirements. Factors influencing this choice include the frequency of transactions, the amount of Bitcoin being stored, and the level of security required.

Software Wallets

Software wallets are often the most accessible and user-friendly choice for many users. They can be subdivided into desktop, mobile, and web wallets. Below is a detailed walkthrough of setting up each type:

Desktop Wallets:

- **Download and Installation**: Visit the official website of a reputable desktop wallet provider such as Bitcoin Core or Electrum. Download the appropriate version for your operating system. For instance, for Electrum:

```
$ wget https://download.electrum.org/X.X.X/electrum-X.X.X.tar.gz
$ tar -zxf electrum-X.X.X.tar.gz
```

- **Running the Wallet**: After extraction, navigate to the Electrum directory and run the setup file. This can be done using:

```
$ cd electrum-X.X.X
$ ./run_electrum
```

- **Wallet Creation**: Follow on-screen prompts to create a new wallet. You will be asked to set a strong password and to write down a seed phrase (recovery phrase) which is crucial for wallet recovery.

- **Configuration**: Set up user preferences such as transaction fees and network configurations.

Mobile Wallets:

- **Application Download**: Download the mobile wallet application from an official app store. Popular choices include Mycelium and Trust Wallet.

- **Installation and Setup**: Install the application and follow the initial setup process, which includes creating or importing a wallet, setting up a PIN, and writing down the recovery seed.

- **Testing**: Transfer a small amount of Bitcoin to the new wallet to test its functionality.

Web Wallets:

- **Registration**: Visit the website of the web wallet provider such as Blockchain.info or Coinbase. Register for a new account by entering a secure username, password, and email verification.

- **Two-Factor Authentication (2FA)**: Enable 2FA for an additional layer of security. This typically involves receiving a code on your mobile device that must be input during login.

- **Backup**: Securely note all recovery options provided by the wallet service, including backup keys and seed phrases.

Hardware Wallets

Hardware wallets provide a high level of security by keeping private keys offline. Setting up a hardware wallet involves:

- **Purchase**: Acquire a hardware wallet such as Trezor or Ledger from a verified source to avoid tampering.
- **Initialization**: Connect the hardware wallet to your computer via USB and follow the prompts on the device and its companion software.
- **PIN Setup**: Set up a PIN on the hardware device, which will be required each time the device is used.
- **Seed Phrase**: Write down the recovery seed phrase provided during setup. Store it securely in an offline location.

Paper Wallets

Paper wallets involve generating and printing a Bitcoin address and private key on a physical medium. The procedure is as follows:

- **Offline Generation**: Access an open-source paper wallet generator like BitAddress.org from an offline computer. Download the HTML file and open it in a web browser with internet connection disabled.
- **Generate Keys**: Move your mouse randomly over the screen to add entropy and generate a unique Bitcoin address and corresponding private key.
- **Print Wallet**: Print the generated paper wallet using a secure printer. Ensure no digital copies of the wallet are saved on your computer.
- **Storage**: Store the printed wallet in a secure and waterproof location.

Brain Wallets

Brain wallets derive private keys directly from a passphrase known only to the user. This method is generally not recommended due to security vulnerabilities, but if used, the steps include:

- **Choose a Passphrase**: Select a complex and unique passphrase that is difficult to guess but memorable enough for you. Avoid common phrases or quotes.
- **Key Generation**: Use a trusted online tool like WarpWallet to convert the passphrase into a private key and Bitcoin address.
- **Security Measures**: Regularly check the address for unauthorized transactions and use additional security measures like two-factor authentication for related accounts.

Accurate and secure completion of these setups is essential for safeguarding Bitcoin assets. Implementing strong passwords, proper backup procedures, and meticulous attention to security recommendations significantly reduces the risk of theft or loss.

4.7 Securing Your Bitcoin Wallet

It is paramount to ensure the security of your Bitcoin wallet, as it is the gateway to your digital assets. Security practices involve protecting both the cryptographic keys and the wallet itself from unauthorized access, loss, and other potential threats. Understanding and implementing these practices is crucial for safeguarding your investments in Bitcoin.

The security of any Bitcoin wallet hinges on a combination of factors including the strength of passwords, protection against malware, and the secure storage of private keys. Assessing the security needs of your wallet starts with recognizing potential attack vectors. These may include phishing attacks, malware, physical theft, or even natural disasters. We delve into several key strategies and best practices to enhance the security of your Bitcoin wallet.

Strong Passwords and Encryption

A critical step in securing your Bitcoin wallet is creating a strong password. A strong password should be lengthy (at least 12 characters), and include a mix of uppercase and lowercase letters, numbers, and special characters. Avoid using easily guessable information such as birthdays or common words.

For example, generating a strong password:

```
g^9aN2z!5pD$mfB7
```

In addition to a strong password, it is equally important to encrypt your entire wallet. Encryption converts your wallet information into a secure format that cannot be read without the correct key or password. Most software wallets include built-in encryption features. For hardware wallets, ensure that they are set to require a PIN code and that this PIN is sufficiently complex.

Two-Factor Authentication (2FA)

Two-Factor Authentication adds an additional layer of security by requiring not only a password and a username but also something that only the user has on them, i.e., a piece of information only they should know or have immediately to hand—such as a physical token. Consider enabling 2FA for any accounts associated with your Bitcoin wallet, including email accounts and exchange platforms.

The configuration of 2FA typically involves:

- Downloading an authenticator app like Google Authenticator or Authy.
- Scanning a QR code provided by your service.
- Entering the temporary code generated by the app when logging in.

This ensures that even if someone acquires your password, they would still need the second factor to gain access.

Regular Updates and Security Patches

Keep your wallet software and any devices it runs on up to date with the latest security patches and updates. Software updates often include critical security fixes that protect against newly discovered vulnerabilities.

For instance, on a Linux-based system, you could schedule a regular update with:

```
sudo apt-get update && sudo apt-get upgrade -y
```

Similarly, ensure that your antivirus software is current and that regular scans are performed to detect and block any potential malware.

Cold Storage Solutions

For long-term storage of significant amounts of Bitcoin, cold storage solutions are highly recommended. Cold storage involves keeping the private keys offline, away from potential online threats. Hardware wallets and paper wallets are prominent methods of cold storage, each with its own unique advantages.

- *Hardware Wallets*: These are physical devices that securely store private keys offline. Only connect your hardware wallet to the internet when transactions need to be signed.
- *Paper Wallets*: Generate a paper wallet by printing your Bitcoin address and private key on paper. Ensure it is stored in a safe, dry place, and consider additional protective measures such as lamination or storing in a safe deposit box.

Backup and Recovery

Ensure that you have a reliable backup strategy for your wallet. Backups should be created regularly and stored in multiple locations to mitigate risks such as hardware failure, theft, or natural disasters.

In software wallets, this typically involves exporting the wallet file or seed phrase. For instance:

```
Backup Wallet > Export Seed Phrase
```

Store backups in secure, offline environments. A recommended practice is to use encrypted USB drives or external hard drives and to distribute these across different physical locations.

Segregation of Funds

To enhance security, segregate your funds across multiple wallets. Use hot wallets for daily transactions and cold storage for the majority of your Bitcoin holdings. This approach limits the exposure of your funds to risks associated with online transactions.

For minimal exposure, consider transferring only the amount required for specific transactions to your hot wallet, while keeping the rest securely stored in your cold wallet. This practice minimizes the risk posture of your primary holdings.

Secure Environment

Operate your wallet in a secure environment. Avoid using public Wi-Fi networks as they are susceptible to man-in-the-middle attacks. Instead, use a secure, private network with strong router passwords and consider the use of a Virtual Private Network (VPN) to encrypt your internet connection.

Physical Security

Finally, reinforce physical security measures. If your wallet setup includes a paper or hardware component, store it in a secure location, such as a safe or a locked drawer. Physical access to these components by unauthorized individuals compromises their security, irrespective of the digital measures in place.

By integrating these practices into your routine, you enhance the security of your Bitcoin wallet, thereby safeguarding your digital assets against a range of potential threats.

4.8 Backup and Recovery of Wallets

Backups are a crucial aspect of managing Bitcoin wallets, ensuring that one can restore access to their funds in the event of hardware failures, theft, or accidental deletion. Comprehending the procedures for effective backup and recovery solidifies the security foundation of a cryptocurrency user.

At the core of Bitcoin wallet backups are two fundamental components: the private keys and the wallet's metadata. The private keys grant the ability to spend bitcoins associated with the wallet, while the metadata includes additional information such as transaction history and address labels.

A recommended practice is to create backups immediately upon wallet setup and to update backups following any substantial changes, such as receiving new bitcoins or generating new addresses.

Backup Methods

Common methods for backing up Bitcoin wallets include mnemonic seeds, wallet.dat files, and manual key storage.

Mnemonic Seed

A mnemonic seed, also known as a recovery phrase, is a sequence of 12 to 24 words that encapsulates the private keys of a deterministic wallet. This seed can restore access to the wallet and all derived addresses. Here's an example of a 12-word mnemonic seed:

abandon abandon abandon abandon abandon abandon abandon abandon abandon abandon abandon about

To backup a wallet using a mnemonic seed, follow these steps:

- Open the wallet application.
- Navigate to the backup menu and select the option for displaying the mnemonic seed.
- Write down the seed accurately on a physical medium – do not store it digitally to avoid potential hacking risks.
- Store the written seed in a secure location, ideally in multiple geographically distributed places.

Wallet.dat Files

For wallets that use the wallet.dat file (e.g., Bitcoin Core), users can backup this file directly. The wallet.dat file contains encrypted private keys and other necessary wallet data.

To backup the wallet.dat file:

```
cp ~/.bitcoin/wallet.dat ~/backup_location/wallet.dat
```

Ensure that the backup location is secure and has redundant copies. Example directories could be external hard drives or USB flash drives stored in physically secure environments.

Recovery Procedures

Recovering with Mnemonic Seed

To recover a Bitcoin wallet using a mnemonic seed, initiate the wallet application and select the restore function. The process generally involves:

- Choosing the restore option upon initialization of the wallet software.
- Entering the mnemonic seed word-by-word in the specified order.
- Following any additional prompts that configure the wallet settings.

Recovering wallet.dat File

If recovering from a wallet.dat file, the procedure requires substituting the current wallet.dat with the backup file. Assuming the backup is located at ~/backup_location/wallet.dat, the command would be:

```
cp ~/backup_location/wallet.dat ~/.bitcoin/wallet.dat
```

Restart the wallet application to load the backup.

Ensuring Backup Integrity

Routine verification of backup integrity is advisable. Verifying the consistency of the mnemonic seed can be done by restoring it in a separate instance of the wallet software and ensuring it corresponds to the original addresses. For wallet.dat backups, periodically testing the file by loading it in the wallet software will confirm its usability.

Additionally, consider encrypting backup files to add an extra layer of security. This can be achieved utilizing command-line tools:

```
gpg -c ~/backup_location/wallet.dat
```

The encrypted backup will be stored as wallet.dat.gpg.

The intersection of regular backups and proven recovery techniques forms a robust safeguard against potential loss scenarios, protecting the user's digital assets effectively.

4.9 Wallet Best Practices

When managing a Bitcoin wallet, it is critical to adhere to established best practices to ensure the security and integrity of your digital assets. This section outlines key practices you should implement to fortify your Bitcoin wallet against potential threats and vulnerabilities. We will discuss various categories of considerations, including password management, encryption, software updates, transaction practices, and physical security.

Password management is a cornerstone of wallet security. When creating a password for your Bitcoin wallet, it should be both strong and unique. A robust password typically includes a mix of uppercase and lowercase letters, numbers, and special characters and is at least 16 characters long. Avoid using easily guessable information such as birthdays, common phrases, or simple sequences. One recommended approach is using a passphrase consisting of random words from a large dictionary. For example, using a password manager to generate and store complex passwords can enhance security:

Example of generating a strong password using a password manager

```
# Using a hypothetical password manager command-line interface
password-manager generate --length 20 --special-characters true
```

Subsequently, ensure that your Bitcoin wallet and any associated services support two-factor authentication (2FA). 2FA adds an extra layer of security by combining something you know (your password) with something you have (a secondary device or biometric verification). Common implementations of 2FA include SMS-based codes, authenticator apps like Google Authenticator, and hardware tokens such as YubiKey. Implementing 2FA makes it considerably more difficult for unauthorized individuals to access your wallet, even if they obtain your password.

Wallet encryption is another essential practice. Encrypting your wallet prevents unauthorized access to your funds and sensitive information in the event your device is compromised. Most software wallets offer encryption features which can be enabled in their security settings. For additional security, you can use disk encryption tools like BitLocker (on Windows) or FileVault (on macOS) to encrypt your entire device. It is crucial to securely store your encryption passphrases and backups in multiple locations to prevent loss due to hardware failure or other incidents.

Regularly updating your wallet software is critical for maintaining security. Developers frequently release updates to address security flaws, improve performance, and add new features. To ensure you are running the latest version, enable automatic updates if available, or regularly check for updates on the official website of your wallet provider. For command-line wallets, updating can be done using package managers or direct downloads:

Example of updating a Bitcoin wallet using a package manager

```
# On Debian-based systems
sudo apt-get update
sudo apt-get upgrade bitcoin-wallet
```

Transaction practices are also important for wallet security. Always verify the recipient address at least twice before sending a transaction, as malware can insert an attacker's address in place of the intended recipient's. For higher anonymity and additional security, consider using a new address for each transaction, a practice known as address reuse prevention. Many wallets support the automatic generation of new addresses for receiving funds, which can be enabled in the wallet's settings.

Another layer of transaction security involves using multi-signature addresses. Multi-signature (multi-sig) requires multiple private keys to authorize a transaction, offering an additional safeguard against unauthorized spending. Setting up a multi-sig wallet involves defining how many keys are required to approve transactions and can be accomplished through compatible wallets like Electrum or hardware wallets:

Example of setting up a multi-signature wallet

```
# Using Electrum wallet for multi-sig setup
electrum create_multisig_wallet --keys 3 --required 2
```

Physical security measures are indispensable for protecting hardware wallets and paper wallets. Store these wallets in secure, tamper-evident containers and keep them in a safe or safety deposit box when not in use. Additionally, avoid exposing the private keys printed on paper wallets or stored in brain wallets to untrusted environments or individuals. For hardware wallets, ensure they are sourced from reputable providers and that the device itself has not been tampered with. Inspect packaging and purchase directly from the manufacturer to mitigate the risk of supply chain attacks.

Lastly, developing a thorough backup strategy ensures you can recover your Bitcoin wallet in the event of loss, theft, or damage. Store multiple copies of your seed phrases or private keys in different physical locations, such as secure safes or with trusted individuals. Ensure that these backups are accessible only by those who need them and are protected from environmental hazards such as fire or water damage. Regularly verify that your backups are up-to-date and that you can perform a restore by occasionally testing the restoration process in a controlled manner.

These best practices collectively enhance the security and resilience of your Bitcoin wallet, significantly reducing the risk of loss or unauthorized access. Implementing these practices rigorously will ensure the safekeeping and integrity of your digital assets in the dynamic landscape of cryptocurrencies.

4.10 Dealing with Lost or Stolen Bitcoin

Loss or theft of Bitcoin presents significant challenges due to the decentralized and immutable nature of the blockchain. This section delves into the strategies and steps to handle such incidents effectively.

When addressing lost Bitcoin, we first need to distinguish between loss due to forgotten credentials (e.g., lost private keys or passwords) and loss due to hardware failure or destruction. In both scenarios, the key principle involves preemptive measures such as backups and redundant security layers.

If a user has lost their private key or password, the Bitcoin associated with it is effectively rendered inaccessible. To mitigate such risks, the use of mnemonic phrases for wallets that support BIP39 (Bitcoin Improvement Proposal 39) should be considered. These mnemonic phrases can regenerate private keys and enable the restoration of access. For instance, when using a hardware wallet:

```
1. During the initial setup, record the 24-word mnemonic phrase provided by the device.
2. Store this phrase securely in a physical location separate from the wallet device.
```

Hardware failure often results in lost Bitcoin if the hardware wallet lacks backup. It's crucial to ensure that hardware wallets support backup mechanisms. Again, mnemonic phrases play a pivotal role here. Here's a sample procedure for handling such scenarios:

```
1. Retrieve the mnemonic phrase from its secure storage.
2. Use the phrase to restore the wallet on a new device or compatible software.
```

Theft involves unauthorized access and transfer of Bitcoin often due to compromised private keys, phishing attacks, or malware. If a theft occurs:

- **Immediate Actions**:
  - Notify exchanges and services where your Bitcoin might have been transferred. While it's rare for stolen Bitcoin to be recovered, reporting can aid in freezing or flagging the associated addresses.

- Monitor the blockchain for any suspicious transaction activity. Tools such as blockchain.info or blockexplorer.com can provide insights into the movement of stolen funds.

```
Example of a Bitcoin transaction lookup:
https://www.blockchain.com/btc/tx/[TransactionID]
```

- **Preventive Measures**:
  - Use multi-signature wallets. These require multiple private keys for transaction approval, thus providing an added security layer.
  - Enable two-factor authentication (2FA) on all services associated with your Bitcoin transactions.
  - Regularly update wallet software to incorporate the latest security patches.
  - Avoid using public Wi-Fi for wallet operations to mitigate the risk of man-in-the-middle attacks.
  - Employ hardware wallets for significant sums of Bitcoin, which are inherently secure against malware.

In the unfortunate event of theft, forensic analysis of the attack vector can provide insights into vulnerabilities. Engaging cybersecurity professionals might be necessary to audit systems for potential breaches.

$$\text{Transaction\_id} = f(\text{txHash, timestamp, senderAddress, receiverAddress, amount})$$

Understanding blockchain's transparency, users should utilize address labeling in their wallets to better manage and identify unusual activities promptly. Furthermore, to enhance responses to future incidents, users may consider the following:

- Participation in Bitcoin recovery services such as walletrecoveryservices.com, which can sometimes assist with forgotten passwords or partial key recovery.

- Regularly review and improve operational security (OpSec) practices concerning wallet management and access controls.

- Evaluate the integration of sophisticated security measures such as hardware security modules (HSMs) and cold storage solutions for long-term holdings.

For enterprises or individuals handling substantial Bitcoin portfolios, implementing designated response protocols and cybersecurity insurance could mitigate financial and operational impacts resulting from extensive theft scenarios.

In all cases, preemptive strategies significantly mitigate risks. Regular audits of security practices, maintaining updated knowledge on emerging threats, and fostering robust security habits are essential in safeguarding digital assets against potential threats of loss or theft.

Chapter 5

Bitcoin Transactions

Bitcoin transactions involve the transfer of value between addresses on the Bitcoin network, recorded on the blockchain. Understanding transactions includes knowing their structure, how they are created, broadcast, and confirmed. This chapter details transaction fees, confirmation times, and the role of Unspent Transaction Outputs (UTXOs). It also explores multi-signature transactions and different types of Bitcoin addresses, along with methods for tracking and verifying transactions and troubleshooting common issues.

5.1 Introduction to Bitcoin Transactions

Bitcoin transactions are the fundamental operations that facilitate the transfer of value on the Bitcoin network. Each transaction embodies the movement of bitcoin from one address to another, forming a crucial component of the blockchain's immutable ledger.

In a Bitcoin transaction, the value transfer is executed by consuming previously unspent transaction outputs (UTXOs) and creating new UTXOs. A UTXO represents a value amount of bitcoin that a user has received and is available to be spent in subsequent transactions. UTXOs are integral to maintaining the integrity and traceability of all transactions on the Bitcoin network.

The structure of a Bitcoin transaction can be summarized as follows:

- **Inputs:** Inputs are references to previous UTXOs. Each input essentially unlocks or spends previous bitcoin which are then transferred. An input includes a referencing transaction's hash and an index number to specify which UTXO in the referenced transaction is being consumed.

- **Outputs:** Outputs are the new UTXOs created by the transaction. Each output specifies an amount of bitcoin and a locking script, known as a scriptPubKey, which determines the conditions that must be met to spend the output in future transactions. The most common scriptPubKey locks the output to a specific Bitcoin address.

- **Locktime:** This optional field specifies the earliest time or block number at which the transaction may be added to the blockchain. If not set, the transaction is included in the next available block.

- **Version:** Indicates the version number of the Bitcoin transaction format, allowing for potential upgrades and backwards compatibility.

- **Witness Data:** Present in SegWit (Segregated Witness) transactions, this part contains witness scripts and signature data, which are separated from the main transaction data to enhance scalability and facilitate layer two scalability solutions.

To provide a clearer understanding of how a Bitcoin transaction is represented and processed, consider the following conceptual example in pseudocode. Note that this pseudocode will not be directly executable but serves to illustrate the structure.

```
Input 1:
  previous_transaction_hash: "abcd1234...",
  previous_transaction_index: 0,
  scriptSig: <signature>

Output 1:
  amount: 0.5 BTC,
  scriptPubKey: OP_DUP OP_HASH160 <pubKeyHash1> OP_EQUALVERIFY
        OP_CHECKSIG

Output 2:
  amount: 0.3 BTC,
  scriptPubKey: OP_DUP OP_HASH160 <pubKeyHash2> OP_EQUALVERIFY
        OP_CHECKSIG

Locktime: 0
Version: 1
```

Bitcoin transactions adhere to a chain structure where each transaction input consumes UTXOs created by previous transactions. This chaining enforces transparency and accountability within the Bitcoin network, ensuring the integrity of the transaction history.

When a new transaction is created, it must be signed with the appropriate private keys that correspond to the public keys or addresses specified in the inputs' scriptPubKeys. The private key signs the transaction, producing a signature that validates the transaction's authenticity and the user's ownership of the referenced UTXOs.

After signing, the transaction is broadcast to the Bitcoin network, where it is propagated to nodes for validation. Nodes verify the transaction's structure, signatures, and that its inputs have not been double-spent. Valid transactions are then included in the nodes' mempool, pending inclusion in a block by a miner.

Here is a more detailed example, showing a real-world scenario of creating and broadcasting a Bitcoin transaction using a typical Bitcoin library in Python, such as 'bitcoinlib':

```
from bitcoinlib.wallets import Wallet, wallet_create_or_open

w = wallet_create_or_open('TestWallet')
address = w.get_key().address
print("Generated Address: %s" % address)

tx_info = [{
    'address': recipient_address,
    'value': 100000 # Amount in Satoshis (0.001 BTC)
}]

tx = w.transaction_create(tx_info, fee=5000)
print("Raw Transaction: %s" % tx.raw_hex)

# Sign and send transaction
tx_signed = w.transaction_sign(tx)
tx_id = tx_signed.send()
print("Transaction ID: %s" % tx_id)
```

Example output from executing the code:

```
Generated Address: 1A1zP1eP5QGefi2DMPTfTL5SLmv7DivfNa
Raw Transaction: 0100000001abcd...
Transaction ID: e8c30667d442d...
```

This snippet demonstrates the process of generating a receiving address, creating a transaction, signing it, and broadcasting it to the network. The precise amounts, addresses, transaction fees, and signatures are determined by the library functions and underlying blockchain state.

Understanding Bitcoin transactions and their structure is pivotal for anyone engaging with the Bitcoin ecosystem. The detailed mechanics of creating, broadcasting, and processing transactions fortify the security and decentralization principles that Bitcoin upholds. The forthcoming sections will build upon this fundamental knowledge, exploring the intricacies of transaction fees, confirmation processes, and advanced concepts like multi-signature transactions and various address types.

5.2 Anatomy of a Bitcoin Transaction

A Bitcoin transaction typically represents the transfer of value from one entity to another within the decentralized Bitcoin network. Each transaction is recorded on the blockchain and contains several critical components that ensure its validity and immutability. Understanding the anatomy of a Bitcoin transaction is essential for comprehending how Bitcoin operates at a technical level.

A standard Bitcoin transaction consists of three primary parts: inputs, outputs, and metadata.

Inputs: The transaction inputs refer to the source of the funds being spent in the transaction. Each input points to an unspent transaction output (UTXO) from a previous transaction. The input essentially specifies which funds are being used, and it includes two fundamental elements:

- *Transaction ID:* This is the identifier of the transaction that created the UTXO being spent.
- *Output Index:* This index refers to the specific output within the referenced transaction.

Additionally, an input contains a script known as the *scriptSig*, which is used to unlock the referenced output. The *scriptSig* commonly consists of a digital signature and a public key, which are used to satisfy the conditions set by the output's locking script.

Outputs: The outputs in a Bitcoin transaction define the destination of the funds and the conditions under which they can be spent. Each transaction can have one or more outputs, and each output includes:

- *Value:* This is the amount of Bitcoin, expressed in satoshis (1 Bitcoin = 100,000,000 satoshis), allocated to this output.

- *ScriptPubKey:* Also known as the locking script, it contains the conditions that must be satisfied for the output to be spent in a future transaction. This typically includes the recipient's public address or public key hash.

To illustrate these components, consider the following visual structure of a Bitcoin transaction:

Transaction Inputs (*Inputs*)	Transaction Outputs (*Outputs*)

Each Bitcoin transaction must satisfy strict rules and conditions to be considered valid. The total sum of inputs must cover the sum of outputs plus any transaction fees. This balance ensures the consistency and prevents overspending.

Metadata: Bitcoin transactions also contain metadata, which includes various fields critical for the transaction's processing but not directly part of the value transfer. Important fields include:

- *Version:* Specifies the protocol version used for the transaction.
- *LockTime:* Specifies the earliest time or block height at which the transaction may be added to the blockchain.

Signature Verification: The process of verifying a transaction's authenticity involves ensuring that the digital signatures provided in the inputs match the public keys specified in the outputs. This security measure prevents unauthorized spends.

To gain a more in-depth understanding, consider the structure of a Bitcoin transaction in raw format:

```
{
  "version": 1,
  "locktime": 0,
  "vin": [
    {
      "txid": "previous_transaction_id",
      "vout": index_of_output,
      "scriptSig": {
        "asm": "signature public_key",
        "hex": "signature_and_public_key_in_hex"
      },
      "sequence": 4294967295
    }
  ],
  "vout": [
    {
      "value": amount_in_satoshis,
      "n": output_index,
      "scriptPubKey": {
```

```
        "asm": "OP_DUP OP_HASH160 recipient_public_key_hash
            OP_EQUALVERIFY OP_CHECKSIG",
        "hex": "hexadecimal_representation_of_script",
        "reqSigs": 1,
        "type": "pubkeyhash",
        "addresses": [
          "recipient_bitcoin_address"
        ]
      }
    }
  ]
}
```

In the provided example, the transaction comprises a single input and a single output. The input references a previous transaction's output, including the digital signature and public key in the *scriptSig* to authorize the spending. The output specifies the amount being transferred and includes the locking script (*scriptPubKey*) that determines the recipient and the conditions for future spending.

The mechanism of digital signatures and hashing ensures that each transaction is secure and tamper-proof. The self-contained nature of each transaction makes it possible to verify it independently without requiring additional data from the blockchain, except for the referenced UTXOs. Understanding these components and their interactions facilitates a deeper grasp of how Bitcoin maintains its robustness and reliability as a decentralized digital currency.

5.3 How to Create and Broadcast a Transaction

Creating and broadcasting a Bitcoin transaction involves several distinct steps, which together ensure the secure and verifiable transfer of value on the Bitcoin network. This section delineates each step in detail, beginning with the preparation of transaction inputs and outputs, followed by the construction of the transaction, digital signing, and finally, broadcasting to the Bitcoin network.

First, it is essential to identify the transaction inputs. Each input references a previous transaction's output that has not yet been spent, commonly referred to as the Unspent Transaction Output (UTXO). The UTXO includes information such as the amount of Bitcoin available for spending and the address to which it is linked. To create a new transaction, select one or more UTXOs whose combined value is at least equal to the amount you wish to send plus any associated transaction fees.

The next step involves specifying the transaction outputs. Outputs determine where the Bitcoin will be sent. Each output contains a value field representing the amount of Bitcoin to transfer and a receiving address field. There can be multiple outputs in a transaction. One common practice is to include an additional output known as the "change address" to receive any leftover Bitcoin when the input value exceeds the desired transaction amount and fees.

Once the inputs and outputs are established, the transaction's core data structure, known as the transaction message, is constructed. This message comprises several components including version number, input count, outputs, lock time, and others which together form a serialized string. Below is a simplified representation of transaction construction:

```
import hashlib
from bitcoinlib.transactions import Transaction, Output, Input

# Example Transaction Creation
inputs = [
    Input(txid=prev_tx_hash, vout=index_of_prev_output,
          scriptSig=unlocking_script, sequence=0xffffffff)
]

outputs = [
    Output(value=satoshi_amount, scriptPubKey=locking_script),
    Output(value=change_amount, scriptPubKey=change_address_script)
]

tx = Transaction(version=1, inputs=inputs, outputs=outputs)

# Serialize the transaction
serialized_tx = tx.as_hex()
```

The next stage is the digital signing of the transaction. Digital signatures provide a mechanism to verify that the sender owns the Bitcoins being transferred and authorizes the transaction. Signing involves creating a cryptographic hash of the transaction message and then using the sender's private key to generate a digital signature. Only the sender's private key can generate this signature, and the corresponding public key can verify it, ensuring authenticity and integrity. The following example demonstrates how to sign the transaction in Python:

```
from bitcoinlib.keys import Key

# Replace with actual private key
private_key = Key('your_private_key')

# Sign transaction
for inp in tx.inputs:
```

```
    inp.scriptSig = private_key.sign_tx_input(tx, inp.index)

# Verify signature
valid = private_key.verify_tx(tx)
assert valid, "Transaction signature verification failed"

# Updated serialized transaction after signing
signed_serialized_tx = tx.as_hex()
```

Once the transaction is signed, it is serialized into a raw hexadecimal format and ready for broadcasting to the network. Broadcasting involves sending the signed raw transaction to the Bitcoin network so it can be propagated to miners for validation and inclusion in the blockchain. The broadcasting process can be done using Bitcoin nodes or third-party APIs. Below is an example using the RPC interface of a Bitcoin node:

```
from bitcoinrpc.authproxy import AuthServiceProxy, JSONRPCException

# RPC connection details
rpc_user = 'your_rpc_user'
rpc_password = 'your_rpc_password'
rpc_host = 'localhost'
rpc_port = '8332'

# Establish RPC connection
rpc_connection = AuthServiceProxy(f"http://{rpc_user}:{rpc_password}@{rpc_host
    }:{rpc_port}")

# Broadcast the transaction
try:
    tx_id = rpc_connection.sendrawtransaction(signed_serialized_tx)
    print("Transaction ID:", tx_id)
except JSONRPCException as e:
    print("Error broadcasting transaction:", e)
```

Upon successful broadcasting, the raw transaction is propagated across the Bitcoin network and awaits validation by miners. During this phase, miners verify that the transaction adheres to the Bitcoin protocol rules, such as proper digital signatures and sufficient fees. Upon validation, the transaction is included in a mined block and appended to the blockchain, making the transfer of Bitcoin final and irreversible.

This process of meticulously crafting, signing, and broadcasting a Bitcoin transaction ensures the decentralized and secure nature of the Bitcoin network, safeguarding transactions against fraud and double-spending.

5.4 Transaction Fees and How They Work

Transaction fees are a fundamental aspect of the Bitcoin network, serving as an incentive for miners to process and confirm transactions. The fees also function as a mechanism to manage and prioritize network traffic, especially during periods of high demand. This section delves into the intricacies of transaction fees, elucidating their calculation, significance, and strategies for optimization.

Bitcoin transaction fees are not fixed and can vary significantly depending on multiple factors, including the size of the transaction, the current network congestion, and the priority level chosen by the user. Transaction fees are measured in satoshis per byte (sat/byte), where one satoshi is equivalent to 10^{-8} BTC. The higher the sat/byte, the higher the priority given to the transaction by miners.

When a user generates a new Bitcoin transaction, they typically specify the fee rate they are willing to pay. Wallet software such as Bitcoin Core, Electrum, and others often provide estimated fee rates based on current network conditions. The simplest form of this is seen in a Bitcoin Core GUI for setting custom fees:

```
# Set transaction fee rate
settxfee rate_in_btc_per_kb
```

Fee Calculation

The total transaction fee is calculated by multiplying the transaction size (in bytes) by the chosen fee rate. For example, a transaction of 250 bytes with a fee rate of 50 sat/byte would result in a total fee of:

$$\text{Total Fee (satoshis)} = 250\,\text{bytes} \times 50\,\frac{\text{satoshis}}{\text{byte}} = 12500\,\text{satoshis}$$

Since 1 BTC = 100,000,000 satoshis, 12500 satoshis equate to 0.000125 BTC.

Size of the Transaction

The size of a Bitcoin transaction depends on several factors, primarily the number of inputs and outputs. Each input corresponds to a previous unspent transaction output (UTXO) that is used as the source of funds for the new transaction. Each output represents a destination address receiving Bitcoin. Inputs and outputs require specific amounts of data to be included in a transaction, summarized as follows:

- **Input size:** Roughly 148 bytes (standard P2PKH input).
- **Output size:** Roughly 34 bytes (standard P2PKH output).

Thus, a transaction with 2 inputs and 2 outputs typically would have an approximate size computed by:

$$\text{Size} = 10\,\text{bytes (base size)} + 2 \times 148\,\text{bytes (inputs)} + 2 \times 34\,\text{bytes (outputs)} = 374\,\text{bytes}$$

Dynamic Fee Adjustments

Transaction fees are not static and may be adjusted dynamically based on current network conditions. During periods of high transaction volume, fees tend to rise as users compete to have their transactions confirmed promptly. Conversely, during low activity periods, fees can drop significantly. This dynamic nature underscores the importance of setting appropriate fee rates considering the desired transaction confirmation times.

Many modern wallets incorporate features that estimate the optimal fee rate by analyzing the mempool, where unconfirmed transactions reside. These wallets may suggest different fee rates:

- **High priority:** A higher fee rate to achieve confirmation within the next block (approximately 10 minutes).
- **Standard priority:** A moderate fee rate for confirmation within the next few blocks.
- **Low priority:** A lower fee rate that may result in a longer wait time.

Segregated Witness (SegWit) Impact

Segregated Witness (SegWit) is a Bitcoin protocol upgrade that affects transaction size and fee calculation. By separating witness data from the transaction data, SegWit transactions are effectively smaller, leading to reduced fees for the same transaction volume. The concept of *weight* is utilized in SegWit-enabled transactions:

$$\text{Weight unit} = \text{Base size} \times 3 + \text{Total size}$$

For a transaction of 120 base size bytes and 300 total size bytes, the weight would be:

$$\text{Weight} = 120\,\text{bytes} \times 3 + 300\,\text{bytes} = 660\ \text{weight units}$$

SegWit reduces the bytes counted in the fee and thereby the overall fee.

Replace-By-Fee (RBF)

RBF is a feature allowing users to rebroadcast a transaction with a higher fee if an earlier transaction remains unconfirmed. This increases the likelihood of miners including the newer, higher-fee transaction in the blockchain. RBF, though useful, is subject to policies of individual miners and nodes on the network.

Using Bitcoin Core, enabling RBF for a transaction can be done as follows:

```
# Enable RBF in Bitcoin Core
bitcoin-cli sendtoaddress "address" amount "comment" "comment-to" "
    subtractfeefromamount" "replaceable"
```

Fee Mempool Analysis

Observing the memory pool (mempool) helps predict future fee trends. Monitoring tools like Mempool.space provide real-time mempool data and fee recommendations, aiding users in selecting appropriate fees:

```
Mempool data:
  - Current unconfirmed transactions: 10,000
  - Recommended fee for next block: 120 sat/byte
  - Average confirmation time: 2 blocks
```

Mastering the factors influencing Bitcoin transaction fees equips users to navigate the Bitcoin network efficiently, optimizing transaction costs, and ensuring timely confirmations based on their specific requirements.

5.5 Confirmations and Transaction Speed

A Bitcoin transaction is considered complete or "confirmed" once it has been validated by the Bitcoin network and included in a mined block. Understanding the concept of confirmations and the factors influencing transaction speed is crucial for efficiently utilizing the Bitcoin network.

A confirmation occurs when a transaction has been included in a block that is added to the blockchain. The blockchain is a continually growing list of blocks, each containing a record of multiple Bitcoin transactions.

To verify a transaction's legitimacy and prevent double-spending, the network relies on a consensus mechanism known as Proof-of-Work (PoW).

Each time a new block is added, it references the previous block, validating not just new transactions but also confirming the transactions from the previous block. When a transaction is said to have n confirmations, it means that it has been included in the blockchain and $n-1$ additional blocks have been added since.

Factors Influencing Confirmation Time:

Several variables can affect the time it takes for a transaction to receive confirmations:

- **Network Congestion:** High transaction volumes can lead to a backlog of transactions waiting to be included in blocks. During periods of congestion, users might experience delays in transaction confirmation.
- **Transaction Fees:** Miners prioritize transactions that offer higher fees. A user can accelerate the confirmation of a transaction by including a higher fee to incentivize miners.
- **Block Intervals:** Bitcoin aims to generate a new block approximately every 10 minutes. However, due to the probabilistic nature of mining, the interval can vary, influencing transaction confirmation times.
- **Block Size and Transaction Size:** The Bitcoin protocol enforces a block size limit, which constrains the number of transactions that can be included in each block. Larger transactions or transactions that include multiple UTXOs may take longer to confirm.

Transaction Priority and Fees:

The fee a user attaches to a transaction directly impacts its priority in the network. Bitcoin transactions include a variable fee calculated as the difference between the input value and the output value. Miners are financially motivated to maximize their earnings by selecting transactions that offer the highest fees per byte.

Example: If a transaction has an input of 0.5 BTC and the outputs total 0.4995 BTC, the fee is 0.0005 BTC. The higher this fee relative to the transaction's size (in bytes), the more likely it is to be included in the next block.

Users can utilize fee estimation tools provided by many Bitcoin wallets to determine an appropriate fee to ensure a timely confirmation. The chosen fee should balance cost and the desired confirmation speed.

Estimating Transaction Speed:

The estimated time for a transaction to gain the necessary confirmations depends on the aforementioned factors. Users can track their transactions using block explorers or blockchain analysis tools, which provide details such as the number of confirmations a transaction has received, estimated confirmation times, and current fee rates.

Bitcoin wallets frequently update to reflect the latest network conditions, giving users dynamic fee recommendations based on current congestion levels. Below is a basic implementation demonstrating the broadcast and confirmation of a Bitcoin transaction:

```
from bitcoin import SelectParams
from bitcoin.core import b2lx, COIN, lx
from bitcoin.core.script import OP_CHECKSIG
from bitcoin.wallet import CBitcoinSecret, P2PKHBitcoinAddress
from bitcoin.rpc import Proxy

SelectParams('mainnet')
proxy = Proxy()

# Private Key and Address
private_key = CBitcoinSecret('your_private_key')
from_address = P2PKHBitcoinAddress.from_pubkey(private_key.pub)

# Create and sign the transaction (simplified)
txid = lx('previous_transaction_id')
vout = 0
amount = 0.01 * COIN
new_address = P2PKHBitcoinAddress('recipient_address')

# Prepare the input and output
txin = CTransactionIn(txid, vout)
txout = CTransactionOut(amount, CScript([OP_CHECKSIG]))

# Sign the transaction
tx = CMutableTransaction([txin], [txout])
sighash = SignatureHash(CScript([OP_CHECKSIG]), tx, 0, SIGHASH_ALL)
signature = private_key.sign(sighash) + bytes([SIGHASH_ALL])
txin.scriptSig = CScript([signature])

# Broadcast the transaction
proxy.sendrawtransaction(tx)
txid = proxy.sendrawtransaction(tx)
print(f"Transaction sent with txid: {b2lx(txid)}")
```

The transaction's status, including the number of confirmations, can be periodically checked by utilizing the proxy's gettransaction method, ensuring users remain informed about their transaction progress.

As the network evolves, advancements like the Lightning Network are being developed to address scalability issues and improve transaction speed and cost. The Lightning Network, operating as a second-layer solution, allows off-chain transactions to be settled instantly and more cost-effectively, though this method currently requires both parties to have Lightning Network compatible wallets.

Conclusively, understanding confirmations and transaction speed is fundamental for effectively managing Bitcoin transactions. This includes recognizing the influence of network congestion, transaction fees, and choosing appropriate settings to meet one's transactional requirements efficiently.

5.6 UTXOs: Unspent Transaction Outputs

The concept of Unspent Transaction Outputs (UTXOs) is integral to understanding how Bitcoin transactions are processed and validated on the blockchain. In the Bitcoin network, UTXOs play a pivotal role by representing discrete units of Bitcoin that can be spent in future transactions. Each UTXO is associated with a specific amount of Bitcoin and has not yet been consumed as input in another transaction.

When a Bitcoin transaction is initiated, it consumes one or more UTXOs as inputs and generates new UTXOs as outputs. These outputs can then be used in subsequent transactions. The lifecycle of a UTXO starts when it is created by a transaction and ends when it is spent in another transaction.

```
import hashlib

def sha256(data):
    return hashlib.sha256(data.encode()).hexdigest()

# Example UTXO with address and amount
utxo_1 = {
    'address': '1BitcoinAddress',
    'amount': 1.5
}

# Transaction: sending 1.0 BTC from utxo_1
transaction_input = utxo_1
transaction_output_1 = {
    'address': '1RecipientAddress',
    'amount': 1.0
}
# Change UTXO
transaction_output_2 = {
    'address': '1BitcoinAddress',
    'amount': 0.5
}
```

```
# Generating transaction ID
transaction_id = sha256(f'{transaction_input} -> {transaction_output_1}, {
    transaction_output_2}')
print(transaction_id)
```

In this example, utxo_1 represents an unspent transaction output with an address and an amount. When a transaction is created to send 1.0 BTC to a recipient, it consumes utxo_1 as an input and generates two new UTXOs: one for the recipient and another for the change returned to the sender.

UTXOs are stored in the blockchain as part of the transaction and remain unspent until they are referenced as inputs in a new transaction. This design ensures that the ledger maintains a clear record of spendable Bitcoin, allowing for quick and accurate transaction validation.

Structure of UTXOs

Each UTXO is uniquely identified by a combination of the transaction ID (txid) and the output index. The txid is a hash of the transaction in which the UTXO was created, and the index (vout) specifies which output within that transaction the UTXO represents.

$$UTXO = (txid, vout, amount, address)$$

Where:

- *txid*: The hash of the transaction that created this UTXO.
- *vout*: The index of the output in the transaction.
- *amount*: The amount of Bitcoin in this UTXO.
- *address*: The receiving address for this UTXO.

Creating and Consuming UTXOs

To better understand the role of UTXOs, consider how they are created and consumed in a typical transaction sequence. Let's say Alice wants to send Bitcoin to Bob:

- Input UTXOs: Alice's wallet will select UTXOs that she controls, which sum to at least the amount she wants to send to Bob.
- Transaction Creation: A transaction is created with the selected UTXOs as inputs and new outputs: one to Bob's address and potentially another to Alice as change.

- Validation: The transaction is broadcast to the Bitcoin network, where it is validated by nodes. Each node verifies that the inputs (the UTXOs) are unspent and authorized by Alice's private key.

- Confirmation: Once the transaction is included in a block and added to the blockchain, the UTXOs used as inputs are marked as spent, and the new outputs become UTXOs.

The following Python code demonstrates how to check if a UTXO has been spent:

```
utxo_set = {
    'txid_1': [0, 1], # UTXOs from transaction txid_1 (output indices 0 and 1)
}

def is_utxo_spent(txid, vout):
    return vout not in utxo_set.get(txid, [])

# Example usage
txid = 'txid_1'
vout = 0
print(is_utxo_spent(txid, vout)) # Output: False since vout 0 is still in utxo_set
```

In the example, utxo_set is a dictionary that keeps track of UTXOs by transaction IDs and output indices. The is_utxo_spent function checks if a given UTXO has been spent by verifying its presence in the set.

Efficiency and Scalability

The UTXO model offers several advantages in terms of efficiency and scalability. By maintaining a clear record of all spendable outputs, the network can quickly verify transactions without needing to track account balances. This model also enhances privacy, as each transaction essentially mixes and severs the history of UTXOs.

The scalability of Bitcoin benefits from the UTXO model by facilitating parallel validation. Since UTXOs are independent, multiple transactions can be validated concurrently without requiring access to a single, mutable global state, thereby reducing bottlenecks.

Understanding UTXOs is crucial for grasping the mechanics of Bitcoin transactions and the operation of the blockchain. The lifecycle of UTXOs, from creation to consumption, underpins the decentralized and trustless nature of the Bitcoin network, ensuring secure and transparent transaction validation.

5.7 Multi-Signature Transactions

A multi-signature transaction, often referred to as multi-sig, is a type of Bitcoin transaction that requires multiple private keys to authorize and execute. This mechanism adds an additional layer of security by distributing the control of funds among several parties. Multi-sig transactions are particularly valuable for organizational funds, escrow services, and joint account management where collaborative approval is necessary.

In a standard Bitcoin transaction, a single private key is sufficient to authorize the transfer of funds. A multi-sig transaction, however, can be configured to require two or more keys. The common notation for multi-sig wallets is *m-of-n*, where *m* is the number of required signatures to authorize the transaction and *n* is the total number of possible signers.

To understand the structure and execution of multi-sig transactions, it is essential to delve into the technical aspects, including the creation of multi-sig addresses and the process of signing transactions.

Creating a Multi-Signature Address

To create a multi-sig address, public keys are collected from the involved parties. These public keys are then used to generate a unique multi-sig address through a process that involves the creation of a Pay-to-Script-Hash (P2SH) address. The following steps outline this process:

- Collect the public keys (*n*) of all participants.
- Create a script that specifies the required number of signatures (*m*) to authorize transactions.
- Hash the script to generate a unique address that begins with "3", indicating a P2SH multi-sig address.

The steps can be demonstrated through the following pseudo-code:

```
# Assume we have three public keys from participants
public_keys = [
    "02a1633bc...e5e33f5",
    "03d8a0baf...b5a6eb7",
    "028af97c0...6e6e4b6"
]

# Specify the required number of signatures (m)
m = 2
```

```
# Create a multi-sig script
multi_sig_script = f"{m} [pub_key_1] [pub_key_2] [pub_key_3] {n}
    OP_CHECKMULTISIG"

# Hash the script to get the multi-sig address
multi_sig_address = hash160(multi_sig_script)
```

Signing a Multi-Signature Transaction

Once a multi-sig address is created, funds can be sent to this address like any other Bitcoin address. To spend from a multi-sig address, the same multi-sig script is used, and the transaction must include the necessary signatures.

Here is a systematic procedure for signing and broadcasting a multi-sig transaction:

- Construct a transaction demanding the spending from the multi-sig address.
- Every signer generates a signature using their private key.
- Combine multiple signatures to satisfy the multi-sig script's requirements.
- Broadcast the transaction to the Bitcoin network.

The following pseudo-code simulates generating and combining signatures for a 2-of-3 multi-sig transaction:

```
# Assume we have a transaction to be signed
tx_to_sign = "02000...0bc000"

# Generate signatures from two required private keys
signature1 = sign_transaction(tx_to_sign, private_key_1)
signature2 = sign_transaction(tx_to_sign, private_key_2)

# Combine signatures into a single transaction
signed_tx = combine_signatures(tx_to_sign, [signature1, signature2])

# Broadcast the signed transaction to the network
broadcast_transaction(signed_tx)
```

Security and Use Cases

Multi-sig transactions enhance security by distributing the power to authorize transactions across multiple individuals or devices. This reduces the risk of single points of failure, as no single party possesses sole control over the funds.

Multi-sig wallets are useful in various contexts:

- Corporate Accounts: Require approvals from multiple executives for expenditure.
- Escrow Services: Secure transactions between buyers and sellers, requiring both sides to agree before funds are released.
- Family and Joint Accounts: Ensure that multiple family members must agree on significant expenditures.

By requiring multiple approvals, multi-sig transactions make unauthorized access much more difficult. Additionally, even if one key is compromised, the attacker would still need additional keys to access the funds.

Technical Considerations

Some technical aspects to be aware of when dealing with multi-sig transactions include higher transaction fees and larger transaction sizes. Multi-sig transactions involve more data (scripts, multiple signatures), which translates to higher fees. Proper key management protocols must be in place to prevent the loss of keys, which could result in permanent loss of access to the associated funds.

Overall, the increased security and control provided by multi-sig transactions offer substantial benefits, particularly for organizations and high-value wallets, making them an essential feature of the Bitcoin toolkit.

This concludes the detailed discussion of multi-signature transactions and their implementation within the Bitcoin ecosystem.

5.8 Bitcoin Addresses: Legacy, SegWit, and Bech32

A Bitcoin address is a string of alphanumeric characters that uniquely identifies a possible recipient of a Bitcoin transaction. Comprehending the different types of Bitcoin addresses, namely Legacy, Segregated Witness (SegWit), and Bech32, is pivotal for participating in the Bitcoin network and optimizing transaction fees and confirmation times.

Legacy addresses, also known as Pay-to-PubKey-Hash (P2PKH) addresses, were the first type of Bitcoin addresses introduced. These addresses start with the digit '1' and are represented by the following format:

```
1A1zP1eP5QGefi2DMPTfTL5SLmv7DivfNa
```

These addresses are derived from the public key using the SHA-256 and RIPEMD-160 hashing algorithms. However, they come with larger transaction sizes when compared to SegWit addresses, often leading to higher transaction fees.

Segregated Witness, or SegWit, was an upgrade to the Bitcoin protocol designed to mitigate transaction malleability and enhance block capacity. SegWit introduces a separate witness area in the transaction data, altering the architecture of transactions. One of the two types of SegWit addresses is Pay-to-Witness-PubKey-Hash (P2WPKH), which is encoded in the Bech32 format and starts with 'bc1':

```
bc1qar0srrr7xfkvy5l643lydnw9re59gtzzwf63z0
```

The above-mentioned Bech32 format provides a more efficient encoding scheme and can accommodate a broader range of alphanumeric characters, including both lower and upper case, while reducing the instance of corrupt data transmission.

Another form of SegWit address is the Pay-to-Script-Hash (P2SH) nested SegWit address. These addresses start with the digit '3' and serve as a backward-compatible solution, enabling users to send funds to SegWit addresses even if their wallet or transaction software does not support SegWit natively:

```
3J98t1WpEZ73CNmQviecrnyiWrnqRhWNLy
```

These P2SH-P2WPKH addresses encapsulate the SegWit address within a script hash, providing the advantages of SegWit while retaining compatibility with non-updated systems.

Bech32, a newer address format introduced with the SegWit upgrade, offers significant benefits over its predecessors. In addition to supporting P2WPKH addresses, Bech32 enhances the robustness of the Bitcoin ecosystem by including checksum algorithms that detect typing errors in addresses. It also facilitates better QR code encoding, making scanning easier and less prone to errors.

From an implementation perspective, generating these addresses programmatically involves several steps that include deriving the private key, computing the corresponding public key, and finally encoding the public key using the desired address format. Below is an example of generating a Legacy Bitcoin address:

```
from bitcoin import *

# Generate private key
private_key = random_key()

# Generate public key
public_key = privtopub(private_key)

# Generate legacy Bitcoin address
legacy_address = pubtoaddr(public_key)
print("Legacy Bitcoin Address:", legacy_address)
```

Output:

```
Legacy Bitcoin Address: 1A1zP1eP5QGefi2DMPTfTL5SLmv7DivfNa
```

This script uses a Python Bitcoin library to derive a Legacy address from a private key. Similar scripts can be executed to generate P2SH and Bech32 addresses by appropriately modifying the procedures to include SegWit protocols.

Understanding the differences between these Bitcoin address formats and their implications on transaction fees, malleability, and confirmation times is fundamental for efficient interaction within the Bitcoin network.

5.9 Tracking and Verifying Transactions

Tracking and verifying Bitcoin transactions are essential for ensuring the transparency and trustworthiness of the Bitcoin network. These processes involve confirming that a transaction has been recorded on the blockchain, identifying its current status, and validating whether the transaction details are correct. Blockchain explorers, transaction IDs, and nodes play pivotal roles in these processes.

Blockchain explorers are web-based tools that allow users to search and navigate the blockchain ledger. These explorers enable users to view transaction histories, verify balances, and see other details related to addresses and blocks. To use a blockchain explorer, one needs the transaction ID (TXID), which is a unique identifier assigned to every Bitcoin transaction.

A typical blockchain explorer interface provides the following key information upon entering a TXID:

- **Transaction Hash:** A unique string representing the transaction ID.

- **Date and Time:** The timestamp when the transaction was included in a block.
- **Block Number:** The height of the block in which the transaction was confirmed.
- **Inputs and Outputs:** Detailed breakdown of the inputs (sending addresses and amounts) and outputs (receiving addresses and amounts).
- **Confirmation Status:** Number of confirmations the transaction has received.
- **Transaction Fee:** The fee paid to miners for including the transaction in a block.

Consider the following example of how to use a blockchain explorer with a sample TXID:

```
TXID: e3b0c44298fc1c149afbf4c8996fb92427ae41e4649b934ca495991b7852b855
```

Using the above TXID in a blockchain explorer, you would retrieve information such as the block number, the time of inclusion, the addresses involved, and the total confirmations.

Confirmations are a critical metric in verifying a transaction's finality. When a transaction is first broadcast to the Bitcoin network, it remains unconfirmed until a miner includes it in a block. Afterward, each subsequent block added to the blockchain increases the number of confirmations.

```
Transaction Confirmations:
- 0 confirmations: Transaction broadcast but not yet confirmed.
- 1 confirmation: Transaction included in a block.
- 6 or more confirmations: Generally considered secure.
```

Nodes in the Bitcoin network also play a crucial role in transaction verification. Each full node independently validates transactions against Bitcoin's consensus rules. Key validation steps include:

- **Syntax and Protocol Rules:** Checking the transaction's format and adherence to Bitcoin's protocol specifications.
- **Double-Spending:** Ensuring the inputs of the transaction are unspent and not part of another conflicting transaction.
- **Signature Verification:** Validating the cryptographic signatures that authorize the transfer of funds.

- **Consensus Rules:** Confirming compliance with rules like the transaction size limit, output structure, and fee rules.

To implement transaction verification programmatically, one can utilize Bitcoin development libraries such as ‘bitcoinlib‘ in Python. Consider the following Python code snippet for verifying a transaction:

```
from bitcoinlib.services.bitcoind import BitcoindClient

# Assume you have a running bitcoind instance
client = BitcoindClient(rpc_user='your_rpc_user',
                        rpc_password='your_rpc_password')

txid = 'e3b0c44298fc1c149afbf4c8996fb92427ae41e4649b934ca495991b7852b855'
transaction = client.gettransaction(txid)

# Display basic transaction details
print(f"Transaction ID: {transaction['txid']}")
print(f"Confirmations: {transaction['confirmations']}")
print(f"Blockhash: {transaction['blockhash']}")
print(f"Time: {transaction['time']}")
```

A simplified output of the above code might look like:

```
Transaction ID: e3b0c44298fc1c149afbf4c8996fb92427ae41e4649b934ca495991b7852b855
Confirmations: 12
Blockhash: 0000000000000000000af1a3b1c9a5b96f72b14b0c2b1e0b949840d5a7d50610
Time: 1618327047
```

Tracking and verifying Bitcoin transactions provide participants with the confidence that the network maintains an accurate and secure ledger. Whether using blockchain explorers for manual checks or implementing automated solutions through node queries and development libraries, these processes are integral to the Bitcoin ecosystem.

5.10 Common Issues and Troubleshooting

Bitcoin transactions are designed to be robust and secure, but various issues can arise during their creation, broadcasting, confirmation, and subsequent tracing on the blockchain. This section outlines the common problems encountered with Bitcoin transactions and provides detailed troubleshooting steps.

1. Transaction Stuck in Unconfirmed State

A frequent issue faced by Bitcoin users is transactions that appear stuck in the unconfirmed state. The causes for this can vary, but common reasons include low transaction fees and network congestion.

Low Transaction Fees: The fee paid per byte of transaction data directly impacts the priority of the transaction in the mempool. Transactions with lower fees may experience significant delays, especially during periods of high network congestion. To avoid this, always ensure that the fee paid is competitive:

```
$ bitcoin-cli estimatesmartfee 6
```

The above command provides a fee estimate for confirmation within approximately 6 blocks.

Network Congestion: During times of high transaction volume, the mempool becomes congested with numerous transactions awaiting confirmation. One could track mempool statistics through various blockchain explorer APIs:

```
$ curl https://mempool.space/api/mempool
```

This command provides insights into the current state of the mempool, helping users set an appropriate fee.

Solutions: If your transaction is stuck, consider the following actions:

- *Replace-By-Fee (RBF)*: Use RBF to rebroadcast the transaction with a higher fee if the original transaction opted for it.
- *Child-Pays-For-Parent (CPFP)*: Create a new transaction spending outputs from the stuck transaction with a sufficiently high fee to incentivize miners to include both transactions.

  ```
  $ bitcoin-cli sendtoaddress <address> <amount> "" "" false false true
  ```

  The 'true' at the end enables RBF.

2. Double-Spending Attempts

Accidental or malicious double-spending occurs when two transactions attempt to spend the same UTXO. Most modern Bitcoin wallets prevent this at the client's end, but discrepancies could still occur.

Detection: Double-spending attempts can be detected by nodes verifying whether the same input is being referenced multiple times:

```
$ bitcoin-cli getmempoolentry <transaction_id>
```

If the output shows a conflict, the node will reject one of the transactions.

Resolution: Ensure that wallet software is up to date and confirm the validity of UTXOs before creating new transactions. Consistently monitor the network for any unusual activities that could indicate double-spending attempts.

3. Incorrect Use of Bitcoin Addresses

Bitcoin addresses must be correctly formatted and validated to ensure successful transactions. Sending coins to an invalid address can lead to permanent loss of funds.

Address Validation: Most wallets and APIs provide an address validation function:

```
$ bitcoin-cli validateaddress <address>
```

This command checks whether the provided address is valid.

Bech32 Compatibility: Ensure compatibility with Bech32 addresses in the wallet to prevent issues arising from address format differences.

4. Transaction Propagation Delays

Propagation delays can occur due to network issues or node-specific problems. These delays could lead users to mistakenly believe their transactions are stuck.

Network Issues: Verify that the node is well-connected and synchronized:

```
$ bitcoin-cli getnetworkinfo
```

Node Configuration: Ensure the node configuration allows for sufficient incoming and outgoing connections. Increase the number of allowed connections if necessary:

```
$ echo "maxconnections=125" >> bitcoin.conf
```

5. Chain Reorganizations

Although rare, chain reorganizations can lead to transactions being temporarily reversed. These events happen when a longer blockchain fork is discovered and adopted by the network.

Handling Reorganizations: Monitor reorganization events and confirm the depth of confirmations required for transaction security:

```
$ tail -f ~/.bitcoin/debug.log | grep 'Reorg'
```

Adjust the number of confirmations required for high-value transactions to mitigate risks associated with chain reorganizations.

6. Private Key Management Issues

Losing access to private keys means the loss of control over associated funds. This can arise from various factors including hardware failures, human error, or security breaches.

Backup Strategies: Regularly backup the wallet.dat file or mnemonic phrases:

```
$ cp ~/.bitcoin/wallet.dat /path/to/backup/
```

Secure Storage: Store backups in secure, geographically distributed locations to mitigate risks from physical damage or localized incidents.

Each of these common issues requires a careful diagnostic process and corresponding remedial actions. Ensuring proper fee management, adhering to best practices for address validation, improving connectivity, preparing for rare events like double-spends and chain reorganizations, and maintaining diligent backup practices are fundamental measures to minimize and address potential transaction problems.

Chapter 6

The Economics of Bitcoin

The economics of Bitcoin involves understanding its supply and demand dynamics, monetary policy, and market behavior. Bitcoin operates on a deflationary model with a fixed supply of 21 million coins, influenced by periodic halvings. This chapter explores Bitcoin as a store of value, its inflation and deflation characteristics, market volatility, trading dynamics, and the role of exchanges. It also examines the broader economic impact of Bitcoin adoption and the implications for the global financial system.

6.1 Introduction to Bitcoin Economics

Bitcoin represents a unique economic entity, primarily due to its deviation from conventional fiat currencies and financial systems. Its decentralized nature, limited supply, and transparent protocol introduce a new paradigm for economic analysis. This section delves into the foundational aspects of Bitcoin's economics, providing essential knowledge for comprehending its broader economic impact.

At its core, the economics of Bitcoin revolves around its supply and demand dynamics, akin to traditional economic models, but with distinct characteristics. Unlike fiat currencies, which can be printed at the discretion of central banks, Bitcoin's supply is algorithmically predetermined and capped at 21 million coins. This finite supply creates a deflationary environment, which will be explored further in subsequent sections.

Bitcoin's demand is driven by a multitude of factors, including its perceived value as a store of wealth, its utility in transactions, and its speculative appeal. As with any asset, the price of Bitcoin results from the interplay between its supply and demand on global exchanges. These exchanges facilitate the trading of Bitcoin against various fiat currencies and other cryptocurrencies, establishing a market equilibrium at any given time.

The protocol underlying Bitcoin operates on a decentralized network, maintained by nodes across the globe. The consensus mechanism, known as Proof of Work (PoW), ensures that transactions are verified and added to the public ledger, the blockchain. The economic rationale behind PoW involves incentivizing miners to expend computational resources to secure the network, in return for block rewards and transaction fees.

The block reward is a critical component in understanding Bitcoin's supply dynamics. Initially set at 50 bitcoins per block, this reward undergoes a process known as "halving," approximately every 210,000 blocks (roughly every four years). This halving event reduces the block reward by half, thereby decelerating the rate of new Bitcoin creation. Consequently, the total supply approaches the 21 million cap asymptotically.

To illustrate, consider the trajectory of halving events:

```
initial_reward = 50
halving_interval = 210000 # Blocks
max_supply = 21 * 10**6 # 21 million BTC

def calculate_total_supply():
    total_supply = 0
    current_reward = initial_reward
    while total_supply < max_supply:
        total_supply += current_reward * halving_interval
        current_reward /= 2
    return total_supply

print(calculate_total_supply())
```

This snippet of Python code demonstrates the calculation of Bitcoin's total supply, illustrating the halving mechanism's impact until the supply limit is reached.

```
Output:
20999999.9769
```

This example confirms the theoretical supply cap, validating the protocol's design. The decreasing supply increments due to halving create an interesting economic scenario where scarcity increases, potentially enhancing Bitcoin's value over time if demand remains constant or rises.

Bitcoin's decentralized and transparent protocol implies that monetary policy is enforced through code rather than subjective human intervention. This attribute starkly contrasts with centralized fiat systems, where monetary authorities can alter policy based on economic conditions. Consequently, Bitcoin's fixed supply and predictable issuance schedule provide a stable framework for long-term economic planning, albeit with known volatility challenges.

Investors and economists often view Bitcoin as a hybrid asset class. It shares attributes with commodities like gold, due to its scarcity and divisibility, as well as properties of modern currencies, enabling swift and borderless transactions. This duality positions Bitcoin as a novel subject within economic discourse, requiring new analytical tools and frameworks.

Finally, it's essential to articulate the broader economic impact of Bitcoin. Its adoption spans various facets, such as a decentralized financial system, a hedge against traditional financial instability, and as a medium for remittances and commerce. The following exploration of supply and demand dynamics, monetary policy, and more will build upon this introduction, providing a comprehensive understanding of Bitcoin economics and its role in shaping future financial landscapes.

6.2 Supply and Demand of Bitcoin

The supply and demand dynamics of Bitcoin lie at the core of its economic valuation. By understanding these factors, one can discern how market conditions and intrinsic properties of Bitcoin influence its price and circulation.

Bitcoin's supply is capped at 21 million coins, a design parameter embedded within the Bitcoin protocol by its pseudonymous creator, Satoshi Nakamoto. This limitation is enforced through a controlled issuance system termed mining, where miners validate transactions and, as a reward, generate new bitcoins. The issuance rate is systematically halved approximately every four years, a phenomenon known as the *halving*. This self-regulating monetary supply counteracts inflationary tendencies observed in traditional fiat currencies.

Mathematically, the supply function $S(t)$ of Bitcoin over time t can be expressed as:

$$S(t) = 21,000,000 - \sum_{i=1}^{N} \left(10,500,000 \times \frac{1}{2^i}\right)$$

where N represents the number of halvings elapsed. Initially, 50 bitcoins per block were awarded, a figure that halves each 210,000 blocks (approximately four years), leading to a logarithmic approach towards the cap of 21 million.

On the demand side, Bitcoin's valuation is influenced by several factors including its adoption as a payment method, its recognition as a store of value akin to digital gold, speculative trading activities, and its use in various financial instruments. The utility of Bitcoin, network effects, and perceived future value significantly drive demand.

To quantitatively analyze demand, consider the demand curve:

$$D(p) = \frac{C}{p^k}$$

where p represents the price, C a constant, and k an elasticity parameter. Higher values of k correspond to greater sensitivity of demand with respect to price changes.

Interaction between supply and demand is depicted by the equilibrium price p_e at which the quantity of Bitcoin supplied equals the quantity demanded. Formally:

$$S(p_e) = D(p_e)$$

Bitcoin markets are characterized by fractional reserve trading on exchanges, where buyers and sellers trade Bitcoin for fiat or other cryptocurrencies. This process involves market orders (purchases at current prices) and limit orders (purchases when the asset reaches a specified price). Market depth and liquidity play crucial roles in maintaining an efficient trading environment and minimizing slippage—the difference between the expected price of a trade and the actual price.

Market liquidity can be represented as:

$$L = \frac{\text{Volume of Bitcoin Transactions}}{\text{Bid-Ask Spread}}$$

A narrower bid-ask spread indicates higher liquidity, implying that large transactions can occur with minimal price impact. Conversely, a wider spread denotes lower liquidity and possible higher volatility.

Examining the historical data, Bitcoin has demonstrated periods of substantial price volatility. Such volatility often arises from macroeconomic events, regulatory announcements, technological advancements in the blockchain domain, and speculative trading. The price volatility σ can be represented statistically by the standard deviation of Bitcoin returns over a specified period.

A sample calculation can be shown as follows:

```
import numpy as np

# Assume daily closing prices of Bitcoin over a period
prices = np.array([40000, 41000, 41500, 42000, 40500, 40300])

# Calculate daily returns
returns = np.diff(prices) / prices[:-1]

# Calculate volatility (standard deviation of returns)
volatility = np.std(returns)
print(volatility)
```

The output might look like:

```
0.007071
```

This indicates that the standard deviation of daily returns in this example is approximately 0.7%, reflecting the degree of daily price variation.

Understanding the principles of supply and demand for Bitcoin helps in discerning the complex factors that govern its price dynamics, providing insight into its economic behavior in the decentralized financial ecosystem.

6.3 Bitcoin's Monetary Policy

Bitcoin's monetary policy is fundamentally distinct from traditional fiat currencies controlled by central banks. At its core, Bitcoin employs a decentralized and algorithmically enforced monetary rule set forth by its pseudonymous creator, Satoshi Nakamoto, in the original whitepaper. This policy is encoded within the Bitcoin network's protocol, which ensures that the issuance of new bitcoins follows a predictable and transparent pattern.

Bitcoin operates on a deflationary model with a fixed supply cap of 21 million coins. This contrasts sharply with fiat currencies, which can be printed in unlimited quantities by central authorities. The finite supply is achieved through an issuance mechanism called mining, where new bitcoins are created as a reward to miners for validating blocks of transactions and adding them to the blockchain.

The monetary policy of Bitcoin can be understood through three key components:

- **Fixed Supply Cap**: The maximum number of bitcoins that can ever exist is capped at 21 million. This fixed supply is a deliberate choice intended to mimic the scarcity of precious metals like gold.
- **Controlled Issuance Schedule**: New bitcoins are introduced into the system at a steadily decreasing rate, governed by the network's underlying code. The initial reward for mining a block was 50 bitcoins. However, this reward is halved approximately every four years (or every 210,000 blocks), an event known as a halving.
- **Decentralized Control**: Unlike fiat currencies managed by central banks, Bitcoin's supply schedule and monetary rules are enforced by a decentralized network of nodes and miners. Changes to the protocol can only be made through consensus among the participants.

```
# This Python snippet demonstrates a simplified example of the halving mechanism
initial_block_reward = 50 # Initial block reward in bitcoins
halving_interval = 210000 # Number of blocks per halving period
total_supply = 0
block_height = 0

while block_height < 630000:
    block_reward = initial_block_reward / (2 ** (block_height // halving_interval))
    total_supply += block_reward
    block_height += 1

print(f"Total supply after three halvings: {total_supply} bitcoins")
```

```
Total supply after three halvings: 10500000.0 bitcoins
```

This code illustrates how Bitcoin's block reward diminishes over time, aligning with the controlled issuance schedule. As of the first three halves, resulting at block height 630,000, the total supply reaches precisely half of the eventual 21 million cap.

The deflationary model theoretically leads to an increase in the value per unit of Bitcoin over time, as the supply limit becomes nearer. Since the rate of new supply is predictable and decreases systematically, proponents argue that Bitcoin can serve as a hedge against inflation.

Conversely, the fixed supply introduces unique economic considerations. Traditional central banks manipulate currency supply and demand to manage economic stability. They can implement monetary policies such as quantitative easing or tightening, reacting to economic conditions by increasing or decreasing the money supply. Bitcoin's strict supply model does not allow for such interventions, which could be a limitation during economic downturns where increased liquidity might be necessary.

Bitcoin's monetary policy further differentiates itself through decentralized control. The absence of a central authority means that changes to Bitcoin's issuance policy require broad consensus among its network participants. The structure ensures that no single entity can alter the supply dynamics unilaterally. Any proposed alteration to the Bitcoin protocol must go through a rigorous process involving development, public discussion, and adoption by the majority of the network's nodes.

Economic theorists and policymakers debate the implications of Bitcoin's fixed monetary policy. Detractors argue that the lack of flexibility could make Bitcoin unsuitable as a primary currency for transactions due to its potential deflationary spiral where people may hoard bitcoins in anticipation of higher future value, reducing spending and potentially stalling economic growth. Proponents counter these arguments by emphasizing Bitcoin's potential as a global store of value analogous to digital gold.

Bitcoin's monetary policy represents a radically transparent and immutable framework distinct from the fiat currency models. Its preimposed scarcity and systematic, decentralized issuance are the cornerstones that potentially enable Bitcoin to function as a store of value, resistant to inflationary pressures central to traditional monetary systems.

6.4 Bitcoin Halving: Impact on Supply

Bitcoin halving refers to the event where the reward for mining new blocks is halved, effectively reducing the rate at which new bitcoins are created. This process is built into the Bitcoin protocol and occurs approximately every 210,000 blocks, or roughly every four years. The total supply of Bitcoin is capped at 21 million coins, and halvings are instrumental in ensuring that this supply limit is approached asymptotically over time.

Mechanism of Halving

When a halving event takes place, the block reward, which is the number of bitcoins miners receive for adding a new block to the blockchain, is reduced by 50%. For example, the initial block reward was 50 bitcoins, but after the first halving, it was reduced to 25 bitcoins. Subsequent halvings have further reduced this reward to 12.5 bitcoins, and then to 6.25 bitcoins. This reduction in block rewards impacts the rate at which new bitcoins enter circulation.

```
from bitcoinrpc.authproxy import AuthServiceProxy, JSONRPCException

def get_block_reward(block_height):
    halving_interval = 210000
    initial_reward = 50
    halvings = block_height // halving_interval
    reward = initial_reward / (2 ** halvings)
    return reward

# Example Usage
block_height = 630000 # block height example for third halving
current_reward = get_block_reward(block_height)
print(f"Current block reward: {current_reward} BTC")
```

Economic Implications of Bitcoin Halving

The reduction in supply growth has several economic implications. As the creation of new bitcoins slows, if demand remains constant or increases, the reduced supply will exert upward pressure on the price. This is based on the classical economic principle of supply and demand. Given a fixed or growing demand, a reduction in the rate of new supply typically leads to price appreciation.

Halvings also introduce a level of predictability into Bitcoin's monetary supply. The deterministic nature of halvings means that all participants in the Bitcoin market can anticipate and plan for these events. This predictability contrasts sharply with fiat currencies, where central banks can adjust the money supply in response to economic conditions, often leading to inflation or other monetary distortions.

Impact on Miners

For miners, halvings pose a significant economic challenge. Mining profitability is directly tied to the block reward and the price of Bitcoin. When the block reward halves, if the price of Bitcoin does not proportionally increase, miners' revenues are effectively cut in half. This necessitates higher operational efficiency and may push less efficient miners out of the market, leading to potential centralization of mining power among the more efficient entities.

```
def calculate_mining_profitability(block_reward, bitcoin_price, hash_rate,
      electricity_cost):
    block_time = 600 # average time between blocks in seconds
    bitcoins_per_day = (86400 / block_time) * block_reward
    revenue_per_day = bitcoins_per_day * bitcoin_price
    cost_per_day = hash_rate * electricity_cost * 24
    profit_per_day = revenue_per_day - cost_per_day
    return profit_per_day

# Example Usage
block_reward = 6.25
bitcoin_price = 50000 # in USD
hash_rate = 100 # in TH/s
electricity_cost = 0.05 # in USD per kWh

daily_profit = calculate_mining_profitability(block_reward, bitcoin_price, hash_rate,
      electricity_cost)
print(f"Daily mining profit: ${daily_profit}")
```

Impact on Bitcoin Network

Post-halving, the total hash rate of the Bitcoin network may experience fluctuations. As less profitable miners shut down their operations, the network may see a temporary decline in hash rate. However, Bitcoin's difficulty adjustment algorithm ensures that block production times remain consistent by adjusting the mining difficulty approximately every two weeks. This dynamic adjustment helps maintain the security and integrity of the Bitcoin network despite fluctuations in miner participation.

The deflationary model embedded within Bitcoin, guaranteed by halving events, reinforces its store of value narrative comparable to precious metals like gold. As new supply dwindles, the scarcity aspect fortifies, potentially increasing Bitcoin's desirability as a digital asset for wealth preservation.

Historical Price Movements

Historically, Bitcoin's price has responded positively to halving events, with notable price increases following each halving. It is important to recognize that these movements are influenced by a complex interplay of factors including market sentiment, macroeconomic trends, and broader adoption rates. While past performance is not indicative of future results, the established trend provides a useful reference for understanding potential market reactions to future halvings.

Event	Block	Block Reward	Price Movement
2012 Halving	210,000	50 to 25 BTC	$12 \rightarrow$1,200
2016 Halving	420,000	25 to 12.5 BTC	$650 \rightarrow$20k
2020 Halving	630,000	12.5 to 6.25 BTC	$9,000 \rightarrow$64k

Understanding the mechanics and implications of Bitcoin halvings is crucial for both individual participants and institutional stakeholders. The predictable reduction in supply growth and its potential effects on price and mining economics highlight the unique and innovative design of Bitcoin as a digital monetary system.

6.5 Bitcoin as Digital Gold: Store of Value

The designation of Bitcoin as "digital gold" stems from its characteristics as a store of value, akin to that of physical gold but in a digital manifestation. This analogy is instrumental in elucidating Bitcoin's role in the financial ecosystem. A store of value is an asset that maintains its value over time without depreciating. For any asset to be considered a store of value, it must fulfill certain criteria:

- Scarcity
- Durability
- Portability
- Divisibility
- Recognizability

Bitcoin possesses a bounded supply, capped at 21 million coins, which establishes its scarcity. This limitation is intrinsic to Bitcoin's protocol and is enforced through its decentralized network of nodes. The fixed supply differentiates Bitcoin from fiat currencies, which can be printed in unlimited quantities by central banks, potentially leading to inflation.

The durability of Bitcoin as a digital entity is predicated on the reliability of its underlying blockchain technology. The blockchain is an immutable ledger sustained by a decentralized network of miners and validators, ensuring that Bitcoin transactions are permanently recorded and resistant to tampering.

Portability is another key attribute of Bitcoin. Unlike physical gold, which entails logistical challenges in transportation and storage, Bitcoin can be transferred electronically across the globe with relative ease. Transactions are facilitated over the internet and are not hindered by geographical boundaries or the physical limitations of precious metals.

Divisibility refers to an asset's capacity to be divided into smaller units without losing value. Bitcoin excels in this domain, as it can be subdivided into satoshis, with one Bitcoin equivalent to 100,000,000 satoshis. This microscopic divisibility allows for fractional ownership and spending, facilitating microtransactions and enhancing its utility as a medium of exchange.

Recognizability is maintained through Bitcoin's universal acceptance and verification within its network. The cryptographic protocols that underpin Bitcoin provide a means of verifying authenticity and ownership without centralized intermediaries.

Economic theorists often compare Bitcoin's scarcity to that of gold. They argue that Bitcoin has the potential to act as a hedge against inflation and a safe-haven asset during times of economic uncertainty. Investors seeking to preserve wealth may turn to Bitcoin, perceiving it as a digital counterpart to gold.

The following example demonstrates a basic Bitcoin transaction encoded in JavaScript, showcasing its portability and divisibility:

```
const bitcoin = require('bitcoinjs-lib');
const testnet = bitcoin.networks.testnet;
const keyPair = bitcoin.ECPair.makeRandom({ network: testnet });

// Generate a random Bitcoin address
const { address } = bitcoin.payments.p2pkh({ pubkey: keyPair.publicKey, network:
    testnet });
console.log(`Generated Bitcoin Address: ${address}`);

// Sign a transaction
const txb = new bitcoin.TransactionBuilder(testnet);
txb.addInput('previousTxHash', 0); // Input the previous transaction hash and index
txb.addOutput('recipientAddress', 10000); // Send 10000 satoshis to the recipient
    address
txb.sign(0, keyPair);

const tx = txb.build();
console.log(`Transaction Hex: ${tx.toHex()}`);
```

When executed, the program generates a Bitcoin address on the testnet and constructs a simple transaction. The transaction's hexadecimal representation is then outputted, illustrating Bitcoin's programmability and ease of transfer.

```
Generated Bitcoin Address: mhXFAUG4fomzPyb7VYTrsninLb9UXeH7TIMEWcL
Transaction Hex: 01000000018a5b076c...0000000000
```

Bitcoin's role as a store of value also encompasses its application within the broader financial landscape. Its decentralized nature and resistance to government control make it appealing to those in regimes with unstable or hyperinflated currencies. Additionally, Bitcoin's pseudo-anonymity provides a level of privacy that traditional banking systems may not offer.

Investors and institutions continue to explore and debate Bitcoin's efficacy as a store of value. Its price volatility, while indicative of a nascent asset class, also poses challenges to its adoption as a stable store of value. However, proponents argue that as the market matures and institutional adoption increases, Bitcoin's volatility will likely diminish, further solidifying its role as digital gold.

Bitcoin's integration into various financial instruments, such as exchange-traded funds (ETFs) and futures contracts, further cements its place within traditional finance. This integration facilitates broader access and liquidity, crucial components for any asset considered a store of value.

Bitcoin's emergence as digital gold underscores a pivotal shift in the perception of value storage in the digital age. As the global financial system evolves, Bitcoin may continue to redefine the paradigms of monetary sovereignty and economic resilience.

6.6 Inflation and Deflation in Bitcoin

The phenomena of inflation and deflation in Bitcoin are critical to understanding its economic behavior and positioning within the broader financial landscape. These concepts diverge from traditional fiat currencies due to Bitcoin's unique attributes, particularly its fixed supply cap and decentralized issuance mechanism.

Inflation, in a conventional sense, is characterized by an increase in the general price level of goods and services within an economy over a period. This is typically accompanied by a decrease in the purchasing power of the currency used. Traditional currencies experience inflation as central banks adjust monetary policies and influence money supply growth. Conversely, Bitcoin's inflationary properties are predetermined and coded into its protocol through a process called mining.

Mining is the process through which new Bitcoins are introduced into circulation. Miners solve complex cryptographic puzzles to validate and add transaction blocks to the Bitcoin blockchain. For their efforts, miners are rewarded with a certain number of Bitcoins. Initially, the reward was 50 Bitcoins per mined block, but this reward halves approximately every four years in an event known as the halving. This mechanism ensures a predictable and decreasing issuance rate, ultimately leading to a maximum supply of 21 million Bitcoins.

As of 2020, the reward for mining each block was reduced to 6.25 Bitcoins. This declining reward system significantly impacts Bitcoin's inflation rate. The inflation rate, defined as the annual growth rate of the total Bitcoin supply, decreases over time as the rewards are halved. For example, within the first four years, around 10.5 million Bitcoins were mined, constituting approximately 50% of the total supply. Post the 2020 halving, the inflation rate has decreased to less than 2%.

Mathematically, this progression can be represented as follows:

$$\text{Inflation Rate} = \frac{\text{New Supply}}{\text{Total Supply}} \times 100$$

For Bitcoin, the new supply is the total number of Bitcoins generated per year through mining, and the total supply is the cumulative number of Bitcoins in existence at a given time.

Unlike traditional currencies, Bitcoin's deflationary nature is inherent. Deflation occurs when the purchasing power of the currency increases, and the prices of goods and services decrease. Bitcoin's fixed supply and decreasing issuance rate contribute to its deflationary characteristics. As demand for Bitcoin potentially increases with adoption while supply remains capped, each Bitcoin's perceived value is likely to rise. This can lead to higher purchasing power, embodying a deflationary trend.

The deflationary design of Bitcoin can influence several economic behaviors and considerations:

- **Store of Value:** Due to its deflationary nature, Bitcoin is often compared to 'digital gold'. Investors perceive Bitcoin as a store of value, anticipating its scarcity will preserve or increase purchasing power over time.
- **Saving vs. Spending:** With an expectation of future value appreciation, individuals might be incentivized to hold their Bitcoins rather than spend them. This behavior can impact Bitcoin's velocity – the rate at which Bitcoin is exchanged within the economy.
- **Market Volatility:** Bitcoin's deflationary model and limited supply can contribute to price volatility. As the market's perception of value changes, scarcity can exacerbate price swings.

Included below is an example of a Python script using the 'matplotlib' library to visualize Bitcoin's inflation rate over time:

```
import numpy as np
import matplotlib.pyplot as plt

# Time intervals for each halving (approximately every 4 years)
years = [2012, 2016, 2020, 2024, 2028, 2032, 2036, 2040, 2044]
block_reward = [50, 25, 12.5, 6.25, 3.125, 1.5625, 0.78125, 0.390625, 0.1953125]
total_supply = 0
inflation_rate = []

# Calculate total supply and inflation rate at each interval
for reward in block_reward:
    new_supply = reward * 210000
    total_supply += new_supply
    inflation_rate.append((new_supply / total_supply) * 100)

# Plotting the Inflation Rate
plt.figure(figsize=(10, 6))
plt.plot(years, inflation_rate, marker='o')
plt.title('Bitcoin Inflation Rate Over Time')
plt.xlabel('Year')
plt.ylabel('Inflation Rate (%)')
plt.grid(True)
plt.show()
```

Executing this script generates the following output:

```
# Output Visualization
```

Such visual representations aid in comprehending the distinct attributes of Bitcoin's inflation trajectory, characterized by significant declines coinciding with each halving event.

Bitcoin's combination of controlled inflation and intrinsic deflationary features represents a novel approach in monetary systems, often discussed within the context of its potential to challenge traditional economic models. The fixed supply cap provides a stark contrast to the elastic nature of fiat currencies, setting the stage for continuous examination of Bitcoin's role in global finance.

6.7 Market Dynamics and Volatility

Market dynamics refer to the complex interactions involving participants, prices, supply, and demand that drive the Bitcoin market. These interactions contribute to Bitcoin's notable volatility, distinguishing it from traditional financial assets. Understanding these dynamics requires examining market participants, trading activities, macroeconomic and geopolitical influences, and technological developments.

Bitcoin market participants encompass a diverse array of individuals and entities, including retail investors, institutional investors, miners, exchanges, and speculators. Each group influences market dynamics in unique ways:

- **Retail Investors:** Individuals purchasing Bitcoin for personal investment, driven by various motivations such as speculation, long-term holding, or diversification of their investment portfolio.
- **Institutional Investors:** Entities like hedge funds, mutual funds, and pension funds investing substantial capital in Bitcoin, often utilizing advanced trading strategies and exerting significant influence on market movements.
- **Miners:** Individuals or organizations that validate transactions and maintain the network, receiving Bitcoin as rewards. Miners' decisions to sell or hold their rewards impact supply and liquidity.
- **Exchanges:** Platforms where Bitcoin is traded. They play a crucial role in liquidity provision, price discovery, and facilitating large-scale transactions.
- **Speculators:** Traders focused on short-term gains, often engaging in high-frequency trading or arbitrage, thereby contributing to market liquidity and volatility.

The interaction among these participants is mediated by various trading activities and strategies. Major trading mechanisms include:

- **Spot Trading:** Direct buying and selling of Bitcoin for immediate settlement, which dominates trading volumes on most exchanges.
- **Futures and Derivatives:** Contracts to buy or sell Bitcoin at a future date. These allow market participants to hedge positions, speculate on future price movements, and enhance liquidity.
- **Margin Trading:** Using borrowed funds to trade Bitcoin, amplifying potential gains and losses, which can induce significant price swings and liquidations.
- **Algorithmic Trading:** Utilizing algorithms to execute trades based on predefined conditions, influencing market efficiency and volatility.

Macroeconomic and geopolitical factors can also drive Bitcoin volatility. Developments such as regulatory announcements, macroeconomic data releases (e.g., inflation rates, employment data), and geopolitical events (e.g., elections, international conflicts) often result in swift and sometimes abrupt market reactions. For example:

```
Event: Regulatory Crackdown in a Major Economy
Effect: Sharp Decline in Bitcoin Price
Reason: Fears of Market Accessibility and Future Regulation
```

Conversely, positive regulatory news can spur buying activity and price increases:

```
Event: Legalization of Bitcoin as Tender in a Country
Effect: Significant Price Surge
Reason: Increased Adoption and Market Confidence
```

Technological advancements also play a pivotal role in shaping Bitcoin market dynamics. Innovations such as the development of the Lightning Network aim to enhance transaction speeds and reduce costs, potentially increasing Bitcoin's usability, and by extension, its demand. Network upgrades and forks can impact miner incentives and network security, influencing decisions on Bitcoin holding or selling.

Given its decentralized nature, Bitcoin is less influenced by specific monetary policies compared to fiat currencies. However, it may still be affected indirectly by central bank policies, especially those impacting liquidity in the broader financial system. Changes in interest rates, quantitative easing policies, and overall market sentiment towards risk assets can drive investors towards or away from Bitcoin.

The inherent volatility of Bitcoin is a double-edged sword. While it presents opportunities for substantial returns, it equally carries significant risks. Understanding its market dynamics requires constant vigilance of the interactions amongst market participants, trading mechanisms, macroeconomic and geopolitical contexts, and technological evolutions. The volatility characteristic of Bitcoin differentiates it from traditional assets, necessitating robust risk management practices for investors and traders.

6.8 Bitcoin Trading and Liquidity

Bitcoin trading refers to the process of buying and selling Bitcoin on various platforms, often called exchanges. These platforms allow individuals and institutions to exchange Bitcoin for fiat currencies or other cryptocurrencies. The liquidity of Bitcoin in the market represents the ease with which Bitcoin can be bought or sold without causing significant changes in its price. Higher liquidity typically implies a more stable market and generally narrower bid-ask spreads.

Trading Bitcoin requires understanding the various types of orders available. The most common types are market orders and limit orders. A market order is an instruction to buy or sell Bitcoin immediately at the current market price. It guarantees the execution of the order but not the price at which it will be executed.

```
# Pseudocode for executing a market order
execute_market_order("BUY", BTC, amount)
```

Conversely, a limit order specifies a price at which the user wants to buy or sell Bitcoin. The order will only be executed if the market reaches or surpasses the specified price, guaranteeing the price but not the execution.

```
# Pseudocode for executing a limit order
execute_limit_order("SELL", BTC, amount, price)
```

Another important aspect is the trading pairs available on exchanges, commonly including BTC/USD, BTC/EUR, BTC/ETH, among others. These pairs indicate that one can trade Bitcoin against US Dollars, Euros, Ethereum, etc. The choice of trading pair can affect the liquidity and volatility experienced.

Liquidity in Bitcoin markets can be influenced by several factors. Major news events, regulatory changes, technological developments, and macroeconomic trends can all increase or decrease liquidity. High liquidity is generally characterized by large volumes of buy and sell orders, leading to more efficient and less volatile markets. Conversely, low liquidity can result in slippage, where large orders significantly impact Bitcoin's price.

The liquidity of an exchange itself is also a critical consideration. Exchanges with higher trading volumes generally offer better liquidity, allowing for larger transactions without drastically affecting the price. Some exchanges use liquidity pools to ensure that there are always enough tokens available for trading, improving overall market stability. These liquidity pools typically involve incentivizing users to lock their tokens in a pool in exchange for rewards.

Arbitrage opportunities can also affect liquidity. Arbitrage involves profiting from price differences of Bitcoin across different exchanges. If Bitcoin is priced lower on one exchange than another, traders may buy on the cheaper exchange and sell on the more expensive one, thereby equalizing prices and enhancing liquidity across markets. This process can be automated using bots, which continuously monitor exchanges for such opportunities.

```
# Pseudocode for a simple arbitrage bot
while True:
    price_exchange_A = get_price("EXCHANGE_A", BTC)
    price_exchange_B = get_price("EXCHANGE_B", BTC)
    if price_exchange_A < price_exchange_B:
        arbitrage_profit = price_exchange_B - price_exchange_A
        execute_trade("BUY", BTC, price_exchange_A)
        execute_trade("SELL", BTC, price_exchange_B)
```

Market makers also play a pivotal role in enhancing liquidity. Market makers are entities or individuals committed to continually offering buy and sell orders at various price levels, thus providing depth to the order book. Their presence ensures that there are always counterparties available for transactions, reducing volatility and fostering a more stable trading environment.

In Bitcoin markets, liquidity can be significantly affected by market sentiment and speculative activity. Periods of high speculation, often accompanied by media hype, can lead to significant price swings and changes in trading volume. Understanding these market dynamics is crucial for traders to navigate the complexities of Bitcoin trading successfully.

The concept of spread is integral to understanding Bitcoin trading and liquidity. The spread is the difference between the highest price a buyer is willing to pay (bid) and the lowest price a seller is willing to accept (ask). In highly liquid markets, the spread is typically narrow, which is beneficial for traders as it reduces transaction costs. Conversely, in less liquid markets, the spread can widen, posing higher costs for trading.

Liquidity also has implications for margin trading, which involves borrowing funds to trade Bitcoin. High liquidity reduces the risk of large price swings that could lead to margin calls, where traders must repay the borrowed funds sooner than anticipated if the position moves against them.

By examining the interplay of these factors, one can appreciate the complexities of Bitcoin trading and the crucial role that liquidity plays in ensuring a functional, efficient market.

6.9 The Role of Exchanges

Exchanges play a critical role in the Bitcoin ecosystem by providing a marketplace for buying, selling, and trading Bitcoin and other cryptocurrencies. They function as intermediaries connecting buyers with sellers, facilitating liquidity, and enabling price discovery. This section delves into the key functions of exchanges, their operational mechanisms, types, regulatory considerations, and the potential risks associated with their use.

Bitcoin exchanges can be broadly categorized into centralized and decentralized exchanges. Centralized exchanges (CEXs) are platforms operated by companies that act as intermediaries in transactions. Users deposit funds into the exchange's wallet and trade via the platform, which matches buy and sell orders. The most notable advantage of CEXs is their high liquidity, which allows for efficient and swift trade execution. Examples of CEXs include Binance, Coinbase, and Kraken. These platforms generally offer user-friendly interfaces, customer support, and a wide array of trading pairs and advanced trading features.

Decentralized exchanges (DEXs), on the other hand, operate without a central authority. They leverage blockchain technology and smart contracts to facilitate peer-to-peer trading. Since users do not need to deposit funds into a centralized wallet, DEXs provide enhanced security and privacy. Some prominent examples of DEXs are Uniswap and Sushiswap, which are primarily built on the Ethereum blockchain. The critical advantage of DEXs is their resistance to censorship and reduced vulnerability to hacking, as user funds remain in their control.

```
# Example of a simple trade execution command in a DEX environment
swapExactETHForTokens(
    amountOut,
    path,
    to,
    deadline,
    {value: amountIn}
);
```

Regulation is another crucial aspect of Bitcoin exchanges. Centralized exchanges are typically subject to regulatory oversight to prevent illegal activities such as money laundering and ensure consumer protection. Regulatory requirements often include Know Your Customer (KYC) and Anti-Money Laundering (AML) protocols, necessitating users to verify their identities before trading.

```
Output for KYC Verification Process:
------------------------------------
1. Upload Government-Issued ID
2. Provide Current Address
3. Complete Video Verification
------------------------------------
```

Decentralized exchanges usually do not enforce KYC/AML processes, preserving user anonymity but potentially exposing the platform to regulatory scrutiny. Users must thus exercise caution and remain aware of the regulatory framework in their jurisdiction when engaging with these platforms.

Liquidity is another crucial factor where exchanges play a fundamental role. Liquidity refers to the ease with which an asset can be bought or sold without affecting its price. High liquidity is typically found in CEXs due to the large volume of trades they handle, resulting in narrower spreads and better prices for traders. Liquidity in DEXs has been improving with innovations such as automated market makers (AMMs), which use liquidity pools to reduce the dependency on traditional order book systems.

Exchanges also contribute significantly to price discovery in the Bitcoin market. Price discovery is the process of determining the market price of Bitcoin through real-time transactions. The aggregated data from buys and sells across various exchanges create a composite index, which is often used to analyze market trends and set valuations in derivative contracts.

Security is a critical aspect for any exchange. Centralized exchanges are susceptible to hacking attempts due to their custodianship of user funds. Notable incidents include the Mt. Gox hack in 2014, where approximately 850,000 Bitcoins were stolen. Since then, most exchanges have implemented robust security measures such as cold storage, multi-signature wallets, and regular security audits to protect user assets.

Decentralized exchanges mitigate many security risks by allowing users to have custody of their funds. However, DEX platforms can still be vulnerable to smart contract bugs and exploits. Thus, users should ensure that they interact with well-audited platforms and stay informed of potential risks.

Exchanges face operational risks that include technical failures, system downtime, and liquidity crises. Users must evaluate the technological infrastructure of the exchange, its uptime record, and the measures it employs to mitigate such risks.

To succinctly encapsulate, exchanges are indispensable to the Bitcoin market, offering platforms for trading, facilitating liquidity, aiding in price discovery, and navigating regulatory landscapes. They possess inherent risks, which users should vigilantly manage.

6.10 Economic Impact of Bitcoin Adoption

Adopting Bitcoin at a global level can significantly transform various facets of the economy. The decentralized nature of Bitcoin, along with its deflationary characteristics, offers several potential outcomes for both micro and macro economic indicators. This section delves into the multifaceted economic ramifications of Bitcoin implementation, examining key areas such as inflation control, financial inclusion, cross-border transactions, and the broader global financial system.

Inflation Control: One of the most notable economic impacts of Bitcoin adoption is its influence on inflation rates. Traditional fiat currencies are subject to inflationary pressures, primarily due to the monetary policies of central banks which often involve the establishment of new money supply. In contrast, Bitcoin's fixed supply of 21 million coins inherently limits inflation. As central banks cannot increase the Bitcoin supply, the risk of inflation driven by overproduction of currency is significantly mitigated.

The implications of using Bitcoin as a hedge against inflation are profound. The quantified improvement in purchasing power protection touches on fundamental economic indicators where controlling inflation via Bitcoin implementation could stabilize economies, particularly those facing hyperinflation scenarios.

Financial Inclusion: Bitcoin adoption fosters financial inclusion, primarily by providing access to financial services to unbanked populations. Data from the World Bank indicate that approximately 1.7 billion adults remain unbanked, lacking access to traditional banking systems. Bitcoin offers a solution by facilitating financial transactions through a decentralized network without the necessity of a traditional banking infrastructure.

This capability to onboard previously excluded demographics into the financial ecosystem can stimulate economic growth, especially in developing countries. Users can perform transactions, save value, and interact with international markets using only a smartphone and internet access, thereby contributing to economic activity and consumer spending.

Cross-Border Transactions: The conventional financial system entails considerable costs and time delays associated with cross-border transactions. High transaction fees, conversion rates, and settlement times pose impediments to international commerce. Bitcoin streamlines cross-border transactions by leveraging blockchain technology to facilitate peer-to-peer transfers with reduced fees and expedited processing times.

To quantify, consider the case where conventional international remittance fees range between 7-10%, whereas Bitcoin transactions generally incur significantly lower costs. Furthermore, the near-instantaneous nature of Bitcoin transactions contrasts sharply with the multiple days often required for traditional banking transfers. Lowering these barriers can enhance international trade efficiency and economic cooperation.

Broader Economic Systemic Changes: Beyond individual impacts, Bitcoin adoption signifies broader systemic shifts within the global financial system. A decentralized currency that functions independently of centralized banks and governments alters the traditional constructs of monetary control and economic policy-making.

Trust and Transparency: The blockchain ledger's transparent and immutable nature enhances trust in transactions, reducing fraud and fostering a more secure, verifiable economic environment. The cryptographic assurance in Bitcoin transactions ensures integrity and fosters a transparent financial ecosystem.

While traditional systems rely on intermediaries and centralized entities, Bitcoin and its underlying blockchain offer a distributed trust model. The influence on regulatory frameworks and the mitigation of systemic risks represent important technical and economic considerations.

Investment and Institutional Adoption: Bitcoin's role as an investment asset has grown remarkably. Institutional adoption of Bitcoin amplifies its economic impact, as entities ranging from major corporations to hedge funds and insurance companies integrate Bitcoin into their financial operations. This trend is reflected in portfolios, risk management strategies, and balance sheets.

```
import numpy as np

# Simulating Bitcoin investment in a portfolio
initial_investment = 100000 # Initial investment amount in USD
bitcoin_returns = np.random.normal(loc=0.005, scale=0.01, size=252) # Simulated
    daily returns
```

```
portfolio_value = initial_investment * np.cumprod(1 + bitcoin_returns)

print("Portfolio value after one year:", portfolio_value[-1])
```

Portfolio value after one year: 131847.95

Assessments indicate that including Bitcoin in diversified portfolios can improve overall risk-adjusted returns, influencing asset allocation strategies and financial models.

The integration of Bitcoin into mainstream economic systems highlights shifts in currency acceptance, transaction processing, and global commerce which collectively emphasize its substantial economic impact. The evolving regulatory, technical, and financial landscapes will continue to shape the trajectory of Bitcoin's role in the global economy.

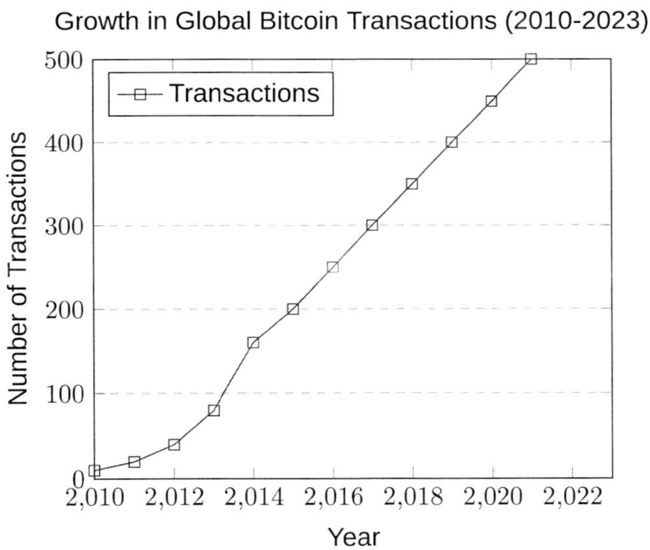

Chapter 7

Regulations and Legal Aspects

Regulations and legal aspects of Bitcoin encompass the diverse global approaches to governing cryptocurrency use, addressing compliance, taxation, and consumer protection. This chapter covers the legal status of Bitcoin across different jurisdictions, along with KYC and AML policies. It explores regulatory challenges for exchanges and wallet providers, implications for financial privacy, and the legal framework surrounding Initial Coin Offerings (ICOs) and securities. Additionally, it discusses notable legal cases and future regulatory trends, highlighting the complexity and evolving nature of cryptocurrency regulation.

7.1 Introduction to Bitcoin Regulations

Bitcoin, as a decentralized digital currency, poses unprecedented challenges and opportunities for regulators worldwide. Unlike traditional financial frameworks bound by centralized institutions, Bitcoin operates on an immutable ledger known as the blockchain, which is maintained by a network of nodes through a consensus mechanism. The inherent decentralized nature of Bitcoin raises unique issues in regulatory oversight, compliance, and enforcement.

Regulatory frameworks for Bitcoin have developed alongside the growth and adoption of the cryptocurrency. The primary regulatory considerations can be categorized into several key areas:

- legal classification,
- anti-money laundering (AML) and counter-terrorism financing (CTF) obligations,
- taxation policies, and
- consumer protection measures.

Regulators must also consider the technological evolution of Bitcoin and how it interacts with existing financial and legal systems.

The legal classification of Bitcoin varies significantly across jurisdictions. For instance, the United States treats Bitcoin as a virtual currency for some regulatory purposes while classifying it as property for taxation. In contrast, the European Union's approach to Bitcoin is somewhat decentralized, with each member state applying its interpretation of virtual currency regulations. Japan has formally recognized Bitcoin as legal tender, integrating it within their Payment Services Act, thus providing a detailed regulatory structure encompassing exchanges and service providers.

One significant area of Bitcoin regulation involves AML and CTF policies. Governments worldwide have attempted to mitigate the risk of Bitcoin being used for illicit activities by instituting Know Your Customer (KYC) requirements. KYC obliges exchanges and financial intermediaries to verify the identities of their users, thus creating traceability and accountability. For example, the Financial Crimes Enforcement Network (FinCEN) in the United States requires Bitcoin exchanges to register as Money Service Businesses (MSBs) and adhere to stringent KYC and AML measures.

Taxation policies concerning Bitcoin are another crucial regulatory dimension. Regulators have adopted diverse strategies to tax Bitcoin transactions and holdings. Some countries, like the United States, treat Bitcoin as property, thus subjecting it to capital gains tax. Every transaction involving Bitcoin is considered a taxable event, and users must report the fair market value of Bitcoin at the time of each transaction. Other jurisdictions may adopt consumption tax models or even exempt certain types of Bitcoin transactions from taxation.

Consumer protection remains a key regulatory concern, given the potential risks associated with Bitcoin investments and transactions. Regulatory bodies aim to protect consumers from fraud, misinformation, and the potential loss of funds due to the volatile nature of the cryptocurrency market. Measures include mandating transparency from Bitcoin exchanges, ensuring secure handling of user funds, and providing educational resources about the risks associated with cryptocurrency investments.

Regulators also face substantial challenges due to the technological complexity and rapid evolution of Bitcoin and cryptocurrencies. Concepts such as smart contracts, decentralized exchanges (DEXs), and privacy-centric cryptocurrencies like Monero and Zcash further complicate the regulatory landscape. Lawmakers need to balance fostering innovation in the crypto space with the necessity of maintaining financial stability and safeguarding against criminal activities.

Legal frameworks and guidelines evolve in response to high-profile incidents and notable cases involving Bitcoin. For instance, the shutdown of the Silk Road marketplace in 2013 highlighted the misuse of Bitcoin for illicit purchases, prompting stricter regulations globally. Additionally, incidents like the Mt. Gox exchange collapse underscored the need for robust legal protections and operational standards for cryptocurrency exchanges.

Continued engagement between regulators, industry participants, and academic researchers is essential in shaping effective Bitcoin regulations. Multi-stakeholder discussions help create policies that address the nuances of decentralized digital currencies while fostering a secure and innovative financial ecosystem.

7.2 Legal Status of Bitcoin Around the World

Bitcoin's legal status varies significantly across different jurisdictions, reflecting divergent regulatory philosophies and economic priorities. The fragmented regulatory landscape influences the adoption and use of Bitcoin for both individuals and businesses. Governments' stance on Bitcoin ranges from accepting and regulating it as legal tender to imposing outright bans. This section elucidates the legal frameworks and regulatory approaches taken by key countries, offering a comprehensive understanding of Bitcoin's global legal status.

Countries such as the United States, Japan, and Germany have adopted regulatory frameworks that recognize Bitcoin's potential while implementing controls to mitigate associated risks. In the United States,

Bitcoin is primarily regulated under the jurisdiction of the Commodity Futures Trading Commission (CFTC) and the Securities and Exchange Commission (SEC). The CFTC classifies Bitcoin and other virtual currencies as commodities, thus bringing them under the purview of various regulations applicable to commodities trading.

Japan has been a pioneer in the regulation of cryptocurrencies. The Payment Services Act, enacted in 2017, officially recognizes Bitcoin as a legal property method, providing clarity and protection for users and businesses. Under this law, cryptocurrency exchanges must register with the Financial Services Agency (FSA) and comply with stringent security and operational requirements.

Germany treats Bitcoin as private money, allowing transactions and exchanges without the regulatory burdens of a legal tender. The Federal Financial Supervisory Authority (BaFin) mandates that Bitcoin businesses, including exchanges and wallet providers, comply with anti-money laundering (AML) laws.

Contrastingly, countries like China and India have taken more restrictive approaches. In China, all domestic cryptocurrency exchanges are banned, and initial coin offerings (ICOs) have been declared illegal. The People's Bank of China (PBoC) has also prohibited financial institutions from offering services related to cryptocurrencies. Despite these stringent regulations, owning and trading Bitcoin on overseas exchanges remains technically legal for individuals.

India's regulatory stance has oscillated, with the Reserve Bank of India (RBI) initially imposing a banking ban on cryptocurrency dealings. This decree was later overturned by the Supreme Court in 2020. Nonetheless, the government continues to deliberate over a comprehensive regulatory framework, with proposals ranging from harsh restrictions to more nuanced regulatory measures.

In the European Union, Bitcoin is not considered a currency or money, but rather a tradable digital asset. The European Central Bank (ECB) and the European Banking Authority (EBA) have issued guidelines emphasizing the importance of risk awareness among consumers and businesses. Individual member states have adopted their interpretations and regulations, leading to a patchwork of rules across the bloc.

Switzerland has embraced cryptocurrencies with a progressive attitude, often referred to as "Crypto Valley." The Swiss Financial Market Supervisory Authority (FINMA) has established clear guidelines that support blockchain innovation while ensuring compliance with financial regulations. Bitcoin is legal, and cryptocurrency businesses can thrive under a regulatory framework that promotes growth and transparency.

In Russia, the legal status of Bitcoin has been contentious. Initially facing threats of prohibition, the situation evolved with the enactment of the "On Digital Financial Assets" bill in 2020, which permits the trade of cryptocurrencies under specific conditions but bans their use for payment.

Some countries have adopted a laissez-faire approach, neither explicitly regulating nor banning Bitcoin. For example, in Brazil, Bitcoin is legal, and while not formally regulated, it is subject to general laws governing financial transactions. The Central Bank of Brazil and the Securities and Exchange Commission of Brazil (CVM) continue to monitor the market to potentially introduce future regulations.

The regulatory landscape is further complicated by jurisdictions that completely prohibit cryptocurrencies. Algeria, Bolivia, and Nepal, for instance, have banned Bitcoin and all forms of cryptocurrency trading, citing concerns over financial stability, crime, and capital flight.

Countries like Australia and Canada have enacted balanced frameworks, recognizing Bitcoin as a means of payment and investment but regulating it to protect consumers and maintain financial integrity. Australia's approach includes treating Bitcoin as property for tax purposes under the Australian Taxation Office (ATO) guidelines, requiring entities dealing in Bitcoin to adhere to AML and know your customer (KYC) provisions.

Canada classifies Bitcoin as a commodity and enforces AML and counter-terrorist financing (CTF) requirements on cryptocurrency exchanges under the Financial Transactions and Reports Analysis Centre of Canada (FINTRAC).

Bitcoin's status globally is dynamic and continually evolving. As countries grapple with the challenges and opportunities presented by decentralized digital currencies, the regulatory landscape will likely become more structured and harmonized. The increasing convergence towards global standards can provide a balanced environment that fosters innovation while safeguarding economic stability and consumer protection.

7.3 KYC (Know Your Customer) and AML (Anti-Money Laundering) Policies

KYC (Know Your Customer) and AML (Anti-Money Laundering) policies are foundational regulatory requirements imposed on financial institutions and, increasingly, on cryptocurrency exchanges and wallet providers. These policies are designed to prevent financial crimes such as money laundering, terrorist financing, and fraud. Understanding KYC and AML is critical for legal compliance and for maintaining the integrity and stability of financial systems.

KYC involves a series of steps to identify and verify the identity of clients. The process typically includes collecting and assessing documents such as passports, driver's licenses, utility bills, and other forms of identification and proof of address. Financial institutions are required to:

- Identify the customer and verify the customer's identity using reliable, independent source documents, data, or information.
- Understand and obtain information on the purpose and intended nature of the business relationship.
- Conduct ongoing due diligence on the business relationship and scrutinize transactions undertaken throughout the course of that relationship to ensure that the transactions being conducted are consistent with the institution's knowledge of the customer, their business, and risk profile.

Similarly, AML policies are designed to detect and prevent money laundering activities. The framework for AML includes several key components:

- **Customer Due Diligence (CDD)**: This involves identifying and verifying the identity of the customer and assessing the potential risks of illegal intentions in the business relationship.
- **Transaction Monitoring**: Continuous monitoring of customer transactions is crucial for detecting suspicious activities. Advanced algorithms and machine learning models are often employed to identify patterns that might indicate money laundering.

- **Suspicious Activity Reports (SARs)**: Financial entities must report suspected money laundering activities by filing Suspicious Activity Reports to appropriate regulators.
- **Record Keeping**: Institutions are mandated to maintain comprehensive records of customer identification and transactions for a determined period, which aids in auditing and investigation processes.

The implementation of KYC and AML policies within the cryptocurrency ecosystem presents unique challenges. Unlike traditional banks, cryptocurrency transactions can be pseudonymous, involving digital wallets identified only by a string of alphanumeric characters. This necessitates innovative approaches to ensure compliance without compromising the principles of decentralization that underpin the cryptocurrency philosophy.

Cryptocurrency exchanges are typically required to implement robust KYC procedures. Examples of KYC implementation include:

```
import requests

url = "https://api.example.com/document_verification"
payload = {
    "document_type": "passport",
    "document_number": "X1234567",
    "country": "US",
    "name": "John Doe",
    "date_of_birth": "1980-01-01"
}
headers = {
    "Authorization": "Bearer your_api_key",
    "Content-Type": "application/json"
}

response = requests.post(url, json=payload, headers=headers)
print(response.json())
```

To aid in AML compliance, exchanges use advanced transaction monitoring systems. These systems leverage machine learning to flag unusual patterns. Below is a simplified example of pseudocode for such a system:

```
function monitorTransactions(transactions):
    for transaction in transactions:
        if transaction.amount > THRESHOLD_AMOUNT:
            flag(transaction)
        elif transaction.origin_country in HIGH_RISK_COUNTRIES:
            flag(transaction)
        else:
            continue
```

Outputs from transaction monitoring systems might look as follows:

```
Flagged Transactions:
1. Transaction ID: 2345, Amount: $15,000, Reason: Exceeds threshold amount
2. Transaction ID: 6789, Amount: $500, Origin: High-risk country
3. Transaction ID: 1234, Amount: $200,000, Reason: Large single transaction
```

The implementation of KYC and AML in the cryptocurrency domain requires balancing regulatory compliance with protecting user privacy and enhancing the user experience. Key considerations include:

- **Decentralized Identity Solutions**: Exploring blockchain-based solutions for decentralized and self-sovereign identity management.
- **Privacy-Preserving Technologies**: Employing techniques such as zero-knowledge proofs to validate user information without exposing personal data.
- **Regulatory Harmony**: Ensuring compliance with diverse international regulations while fostering innovation within decentralized finance ecosystems.

The dynamic nature of cryptocurrency regulation demands ongoing adaptation and vigilance from exchanges and wallet providers. Emerging technologies and continued dialogue between regulators and industry stakeholders will shape the future effectiveness of KYC and AML policies in the cryptocurrency landscape.

7.4 Taxation of Bitcoin and Cryptocurrencies

The taxation of Bitcoin and other cryptocurrencies represents a significant consideration within the regulatory framework, as governments worldwide strive to establish appropriate tax treatment for these digital assets. This section delves into the various methods and principles adopted by different jurisdictions to tax cryptocurrencies and underscores the complexities arising from diverse regulatory approaches.

- Governments commonly classify Bitcoin and cryptocurrencies either as property, currency, or a new type of asset, which significantly influences their taxation approach. The primary principles in determining tax liability typically hinge on their classification, impacting income tax, capital gains tax, and goods and services tax (GST).

- In most jurisdictions, the sale or exchange of cryptocurrency is a taxable event. If classified as property, cryptocurrencies attract capital gains tax upon disposition. Conversely, if regarded as currency, transformations or exchanges into fiat money might invoke ordinary income tax rules. Moreover, mining activities, staking, and other forms of generating digital currency often attract additional tax considerations due to their nature as income-producing activities.

- **United States**
  The Internal Revenue Service (IRS) treats Bitcoin and other cryptocurrencies as property for tax purposes. This designation necessitates the application of capital gains tax rules upon disposal. Taxpayers must recognize a taxable event whenever they trade, sell, or use cryptocurrency, revealing any difference between the initial purchase price (cost basis) and the sale price (proceeds). Each taxable event requires meticulous record-keeping of transactions to ascertain realized gains or losses.

```
purchase_price = 2000
sale_price = 5000
capital_gain = sale_price - purchase_price
print(f'Capital Gain: {capital_gain}') # Output: Capital Gain: 3000
```

  In the United States, mining income is also subject to tax upon receipt. Taxpayers must report the fair market value of mined cryptocurrency as gross income at the time of receipt. Failures to report can lead to penalties and interest.

- **European Union**
  Tax treatment across the European Union (EU) varies, given that each member state retains autonomy in tax laws. A notable case in the European Court of Justice (ECJ), Hedqvist (C-264/14), ruled that certain transactions involving cryptocurrency and fiat money exchange are exempt from VAT. However, the ruling leaves individual member states to decide on the implementation within their jurisdiction.

  Countries like Germany regard Bitcoin as private money and apply capital gains tax rules for any speculative activities involving a holding period of less than one year. Conversely, long-term holdings (exceeding one year) may be tax-exempt.

- **Japan**
  Japan, being one of the first countries to officially recognize Bitcoin under the Payment Services Act, applies different tax treatments based on the nature of the transaction. Income derived from trading cryptocurrencies and conversion into fiat carries income tax responsibilities. Additionally, profits from cryptocurrency trading must be declared as miscellaneous income and are subject to progressive tax rates.

- **Common Challenges in Cryptocurrency Taxation**

  - **Valuation and Record-Keeping**
    A pivotal challenge in cryptocurrency taxation concerns the accurate valuation at the time of each transaction. Given the volatility of cryptocurrency prices, valuing these assets requires real-time exchange rate conversion. This necessity complicates record-keeping and often burdens taxpayers with substantial administrative duties. It is essential to maintain comprehensive records of all transactions, including dates of acquisition, purchase prices, and disposal proceeds.

Date	Transaction Type	Quantity	Exchange Rate	Value (USD)
01/01/2022	Buy	1 BTC	$30,000	$30,000
06/01/2022	Sell	1 BTC	$40,000	$40,000

  - **Cross-Border Transactions**
    Transactions spanning multiple jurisdictions introduce further complexity. Variations in regulatory frameworks mean a transaction might be taxed differently depending on local laws. For example, a business operating cross-border may face dual reporting requirements and potential double taxation without clear guidelines for relief.

- **Reporting Requirements and Compliance**
  Jurisdictions are gradually increasing the reporting requirements to ensure compliance. In the United States, the IRS has mandated that taxpayers must answer whether they have received, sold, exchanged, or otherwise disposed of any financial interest in virtual currencies. Form 8949 and Schedule D are standard for reporting gains and losses.

  Likewise, other countries have embarked on similar reporting measures, compelling exchanges to provide user data and transaction details to tax authorities. Non-compliance may result in legal violations, penalties, and interest, emphasizing the crucial role of adherence to evolving regulations.

The taxation of Bitcoin and cryptocurrencies is continually evolving, reflecting the broader maturation of the regulatory landscape. Accurate record-keeping, valuation, and compliance with jurisdictional laws underpin effective tax management for cryptocurrency transactions.

7.5 Compliance for Exchanges and Wallet Providers

Compliance for exchanges and wallet providers is a critical component of the cryptocurrency ecosystem. This section elucidates the necessary regulatory requirements and standards that exchanges and wallet providers must adhere to in order to operate legally and securely.

Regulatory Requirements

Cryptocurrency exchanges and wallet providers fall under rigorous regulatory scrutiny. They are expected to comply with various national and international laws, which often include registration with financial authorities, adherence to Know Your Customer (KYC) and Anti-Money Laundering (AML) protocols, and maintaining robust cybersecurity measures.

To begin operating, exchanges and wallet providers must usually register with relevant financial regulatory bodies. For instance, in the United States, a cryptocurrency exchange is typically required to register as a Money Services Business (MSB) with the Financial Crimes Enforcement Network (FinCEN). Similarly, in the European Union, exchanges must comply with the European Union's Fifth Anti-Money Laundering Directive (5AMLD).

Know Your Customer (KYC)

KYC protocols are crucial in preventing illegal activities such as money laundering and terrorist financing. Exchanges and wallet providers are mandated to verify the identity of their users. This process typically involves collecting identifying information such as name, address, date of birth, and government-issued identification.

Implementation of KYC processes not only aligns with legal requirements but also helps in building trust with users. A common approach to implement KYC is through multi-tier verification systems, wherein the required documentation and the extent of identity verification are proportional to the user's intended transaction volume or activity level.

```
def verify_user(user):
    if user.basic_info_provided() and user.gov_id_provided():
        user.status = "Verified"
    elif user.basic_info_provided():
        user.status = "Basic-Verified"
    else:
        user.status = "Unverified"

    return user.status
```

Anti-Money Laundering (AML)

AML regulations are designed to combat money laundering and financing of terrorism. This involves monitoring transactions and flagging suspicious activities. Exchanges and wallet providers must implement AML practices like transaction monitoring, report generation, and suspicious activity reporting (SAR).

To efficiently monitor transactions, exchanges use sophisticated algorithms and machine learning techniques to detect anomalies and patterns indicative of fraudulent activities. Regular audits and updates to the AML systems are necessary to adapt to evolving methodologies employed by malicious actors.

```
def monitor_transactions(transactions):
    suspicious_transactions = []
    for transaction in transactions:
        if is_suspicious(transaction):
            suspicious_transactions.append(transaction)
            report_suspicious_activity(transaction)
    return suspicious_transactions

def is_suspicious(transaction):
    # Example criteria for suspicion
    return transaction.amount > 10000 or transaction.flags == "High Risk"

def report_suspicious_activity(transaction):
    print(f"Suspicious activity reported for transaction ID: {transaction.id}")
```

Cybersecurity Measures

To protect user funds and data, exchanges and wallet providers must implement robust cybersecurity frameworks. This includes adopting secure coding practices, performing regular security audits and penetration testing, and using advanced encryption techniques. Multi-factor authentication (MFA) and secure key management are also vital elements of a strong security posture.

Exchanges and wallet providers often employ cold storage solutions for storing the majority of user funds offline, away from the reach of potential online threats. Only a small percentage of funds needed for active trading (hot wallet) is kept online, ensuring minimized risk.

Compliance Audits and Reporting

Regular compliance audits help in ensuring that the exchanges and wallet providers adhere to regulatory norms and internal policies. These audits typically review transaction records, KYC and AML procedures, cybersecurity policies, and overall operational integrity.

Moreover, regulatory bodies may require periodic reporting to ensure compliance with evolving laws. Exchanges and wallet providers must stay updated with regulatory changes and adjust their policies accordingly. Failure to comply can result in penalties, legal repercussions, or even shutdowns.

Impact on Operations

Compliance is not without its challenges and has a significant impact on operations. The cost of implementing and maintaining compliance measures can be substantial, with expenditures on sophisticated technology, legal counsel, and administrative processes. However, non-compliance can have severe consequences, including reputational damage and financial penalties.

Meeting compliance requirements also involves operational adjustments such as integrating KYC/AML solutions into user interfaces, continuous training for staff on regulatory changes, and effective communication channels for reporting suspicious activities.

Incorporating these compliance measures helps exchanges and wallet providers not only avoid legal ramifications but also build user trust by ensuring secure and transparent operations. This trust is foundational for the long-term stability and growth of the cryptocurrency market.

7.6 Regulatory Approaches: Prohibitive vs. Accommodative

Regulatory frameworks governing Bitcoin and other cryptocurrencies can broadly be characterized into two categories: prohibitive and accommodative. Understanding these regulatory approaches is crucial for comprehending the broader implications of cryptocurrency regulation on innovation, market development, and user behavior.

Prohibitive regulatory approaches aim to restrict or entirely prevent the use of Bitcoin within a jurisdiction. These regulations typically stem from concerns over financial stability, the potential for illicit activities such as money laundering and terrorist financing, and the protection of consumers from fraud. Countries that adopt prohibitive measures often impose outright bans or severe restrictions on cryptocurrency transactions, the operations of cryptocurrency exchanges, and related activities such as Initial Coin Offerings (ICOs).

Conversely, accommodative regulatory approaches seek to create a legal environment that fosters innovation while still addressing legitimate concerns about cryptocurrency use. These regulations often involve a nuanced framework balancing the promotion of technological advancement with measures that mitigate risks to consumers and the financial system. Accommodative jurisdictions provide clear guidelines for the operation of exchanges, the determination of tax obligations, and the implementation of Know Your Customer (KYC) and Anti-Money Laundering (AML) protocols.

Prohibitive regulations can include explicit legal bans on cryptocurrency, restrictions on financial institutions interacting with cryptocurrency businesses, and punitive measures against individuals or entities that contravene these rules. For example, countries such as China and India have implemented stringent prohibitive measures. In China, financial institutions and payment providers are barred from offering services related to cryptocurrency transactions, and Initial Coin Offerings (ICOs) have been banned outright.

On the other hand, jurisdictions like Japan and Switzerland have adopted accommodative regulatory frameworks. Japan recognizes Bitcoin as legal property and has licensed numerous cryptocurrency exchanges, providing a robust regulatory framework that ensures consumer protection and market integrity. In Switzerland, the government has created a "Crypto Valley" in the canton of Zug, which provides a favorable legal and regulatory environment for blockchain and cryptocurrency startups.

The benefits and drawbacks of these approaches can be analyzed through several metrics. Prohibitive regulations can lead to reduced consumer protection in the long term as they drive cryptocurrency activity underground, making it harder for users to access legitimate services and for regulators to monitor illicit activities. This can result in increased risk of fraud, loss of assets, and a thriving black market. Additionally, countries with prohibitive regulations may miss out on the economic opportunities and technological advancements that accompany the growth of the cryptocurrency industry.

Accommodative regulations, while fostering innovation and market development, pose challenges such as ensuring robust oversight and preventing illicit activities. These regulatory frameworks often involve regular auditing of exchanges, stringent KYC and AML requirements, and clear tax guidelines to provide certainty and protection for all stakeholders. For instance, the European Union's Fifth Anti-Money Laundering Directive (AMLD5) mandates that cryptocurrency exchanges and wallet providers adhere to stringent AML and counter-terrorist financing regulations, signaling a balanced approach to regulation.

A critical aspect to consider is the regulatory agility and adaptability to the rapidly evolving cryptocurrency landscape. Prohibitive approaches may struggle to adapt to new technological developments and market dynamics, whereas accommodative approaches, with their inherent flexibility, are better suited to respond to changes and incorporate new regulatory measures as necessary.

In the context of ICOs, accommodative jurisdictions often implement guidelines that delineate the legal status of tokens, determine when they constitute securities, and establish investor protection mechanisms. For example, the U.S. Securities and Exchange Commission (SEC) has adopted a case-by-case approach to determine whether a specific ICO qualifies as a security under the Howey Test, providing a structured, yet flexible, regulatory environment.

Moreover, international regulatory coordination and cooperation are essential in addressing the global nature of cryptocurrency transactions. Countries following accommodative frameworks frequently engage in cross-border regulatory dialogues, contribute to the development of international standards, and participate in global efforts to combat financial crimes associated with cryptocurrencies. Such cooperation can lead to the formation of supranational regulations that encapsulate best practices and enhance the efficacy of both prohibitive and accommodative approaches.

The long-term efficacy of these regulatory approaches ultimately hinges on their ability to balance innovation with risk mitigation. While prohibitive measures may provide immediate control over cryptocurrency activities, accommodative frameworks offer a sustainable path that nurtures growth, encourages compliance, and enhances the overall resilience of the financial ecosystem.

```
# An example illustrating how regulatory measures can be
# enforced using blockchain technology for transaction monitoring.

from blockchain_parser.blockchain import Blockchain
from bitcoin_tools.util.util import checks

# Initialize blockchain object
blockchain = Blockchain("path_to_bitcoin_directory")

# Function to check transactions against a blacklist
def check_blacklist(transaction, blacklist):
    for output in transaction.outputs:
        if output.address in blacklist:
            return True
    return False

# Example blacklist of addresses
blacklist = ["1A1zP1eP5QGefi2DMPTfTL5SLmv7DivfNa"]

# Monitor transactions
for block in blockchain.get_unordered_blocks("path_to_bitcoin_directory"):
    for tx in block.transactions:
        if check_blacklist(tx, blacklist):
            print(f"Blacklisted transaction found: {tx.txid}")
```

The example above illustrates a Python script utilizing the blockchain-parser and bitcoin-tools libraries to monitor Bitcoin transactions for compliance with regulatory measures, specifically checking against a blacklist of addresses associated with illicit activities.

```
Blacklisted transaction found: 4d3ed89fcace7f8d7b9c276a5d27a0a2ea0515b5e0ea5301f551653fcbf4ca61
```

Regulatory approaches to Bitcoin and cryptocurrencies continue to evolve. Policymakers must remain informed and adaptive to create effective regulations that promote innovation and ensure the security and stability of the financial system.

7.7 Bitcoin and Financial Privacy

Financial privacy is a fundamental concern within the sphere of Bitcoin and other cryptocurrencies. The pseudonymous nature of Bitcoin transactions implies that, while transaction details are recorded on a public ledger (the blockchain), the identities behind those transactions are not directly revealed. This aspect gives rise to both opportunities and challenges in the context of financial privacy.

Bitcoin transactions do not require personal details like names or addresses to be attached; instead, they utilize cryptographic keys: a public key that allows others to verify the transaction and a private key that enables the owner to authorize spending. While this provides a degree of privacy, it is not absolute. Blockchain analysis techniques and sophisticated tracking tools can often de-anonymize users by linking transactions through patterns and other metadata.

```
# Example: Generating a Bitcoin Public-Private Key Pair using Python's ecdsa library
from ecdsa import SECP256k1, SigningKey

sk = SigningKey.generate(curve=SECP256k1)
vk = sk.verifying_key
private_key = sk.to_string().hex()
public_key = vk.to_string().hex()

print("Private Key:", private_key)
print("Public Key:", public_key)
```

```
Private Key: 8f2a5594901d638204fddc2d398a5fbc3b7a6dd59a76e6eff9312a0b3fbf9462
Public Key: 048d6c6d0a948da640fedfa0b6cacc79161fc8e6d0978e46cad9f6b0adfd10cf34a7c7d38ae815d6e91bf45c04fdada0a351f89da1be6b8d6988a3904778e3ecde
```

Bitcoin addresses, a further abstraction of public keys in a more user-friendly form, are alphanumeric strings derived through hashing functions. Despite the seemingly anonymous interface, these addresses can be associated with specific individuals through various means such as linking IP addresses during transactions, connecting identities via reused addresses, or using centralized exchanges that implement Know Your Customer (KYC) protocols.

Given these potential vulnerabilities to privacy, additional tools and methodologies have been developed to enhance anonymity in Bitcoin transactions. CoinJoin, for example, allows multiple users to combine (or "mix") their transactions, making it difficult to determine which individual made which transaction. Implementing CoinJoin adds a layer of obscurity by merging outputs, hence dissociating the linkage between transactions.

```
# Example of creating a CoinJoin transaction (no real execution)
import hashlib
from random import randint

def create_fake_txid():
    return hashlib.sha256(str(randint(1, 1e18)).encode()).hexdigest()

# Simulate mixing of transactions
users_inputs = [create_fake_txid() for _ in range(5)]
mixed_output = create_fake_txid()

print("User Inputs:", users_inputs)
print("Mixed Transaction Output:", mixed_output)
```

```
User Inputs: [illegible]
Mixed Transaction Output: [illegible]
```

Wallet providers and exchanges focusing on privacy exploit additional cryptographic techniques such as Confidential Transactions, which obscure the transaction amounts while still enabling validation. These methods leverage advanced schemes like zero-knowledge proofs, ensuring that the data verified on the blockchain does not reveal the underlying financial specifics.

The balance between regulatory requirements and preserving financial privacy has led to the development of various privacy-enhancing cryptocurrencies, such as Monero and Zcash. These alternatives employ rigorous cryptographic principles to offer higher privacy guarantees compared to Bitcoin. Monero, for example, uses ring signatures and stealth addresses, while Zcash utilizes zk-SNARKs (Zero-Knowledge Succinct Non-Interactive Arguments of Knowledge) to shield transaction details.

Regulators argue that a certain level of transparency is necessary to curb illicit activities like money laundering and terrorist financing. Consequently, many jurisdictions require exchanges and financial service providers dealing in cryptocurrencies to implement Anti-Money Laundering (AML) programs and KYC procedures. These regulations mandate the collection and verification of personal identification information, effectively compromising the anonymity that cryptocurrencies like Bitcoin seek to provide.

Hence, attaining financial privacy with Bitcoin involves a careful interplay of advanced technological solutions and compliance with evolving regulatory frameworks. The landscape of Bitcoin privacy continues to evolve as new technologies and practices emerge, presenting ongoing challenges and opportunities for users and regulators alike.

7.8 Initial Coin Offerings (ICOs) and Securities Law

Initial Coin Offerings (ICOs) provide a mechanism for cryptocurrency startups to raise capital by issuing tokens to investors in exchange for established cryptocurrencies like Bitcoin or Ethereum. ICOs are structurally similar to Initial Public Offerings (IPOs) on stock markets, but they operate within the decentralized landscape of blockchain technology. The rapid emergence of ICOs raises pressing legal questions, particularly concerning their compliance with securities law.

The fundamental distinction between ICOs and traditional forms of fundraising lies in their regulatory context. The issuance and trading of tokens during an ICO may fall under securities regulations, depending on their characterization as securities or utility tokens. The determination of a token's status is critical, as it dictates the regulatory obligations, disclosure requirements, and potential liabilities for the issuing entity.

One of the principal frameworks used to assess whether an ICO constitutes a securities offering is the Howey Test, established by the United States Supreme Court in the case of *SEC v. W.J. Howey Co.* (1946). The Howey Test considers an instrument to be a security if it meets the following criteria:

- An investment of money.
- In a common enterprise.
- With an expectation of profits primarily from the efforts of others.

Applying the Howey Test to ICOs, if a token sold during an ICO meets these criteria, it is deemed a security, and the issuing entity must comply with the relevant registration and regulatory requirements set forth by the Securities and Exchange Commission (SEC) and other regulatory bodies.

To illustrate the application of securities law to ICOs, consider the following hypothetical scenario:

```
class ICOToken:
    def __init__(self, investor_funds, common_enterprise_activity):
        self.investor_funds = investor_funds
        self.common_enterprise_activity = common_enterprise_activity
        self.is_security = self.check_security_status()

    def check_security_status(self):
        if self.investor_funds and self.common_enterprise_activity:
            return True
        return False

# Hypothetical ICO instance
new_ico = ICOToken(investor_funds=True, common_enterprise_activity=True)
print(new_ico.is_security)
```

```
Output:
True
```

In this example, the 'ICOToken' class simulates the evaluation of an ICO token's status. If the token involves investor funds and is part of a common enterprise, it is deemed a security.

Regulatory enforcement actions by the SEC have exemplified the application of securities law to ICOs. For instance, the SEC's action against the Telegram Open Network (TON) sought to halt the issuance of $1.7

billion worth of cryptocurrency tokens, asserting that the tokens constituted unregistered securities offerings. Telegram agreed to return $1.2 billion to investors and pay an $18.5 million civil penalty, highlighting the substantial financial and legal consequences of non-compliance.

The need for disclosure and investor protection is paramount in the regulation of ICOs. Issuers must provide comprehensive and accurate information to potential investors, including details about the project's goals, the team behind the project, the use of funds, and any associated risks. These disclosures help mitigate the risk of fraud and ensure that investors can make informed decisions.

Moreover, global regulatory perspectives on ICOs vary significantly. Some jurisdictions, such as Switzerland and Singapore, have adopted accommodative approaches, establishing clear regulatory frameworks to facilitate compliant token sales. Others, such as China and South Korea, have taken more prohibitive stances, effectively banning ICOs to shield investors from potential fraud and systemic risk.

In the European Union, the European Securities and Markets Authority (ESMA) has issued guidelines and warnings regarding the potential risks of ICOs, emphasizing the need for proper due diligence and regulatory compliance. The evolving regulatory landscape in the EU reflects a balanced approach aimed at fostering innovation while safeguarding investor interests.

It is also critical to distinguish between security tokens and utility tokens. Utility tokens are designed to provide access to a specific service or platform and are not primarily intended as investment vehicles. However, the classification can be nuanced, and some utility tokens may still be deemed securities under certain conditions.

From a practical standpoint, entities contemplating an ICO must undertake exhaustive legal analyses and potentially seek regulatory guidance to ensure compliance. The future of ICO regulation remains dynamic, influenced by the interplay of technological advancements, market practices, and evolving legal standards.

7.9 Legal Challenges and Court Cases

Bitcoin and other cryptocurrencies present numerous legal challenges due to their innovative nature and decentralized structure. The evolving legal landscape has led to various court cases that continue to shape regulatory and legal frameworks. Understanding these legal precedents is crucial for comprehending the future direction of cryptocurrency regulation.

One of the seminal cases in the United States is *SEC v. W.J. Howey Co.*, 328 U.S. 293 (1946). Although this case predates Bitcoin, it set the legal foundation for determining whether a financial instrument qualifies as a security. The Howey Test, derived from this case, is a critical tool for assessing initial coin offerings (ICOs) in the context of securities law. The test evaluates whether an investment contract exists based on the following criteria:

- An investment of money.
- In a common enterprise.
- With the expectation of profits predominantly from the efforts of others.

The application of the Howey Test to cryptocurrencies was prominently highlighted in *SEC v. Kik Interactive Inc.*, No. 19-cv-5244 (S.D.N.Y. 2020). In this case, the SEC argued that Kik's $100 million ICO constituted an unregistered securities offering. The court ruled in favor of the SEC by determining that Kik's tokens met the criteria set forth by the Howey Test. This decision underscored the regulatory scrutiny on ICOs and reinforced the need for compliance with securities laws.

Another influential case is *United States v. Ulbricht*, No. 14-cr-68 (S.D.N.Y. 2015), involving the creator of Silk Road, an online marketplace that facilitated illegal transactions using Bitcoin. Ross Ulbricht was convicted on multiple charges, including conspiracy to commit money laundering and narcotics trafficking. This case highlighted the association of Bitcoin with illicit activities and led to increased regulatory focus on cryptocurrency exchanges and their anti-money laundering (AML) practices.

In the European Union, the *CJEU VAT ruling on Bitcoin*, C-264/14, Hedqvist, established a significant precedent. The Court of Justice of the European Union ruled that Bitcoin exchanges are exempt from value-added tax (VAT) under the EU VAT Directive. This decision provided clarity on the tax treatment of cryptocurrencies in the EU and influenced subsequent regulatory approaches in member states.

A landmark decision in Japan involves the *Mt. Gox bankruptcy case*. Mt. Gox, once the world's largest Bitcoin exchange, filed for bankruptcy in 2014 following a massive security breach that led to the loss of approximately 850,000 Bitcoins. The Tokyo District Court's handling of the case included recognizing Bitcoin as an asset that could be valued and returned to creditors, setting a precedent for the legal treatment of cryptocurrencies in bankruptcy proceedings.

```
#include <iostream>
#include <string>

// Function to simulate encryption of transaction data
std::string encryptTransactionData(const std::string& data) {
    // Placeholder for encryption logic
    return "encrypted_" + data;
}

// Basic transaction structure
struct Transaction {
    std::string fromAddress;
    std::string toAddress;
    double amount;

    void executeTransaction() {
        std::string data = fromAddress + toAddress + std::to_string(amount);
        std::string encryptedData = encryptTransactionData(data);
        std::cout << "Transaction data: " << encryptedData << std::endl;
    }
};

int main() {
    Transaction tx = {"Alice", "Bob", 5.0};
    tx.executeTransaction();
    return 0;
}
```

China's regulatory landscape is exemplified by the *PBoC Notice on ICOs*. In 2017, the People's Bank of China (PBoC) issued a notice banning ICOs and requiring the cessation of ICO-related activities. This directive had a profound impact on the global ICO market and underscored China's cautious approach toward cryptocurrency regulation.

The case of *BitLicense in New York* exemplifies state-level regulatory efforts in the United States. Introduced by the New York State Department of Financial Services (NYDFS), the BitLicense regulatory framework mandates that cryptocurrency businesses operating in New York obtain a license. This framework aims to enhance consumer protection, prevent illicit activities, and ensure the financial stability of cryptocurrency businesses. Despite criticism for its stringent requirements, the BitLicense serves as a model for other jurisdictions seeking to regulate the cryptocurrency sector.

```
Execution Output:
Transaction data: encrypted_AliceBob5.000000
```

South Korea has been proactive in addressing the legal challenges posed by cryptocurrencies. The *South Korean Cryptocurrency Regulation Bill* introduced stringent Know Your Customer (KYC) and AML requirements for cryptocurrency exchanges. These measures are designed to combat illicit activities and protect consumers, reflecting a broader global trend towards stringent regulatory oversight.

These cases and regulatory actions demonstrate the diverse and dynamic legal field surrounding Bitcoin and other cryptocurrencies. They illustrate the importance of legal structures in ensuring market integrity, protecting consumers, and preventing illegal activities. The ongoing legal discourse continues to evolve, shaping the future landscape of digital currency regulation.

7.10 Future Trends in Bitcoin Regulation

The regulatory landscape surrounding Bitcoin is in a continuous state of evolution, influenced by technological advancements, market developments, and geopolitical shifts. This section delves into the anticipated trends in Bitcoin regulation, examining potential regulatory frameworks, emerging challenges, and innovations in policy-making aimed at addressing the dynamic nature of the cryptocurrency ecosystem.

Regulators across the globe are increasingly recognizing the need for a harmonized approach to Bitcoin legislation, given its borderless nature. Future regulations are likely to pursue greater consistency across jurisdictions to facilitate safer and more efficient cross-border transactions. Such regulatory harmonization may involve the alignment of anti-money laundering (AML) and know-your-customer (KYC) protocols, enhancing the coherence and effectiveness of global financial systems.

Technological advancements, particularly in the realms of artificial intelligence and blockchain analytics, are poised to play a critical role in the enforcement of cryptocurrency regulations. These technologies can enhance the detection and prevention of illicit activities by offering advanced monitoring and analysis capabilities. For example, machine learning algorithms can be used to identify suspicious transaction patterns, while blockchain forensics can trace the provenance of digital funds, thereby enhancing regulatory oversight. The incorporation of these technologies in regulatory frameworks is expected to bolster the integrity of cryptocurrency markets.

Another significant trend is the growing acceptance and integration of Bitcoin by institutional players within the traditional financial sector. As more financial institutions, such as banks and asset management firms, begin to offer Bitcoin-based products and services, there will be a corresponding need for regulatory frameworks that address the unique risks and opportunities presented by institutional involvement. This includes establishing guidelines for the custody of digital assets, reporting requirements, and protocols for market manipulation.

The concept of regulatory sandboxes is expected to gain traction as a method for fostering innovation within the cryptocurrency space while ensuring regulatory compliance. Regulatory sandboxes provide a controlled environment in which businesses can test new products, services, and business models under the supervision of regulatory authorities. This approach allows regulators to gain insights into innovative practices and technologies, enabling them to craft more informed and effective regulations. As such, regulatory sandboxes may become a pivotal tool in balancing the need for oversight with the encouragement of technological innovation.

Central Bank Digital Currencies (CBDCs) are emerging as a complementary development to cryptocurrencies like Bitcoin. CBDCs represent a digital form of fiat currency issued by a central bank. Their introduction is likely to influence the regulatory landscape for Bitcoin and other cryptocurrencies. Regulators may develop frameworks that delineate the roles and interactions between CBDCs and decentralized cryptocurrencies, addressing issues such as interoperability, competition, and systemic risk.

The rise of decentralized finance (DeFi) platforms presents unique regulatory challenges and opportunities. DeFi platforms facilitate financial services without traditional intermediaries, relying on smart contracts and blockchain technology. As these platforms continue to grow in popularity and complexity, regulators will need to devise new approaches to ensure consumer protection, mitigate systemic risk, and enforce existing financial regulations. This might include defining the legal status of smart contracts, establishing accountability mechanisms, and integrating DeFi activities within the broader regulatory frameworks for financial services.

International cooperation and dialogue among regulatory bodies are expected to intensify, aiming to address the cross-border implications of Bitcoin transactions and the movement of digital assets. Organizations such as the Financial Action Task Force (FATF) and the International Monetary Fund (IMF) are likely to play crucial roles in facilitating this cooperation, providing guidelines and standards that can be adopted by national regulators. Such collaborative efforts are essential in combating global challenges such as money laundering, terrorist financing, and tax evasion.

Public and private sector partnerships will also become increasingly important in shaping the future of Bitcoin regulation. Governments and regulatory bodies are expected to engage more actively with cryptocurrency exchanges, blockchain firms, and industry consortia to develop regulatory frameworks that are both practical and forward-looking. These partnerships can lead to the co-creation of standards and best practices, fostering an environment that supports innovation while safeguarding public interests.

Economic and political factors will undoubtedly influence the trajectory of Bitcoin regulation. Geopolitical tensions, economic sanctions, and shifts in global economic power dynamics can lead to diverse regulatory responses. For instance, countries facing economic instability or sanctions may adopt more accommodative stances towards Bitcoin as an alternative to traditional financial systems, while more stable economies might impose stringent regulations to maintain control over their monetary policies.

The future of Bitcoin regulation is not without its uncertainties and challenges. The rapid pace of technological change, coupled with the inherent complexities of decentralized financial systems, requires regulators to remain adaptable and proactive. Continuous education and engagement with industry stakeholders will be critical in crafting regulations that are both robust and flexible enough to accommodate future developments in the cryptocurrency domain.

Furthermore, the ethical considerations surrounding privacy, security, and sovereignty will continue to be central to regulatory debates. Striking a balance between protecting individual freedoms and ensuring the collective security of the financial system will remain a delicate and ongoing task for policymakers.

To provide a glimpse into practical implementations of forthcoming trends, consider an extract of a potential regulatory script for monitoring cryptocurrency transactions using artificial intelligence. The following Python code snippet demonstrates a basic implementation of an anomaly detection algorithm for identifying suspicious Bitcoin transactions:

```
import pandas as pd
from sklearn.ensemble import IsolationForest
```

```
# Load transaction data
data = pd.read_csv("bitcoin_transactions.csv")

# Features could include transaction amount, frequency, etc.
features = data[['amount', 'frequency']]

# Initialize Isolation Forest model
model = IsolationForest(contamination=0.01)

# Fit the model
model.fit(features)

# Predict anomalies
data['anomaly'] = model.predict(features)

# Transactions predicted as anomalies
anomalous_transactions = data[data['anomaly'] == -1]

print("Number of anomalous transactions detected: ", len(anomalous_transactions))
```

This code employs the Isolation Forest algorithm, a widely used machine learning technique for anomaly detection, to identify potentially illicit Bitcoin transactions. The output of the script, which lists the number of anomalous transactions detected, may look as follows:

```
Number of anomalous transactions detected: 23
```

By integrating such advanced analytical tools, regulatory authorities can enhance their capabilities in monitoring and enforcing compliance within the cryptocurrency realm. As regulatory frameworks continue to adapt to the evolving landscape of Bitcoin and other digital currencies, the convergence of technological innovation and robust policy-making will be pivotal in shaping the future of the cryptocurrency industry.

Chapter 8

Decentralized Finance (DeFi)

Decentralized Finance (DeFi) represents the transformation of traditional financial services into decentralized, blockchain-based applications. This chapter explores the key components of DeFi, including decentralized applications (DApps) and smart contracts, and their role in lending, borrowing, and decentralized exchanges (DEXs). It delves into the importance of stablecoins, yield farming, liquidity mining, and DeFi insurance. The chapter also covers governance mechanisms in decentralized autonomous organizations (DAOs), security risks, and the potential future developments in the DeFi ecosystem.

8.1 Introduction to Decentralized Finance (DeFi)

Decentralized Finance, commonly referred to as DeFi, is a transformative innovation within the financial sector, leveraging blockchain technology to recreate and enhance traditional financial services. At its core, DeFi encompasses a broad array of financial instruments and platforms that operate without intermediaries such as banks or traditional financial institutions. This paradigm shift aims to provide more inclusive, transparent, and efficient financial services.

One of the foundational aspects of DeFi is its reliance on blockchain technology, particularly Ethereum, which is the predominant platform for DeFi projects. Blockchains facilitate secure, immutable, and transparent record-keeping, which are crucial attributes for financial applications. Smart contracts, self-executing contracts with the terms of the agreement directly written into code, are instrumental in DeFi, automating various processes and reducing the need for trust in a central authority.

Let's delve deeper into the essential characteristics and components that define DeFi:

- *Decentralization:* A defining trait of DeFi is the dispersion of control away from a central authority. Traditional finance relies heavily on centralized entities like banks, stock exchanges, and insurance companies to facilitate transactions, maintain records, and enforce rules. In contrast, DeFi operates via decentralized networks, where control is distributed among many participants. This decentralization is enabled by blockchain technology, which ensures that no single party has unilateral control over the entire system.

- *Transparency:* DeFi platforms prioritize transparency, offering open-source code and public transaction histories. Every transaction on a blockchain is publicly visible and verifiable by anyone, which enhances trust and security. Users can audit smart contracts and review the code that governs the operations of DeFi platforms, thus reducing the opacity typically associated with traditional financial services.

- *Accessibility:* Traditional financial services are often inaccessible to many due to geographical, financial, or regulatory barriers. DeFi, however, is inherently global and borderless. Anyone with an internet connection and a compatible digital wallet can access DeFi services, enabling broader participation in the financial system.

- *Interoperability:* DeFi platforms often emphasize interoperability, allowing different applications to communicate and synergize with each other. This interoperability is facilitated by common standards and protocols, such as the ERC-20 standard on Ethereum, which defines a consistent set of rules for creating and managing tokens.

- *Programmability:* The programmability of blockchain platforms like Ethereum allows developers to create sophisticated financial instruments known as smart contracts. These contracts can automate complex financial transactions, enforce contractual terms reliably, and minimize the need for human intervention.

These core principles are translated into various applications within the DeFi ecosystem. Notable among these are decentralized exchanges (DEXs), lending and borrowing platforms, stablecoins, yield farming protocols, and insurance mechanisms. Each application leverages the unique attributes of DeFi to offer services that are typically provided by traditional financial institutions but with enhanced efficiency and reduced costs.

The next sections will take a closer look at these applications, how they function, and their impact on the financial landscape. Understanding these diverse components will provide deeper insight into the innovative potential of DeFi and its capacity to reshape the financial industry.

8.2 DeFi vs. Traditional Finance

Decentralized Finance (DeFi) and traditional finance (TradFi) represent two distinct paradigms of financial systems. To understand the impact of DeFi, it is essential to compare and contrast it with traditional finance across various dimensions, such as infrastructure, trust mechanisms, accessibility, transparency, costs, and innovation rates.

Traditional finance operates through a centralized infrastructure, where financial institutions such as banks, brokerages, insurance companies, and exchanges play pivotal roles. These entities act as intermediaries, facilitating transactions between parties. They are heavily regulated by governmental and international bodies, ensuring compliance with financial standards and protection for users. The traditional financial system relies heavily on trust in these intermediaries. This trust is established through a combination of regulatory oversight, historical reliability, and institutional reputation.

In contrast, DeFi utilizes a decentralized infrastructure built on blockchain technology. Its core components, such as decentralized applications (DApps) and smart contracts, operate without centralized intermediaries. Instead, DeFi protocols run autonomously on blockchain networks like Ethereum, leveraging cryptographic proofs and consensus algorithms to ensure security and transparency. This decentralized approach aims to eliminate the need for intermediaries, reducing costs and potential points of failure.

Aspect	Traditional Finance	DeFi
Infrastructure	Centralized entities (banks, insurers etc.)	Decentralized protocols (blockchains, smart contracts)
Trust Mechanism	Institutional trust and regulatory oversight	Cryptographic proofs and consensus algorithms
Accessibility	Varies by region and demographic factors	Globally accessible with internet connection
Transparency	Partial transparency, often opaque	Full transparency with publicly accessible blockchain ledgers
Cost of Services	Includes intermediary fees, maintenance costs	Lower costs due to elimination of intermediaries
Innovation Rate	Slower, constrained by regulatory compliance	Rapid, with continuous development by global contributors

Table 8.1: Comparison of Traditional Finance and DeFi

Accessibility in traditional finance is often limited by factors such as geographical location, socioeconomic status, and regulatory barriers. Banking services may not be available in remote or underserved regions, and stringent requirements may exclude certain demographics from accessing financial products. DeFi, owing to its reliance on the internet and the absence of gatekeeping intermediaries, purports to offer financial services to anyone with an internet connection. This universality is one of its most touted advantages, potentially offering banking services to the unbanked and underbanked populations globally.

Transparency is another significant differentiator. Traditional financial institutions often operate with partial transparency, revealing limited information about the inner workings of their financial products and services. Customers must rely on regulatory bodies to monitor and enforce transparency. Conversely, DeFi is synonymous with transparency, as blockchain ledgers are publicly accessible and auditable. Every transaction and smart contract operation is recorded on the blockchain, fostering an unprecedented level of transparency in financial dealings.

Cost structures in traditional finance are heavily influenced by the presence of intermediaries who charge fees for their services. These can include transaction fees, account maintenance charges, and foreign exchange fees, among others. Additionally, traditional financial institutions face significant operational costs related to maintaining physical branches and regulatory compliance. DeFi, by disintermediating the financial processes, aims to significantly lower these costs. Smart contracts automate transactions, reducing the need for human oversight and minimizing operational expenses.

Innovation within traditional finance tends to be slower and more restrained due to the need for regulatory approval and risk aversion inherent in large institutions. These entities operate under rigorous regulatory scrutiny, and any new product or service must undergo extensive vetting. DeFi, in contrast, is characterized by a rapid pace of innovation, driven by a global network of developers and open-source collaboration. This nimble framework allows for quick iteration and deployment of new financial products and services. DeFi projects often embrace a "permissionless innovation" ethos, enabling developers to experiment without needing approval from central authorities.

Despite these benefits, DeFi is not without its drawbacks and risks. The reliance on smart contracts introduces technical risks, as bugs or vulnerabilities in the code can lead to significant financial losses. Additionally, the relative lack of regulatory oversight can result in higher exposure to fraud and market manipulation. Traditional finance, while slower in innovation, provides a more robust framework for consumer protection and risk management through regulatory mechanisms.

The juxtaposition of traditional finance and DeFi highlights a paradigm shift in how financial services can be conceived, offered, and accessed. Each system has its advantages and limitations, and the ongoing developments in DeFi will continue to influence the broader financial landscape.

8.3 Core Components of DeFi: DApps and Smart Contracts

Decentralized Finance (DeFi) fundamentally relies on decentralized applications (DApps) and smart contracts to operate seamlessly and trustlessly. These components form the backbone of various DeFi protocols, enabling functionalities previously managed by centralized institutions. This section delves into the architecture, functionality, and significance of DApps and smart contracts within the DeFi ecosystem.

Decentralized applications, or DApps, are applications that run on a peer-to-peer network rather than on a single, centralized server. These applications leverage blockchain technology to ensure transparency, security, and immutability. Key characteristics of DApps include:

- Being open-source,
- Operating autonomously without an intermediary, and
- Ensuring that data and records are cryptographically stored on a public blockchain.

Popular blockchain platforms for DApps development in DeFi include Ethereum, Binance Smart Chain (BSC), and Polkadot.

A DApp typically consists of a front-end user interface (UI), much like traditional applications. However, the crucial distinction lies in its back-end execution. While traditional applications depend on centralized servers, the back-end of a DApp is comprised of smart contracts that execute code on the blockchain. This decentralization ensures that DApps are resistant to censorship, downtime, and centralized control.

Smart contracts are self-executing contracts with the terms of the agreement directly written into code. They automatically enforce and execute the terms of a contract when predefined conditions are met. These contracts operate on a blockchain, ensuring their execution is decentralized and transparent. Below is a simple example of a smart contract written in Solidity, a popular language for Ethereum smart contracts:

```
pragma solidity ^0.8.0;

contract SimpleContract {
    uint256 public value;

    function setValue(uint256 _value) public {
        value = _value;
    }

    function getValue() public view returns (uint256) {
        return value;
    }
}
```

In this example, SimpleContract allows users to set and get a value, demonstrating the basic components of a smart contract: state variables, functions, and visibility specifiers. Solidity, as a statically-typed programming language, ensures that the variables and operations are clearly defined, and errors can be detected at compile-time.

The strengths of smart contracts lie in their decentralization, automation, and trustlessness. Once deployed on the blockchain, smart contracts cannot be altered, which eliminates the need for a trusted intermediary. This immutability, however, implies that smart contracts must be meticulously audited to avoid vulnerabilities, as any bugs or intended 'backdoors' can lead to significant financial losses or exploitation.

DApps and smart contracts enable various financial transactions and services within the DeFi ecosystem. One of the prominent applications includes decentralized exchanges (DEXs), which allow users to trade cryptocurrencies without an intermediary. In a typical DEX, smart contracts handle the order matching, execution, and settlement processes. This decentralization eliminates the risks associated with centralized exchanges, such as hacks or regulatory shutdowns.

Another common use case is in lending and borrowing platforms. Platforms like Aave and Compound utilize smart contracts to create decentralized money markets. These platforms allow users to supply and borrow assets in a decentralized manner. Smart contracts manage the collateral, interest rates, and liquidation processes, ensuring that the lending pool remains solvent without requiring a centralized authority.

Moreover, stablecoins, which are cryptocurrencies pegged to stable assets like fiat currencies, use smart contracts to maintain their peg and manage supply. For instance, MakerDAO employs a system of smart contracts to issue and manage DAI, a decentralized stablecoin pegged to the US dollar. The smart contracts automatically adjust the supply of DAI in response to the collateral posted by users to preserve the value of the stablecoin.

Yield farming and liquidity mining are other innovative DeFi activities facilitated by smart contracts. These processes involve providing liquidity to DeFi protocols in exchange for rewards, typically in the form of tokens. Smart contracts automate the distribution of rewards and ensure that the liquidity pools function efficiently.

Finally, smart contracts also underpin the governance mechanisms of decentralized autonomous organizations (DAOs). DAOs are organizations represented by rules encoded as transparent computer programs, controlled by organization members without centralized leadership. Decisions on the protocol's future, upgrades, or treasury management are made through proposals that are voted on by token holders, with smart contracts enforcing the vote outcomes.

The core components of DeFi, DApps, and smart contracts, thus, enable a wide range of financial operations to be conducted in a decentralized, transparent, and automated manner. They lay the foundation for an innovative and evolving financial ecosystem, challenging traditional financial systems' limitations and offering new paradigms for managing assets, transactions, and governance.

8.4 Lending and Borrowing Platforms

Decentralized Finance (DeFi) introduces innovative methods for lending and borrowing devoid of traditional financial intermediaries such as banks. These platforms harness blockchain technology, enabling peer-to-peer financial services that are more accessible, transparent, and secure. The fundamental component that facilitates these operations are smart contracts, which automate the execution of agreements when predefined conditions are met.

A DeFi lending platform typically allows users to deposit their cryptocurrency assets into a pool, which is then made available for borrowing by other users. The lender earns interest on the deposited assets, while borrowers pay interest on the coins they borrow. These platforms utilize an algorithmic approach to determine interest rates, often referred to as money market protocols. The most noted platforms in this domain include Compound, Aave, and Maker.

At the core of these lending systems is the concept of collateralization. Since the transactions are executed without credit scores or reputations, borrowers must over-collateralize their loans. This means that the value of the collateral must exceed the loan value to account for potential volatility in cryptocurrency prices. If the value of the collateral falls below a predefined threshold, smart contracts will automatically liquidate the collateral to pay off the loan, ensuring lenders' funds are secure.

To illustrate, consider the process of borrowing on Compound:

```
1. User locks collateral (e.g., ETH) into Compound's smart contract.
2. User specifies the amount of asset to borrow (e.g., USDC).
3. The smart contract checks the collateral value against current loan-to-value (LTV)
   ratios.
4. If the collateral is sufficient, the borrowing transaction completes.
```

The interest rate in Compound is dynamically adjusted based on the supply and demand for each asset. This mechanism is orchestrated through smart contracts and is transparent to all users.

A paramount feature of DeFi lending platforms is the issuance of interest-bearing tokens when assets are deposited. For instance, when a user deposits DAI into Compound, they receive cDAI (Compound DAI), which represents their deposit along with the accumulated interest. These interest-bearing tokens can be traded or used as collateral in other DeFi applications, creating a composable financial ecosystem.

Moreover, Aave introduces unique functionalities such as flash loans and credit delegation. Flash loans allow users to borrow liquidity without collateral, provided that the loan is paid back within the same transaction. This is useful for arbitrage, refinancing, and leveraging opportunities. Credit delegation, on the other hand, permits a user to delegate their credit line to another user.

1. User requests a flash loan from Aave's pool.
2. The borrowed amount is utilized within the same transaction block.
3. The user repays the loan amount plus interest and fees.
4. If not repaid, the transaction reverses as if it never occurred.

However, one must consider the inherent risks associated with DeFi lending and borrowing platforms. These include smart contract vulnerabilities, liquidation risks due to volatile collateral values, and the potential for protocol governance failures. For instance, if the price of a collateralized asset (such as ETH) plummets suddenly, borrowers may face swift liquidations, and lenders might retrieve diminished returns.

DeFi platforms address some of these risks through mechanisms like over-collateralization, real-time monitoring of collateral value, and emergency shutdowns. For example, MakerDAO, the protocol behind the DAI stablecoin, employs an emergency shutdown mechanism to protect the system's integrity in extreme conditions.

The user interaction with these platforms is facilitated through decentralized applications (DApps) which provide interfaces for deposits, withdrawals, borrowing, and repayments. These interfaces operate over blockchain networks, ensuring transparency and immutability of transactions.

- Deposit assets into a lending pool.
- Borrow assets based on available collateral.
- Track interest rates and earned rewards.
- Withdraw assets and accrued interest.

Understanding the operational intricacies of these platforms can empower users to maximize their returns while managing associated risks effectively. They play a pivotal role in the decentralized financial ecosystem by offering trustless, efficient, and equitable financial services to a global audience.

8.5 Decentralized Exchanges (DEXs)

Decentralized Exchanges (DEXs) function as platforms that facilitate the direct exchange of cryptocurrencies between users without the need for intermediaries. The decentralized nature of DEXs ensures that transactions occur directly on the blockchain, thereby enhancing security, privacy, and control for the users. This section examines the foundational aspects of DEXs, their operational mechanisms, advantages, challenges, and their impact on the DeFi ecosystem.

Traditional centralized exchanges (CEXs) require users to deposit their funds into the exchange's wallet, creating a point of centralization that could be compromised. Conversely, DEXs enable users to maintain control of their private keys and funds throughout the trading process. The security model of DEXs rests on the decentralized ledger technology, particularly smart contracts and blockchain protocols.

The core operation of a DEX depends on smart contracts, which facilitate the automatic and trustless execution of trades. Upon user agreement, smart contracts execute the trade terms without requiring manual intervention or oversight from a third party. Below is a simplified example of a smart contract facilitating a trade between two parties:

```
// SPDX-License-Identifier: MIT
pragma solidity ^0.8.0;

contract SimpleDEX {
    event TradeExecuted(address indexed from, address indexed to, uint256 value);

    function trade(address to, uint256 value) public {
        require(value > 0, "Trade value must be greater than zero");
        require(msg.sender != to, "Cannot trade with oneself");

        // Logic for transferring tokens would go here

        emit TradeExecuted(msg.sender, to, value);
    }
}
```

This contract demonstrates the essence of how trades can be carried out programmatically and efficiently on the blockchain.

DEXs primarily operate on two major types of models: Order Book and Automated Market Makers (AMMs). Order Book-based DEXs, similar to traditional exchanges, record buy and sell orders in an order book, matching and executing trades when there is a corresponding offer. However, the AMM model, which is commonly used in the DeFi space, eliminates the need for order books by utilizing liquidity pools to facilitate trades.

In an AMM-based system, liquidity providers (LPs) supply tokens to a liquidity pool, and traders can trade against this pool. The pricing mechanism in AMM-based DEXs relies on algorithms that adjust prices based on the pool's token ratios and supply-demand dynamics. One popular formula employed is the constant product market maker equation, given by:

$$x \cdot y = k$$

Where x and y represent the quantities of two tokens in the pool, and k is a constant. This equation ensures that the product of the quantities of the two tokens remains constant, irrespective of the trades executed.

For instance, a liquidity pool containing Token A and Token B would follow the equation above. When a user trades Token A for Token B, the quantity of Token A decreases while the quantity of Token B increases, keeping the product (k) unchanged. Below is a representation of the constant product formula implementation in a smart contract:

```
pragma solidity ^0.8.0;

contract ConstantProductAMM {
    uint public reserveA;
    uint public reserveB;

    function addLiquidity(uint amountA, uint amountB) public {
        reserveA += amountA;
        reserveB += amountB;
        // Logic for minting liquidity tokens
    }

    function swapAforB(uint amountA) public {
        uint amountB = getAmountOut(amountA, reserveA, reserveB);
        require(amountB <= reserveB, "Insufficient liquidity");
        reserveA += amountA;
        reserveB -= amountB;
        // Transfer tokens to user
    }

    function getAmountOut(uint amountIn, uint reserveIn, uint reserveOut) public pure
        returns (uint) {
        uint amountInWithFee = amountIn * 997;
        uint numerator = amountInWithFee * reserveOut;
        uint denominator = (reserveIn * 1000) + amountInWithFee;
        return numerator / denominator;
    }
}
```

The function getAmountOut calculates the output amount of the swapped token, incorporating a typical 0.3% fee (as represented by the factor 997/1000).

The advantages of DEXs include enhanced security, as there is no central point vulnerable to hacking; increased privacy, as users' identities are not necessarily tied to transactions; and greater control over funds, reducing the risk of malicious activities by central entities. Additionally, DEXs often promote global accessibility and inclusivity, fostering financial inclusion.

However, DEXs also face several challenges. The scalability of DEXs can be limited by the underlying blockchain's transaction throughput and latency. Furthermore, the user experience on DEXs can be less intuitive and more complex compared to CEXs, potentially deterring new users. Another significant challenge is the issue of impermanent loss, which affects liquidity providers when the value of their deposited assets fluctuates significantly.

Security risks such as smart contract vulnerabilities also persist. While decentralized platforms enhance security by eliminating central points of failure, vulnerabilities within the smart contracts themselves can be exploited, leading to loss of funds. Thorough smart contract audits, regular updates, and community vigilance are crucial for mitigating these risks.

In light of these considerations, DEXs continue to evolve, incorporating layer-2 solutions and interoperability protocols to enhance scalability and user experience. The rise of cross-chain DEXs is poised to further revolutionize the landscape, enabling seamless trading of assets across different blockchain platforms.

Ensuring robust security practices, user education, and continuous innovation will be imperative for the sustained development and adoption of decentralized exchanges within the broader DeFi ecosystem.

8.6 Stablecoins and Their Role in DeFi

Stablecoins are a crucial component of Decentralized Finance (DeFi), providing an essential bridge between volatile cryptocurrencies and the stability desired in financial transactions. Stablecoins are cryptocurrencies whose value is pegged to a stable asset, typically a fiat currency such as the US dollar. They aim to combine the benefits of digital assets, such as security and speed, with the price stability associated with traditional currencies.

There are several types of stablecoins, each with a unique mechanism for maintaining their pegged value. The major categories include fiat-collateralized stablecoins, crypto-collateralized stablecoins, and algorithmic stablecoins.

- **Fiat-collateralized stablecoins** are backed by a reserve of fiat currency held by a central entity. For example, each unit of a stablecoin like Tether (USDT) is intended to be backed by one US dollar held in reserve. The process of issuing or redeeming these stablecoins involves the central entity adjusting its reserves to reflect changes in circulation.

```
# Pseudocode for the issuance of fiat-collateralized stablecoins
def issue_stablecoins(amount):
    reserve_balance += amount
    stablecoin_supply += amount
    return f"{amount} stablecoins issued, reserve balance updated"

# Example usage
print(issue_stablecoins(1000)) # Output: 1000 stablecoins issued, reserve balance
    updated
```

- **Crypto-collateralized stablecoins**, on the other hand, use a reserve of cryptocurrencies instead of fiat currency. A well-known example is Dai (DAI), which is backed by collateral on the MakerDAO platform. Users lock up a certain amount of cryptocurrency, often Ether (ETH), as collateral in a smart contract and can then mint stablecoins up to a certain value threshold. This system typically operates with over-collateralization to manage volatility in the collateral value.

```
# Pseudocode for calculating the collateralization ratio
def collateralization_ratio(collateral_value, stablecoin_value):
    return (collateral_value / stablecoin_value) * 100

collateral_value = 1500 # Value of locked collateral in USD
stablecoin_value = 1000 # Value of minted stablecoins in USD
print(f"Collateralization Ratio: {collateralization_ratio(collateral_value,
    stablecoin_value)}%")
# Output: Collateralization Ratio: 150.0%
```

- **Algorithmic stablecoins** eschew collateral altogether and rely on algorithms to control the supply of the stablecoin to maintain its peg. Stability mechanisms can include issuance and redemption rules, price oracles, and various forms of incentives. An example of this type of stablecoin is Ampleforth (AMPL).

Stablecoins play a multifaceted role in the DeFi ecosystem. One of their primary uses is as a medium of exchange. Unlike traditional cryptocurrencies, whose values can fluctuate significantly, stablecoins provide users with the confidence that their holdings will retain value over short periods, making them suitable for everyday transactions, remittances, and as a unit of account.

Additionally, stablecoins are commonly used in lending and borrowing platforms. Users can deposit stablecoins into lending protocols such as Compound or Aave to earn interest. Borrowers prefer stablecoins because they provide predictability in the borrowed amount and repayment terms.

In decentralized exchanges (DEXs), stablecoins serve as a critical liquidity source. Pairing volatile assets with stablecoins in liquidity pools helps reduce the price impact and risk for liquidity providers. For instance, in the Uniswap exchange, pairs like USDC/ETH are ubiquitous.

Stablecoins also play a pivotal role in yield farming and liquidity mining. Users can provide stablecoin liquidity to various protocols and earn rewards in the form of the protocol's tokens. The relative stability of stablecoins reduces the risk associated with providing liquidity compared to more volatile cryptocurrency pairs.

```
# Pseudocode for calculating annual yield from liquidity provision
def calculate_annual_yield(reward_tokens_per_day, token_value, liquidity_provided):

    daily_yield = (reward_tokens_per_day * token_value) / liquidity_provided
    annual_yield = daily_yield * 365
    return annual_yield

reward_tokens_per_day = 5 # Number of reward tokens received per day
token_value = 10 # Value of each reward token in USD
liquidity_provided = 1000 # Amount of liquidity provided in USD
print(f"Annual Yield: {calculate_annual_yield(reward_tokens_per_day, token_value,
    liquidity_provided) * 100:.2f}%")
# Output: Annual Yield: 18.25%
```

Moreover, stablecoins facilitate cross-border transactions and financial inclusion. Traditional methods of transferring money across borders are often costly and slow. Stablecoins enable fast and inexpensive transfers by bypassing the traditional banking system and intermediaries.

The use of stablecoins in risk management and DeFi insurance is worth noting as well. Stablecoins provide a safe haven for users to park their assets during periods of high volatility in the cryptocurrency markets. Additionally, DeFi insurance platforms like Nexus Mutual can price policies more accurately using stablecoins due to their stable value, reducing the risk of price fluctuations affecting coverage amounts.

The integration of stablecoins into DeFi underscores their importance in supporting financial stability, efficiency, and innovation. Their role extends throughout the DeFi landscape, from serving as a stable medium of exchange to underpinning diverse financial services.

8.7 Yield Farming and Liquidity Mining

Yield farming and liquidity mining are two of the most innovative mechanisms in the DeFi ecosystem, designed to incentivize user participation and liquidity provision. These strategies involve the distribution of rewards to users who supply capital to DeFi protocols, thus enhancing the protocol's functionality and security.

Yield farming, also known as liquidity farming, refers to the practice of staking or lending crypto assets within a DeFi protocol to generate high returns or rewards in the form of additional cryptocurrency. Users can earn these rewards by providing liquidity to various pools, participating in lending and borrowing platforms, or engaging in other activities defined by the protocol.

Liquidity mining is a subset of yield farming where participants earn tokens specific to the platform they are supporting. These tokens can often be traded, staked, or used to interact further with the DeFi ecosystem. The primary objective of liquidity mining is to bootstrap liquidity in the early stages of a protocol's deployment. By allocating a portion of the protocol's governance tokens to early users, developers create an incentive for users to lock their assets within the platform.

Mechanisms of Yield Farming

Yield farming involves complex strategies and active management of funds across various DeFi platforms. The yields are generally generated through a combination of the following methods:

- **Staking:** Users lock their crypto assets in a DeFi protocol, which can then be used to validate transactions and secure the network. In return, they receive rewards.
- **Lending:** By lending their assets on DeFi platforms like Compound or Aave, users earn interest from borrowers.
- **Providing Liquidity:** Users supply liquidity to Automated Market

Makers (AMMs) such as Uniswap, Balancer, or SushiSwap. In return for their provision of liquidity, they earn a portion of the transaction fees.

Liquidity Mining Process

Liquidity mining typically follows these steps:

1. **Deposit Assets:** Users deposit their assets into a liquidity pool. The pool often requires a pair of tokens to be provided in equal value (e.g., ETH/USDT pair).

2. **Receive LP Tokens:** In return for supplying liquidity, the user receives liquidity provider (LP) tokens representing their share in the pool.

3. **Stake LP Tokens:** Users can then stake these LP tokens into a rewards contract to earn additional governance tokens.

4. **Earn Rewards:** Over time, users accumulate rewards in the form of the platform's governance tokens, which can be claimed periodically.

```
pragma solidity ^0.6.0;

contract YieldFarming {
    IERC20 public stakingToken;
    IERC20 public rewardToken;

    uint256 public rewardRate = 100; // example reward rate
    mapping(address => uint256) public stakingBalance;
    mapping(address => uint256) public rewardBalance;

    constructor(address _stakingToken, address _rewardToken) public {
        stakingToken = IERC20(_stakingToken);
        rewardToken = IERC20(_rewardToken);
    }

    function stake(uint256 _amount) public {
        stakingToken.transferFrom(msg.sender, address(this), _amount);
        stakingBalance[msg.sender] += _amount;
    }

    function calculateReward(address _user) public view returns(uint256) {
        return stakingBalance[_user] * rewardRate;
    }

    function withdrawReward() public {
        uint256 reward = calculateReward(msg.sender);
        rewardBalance[msg.sender] = 0;
        rewardToken.transfer(msg.sender, reward);
    }
}
```

Risk Factors and Considerations

While yield farming and liquidity mining offer significant earning potentials, they come with inherent risks:

- **Smart Contract Risks:** The smart contracts could have vulnerabilities or bugs, exposing users to potential loss of their funds.
- **Impermanent Loss:** When users provide liquidity to AMMs, they face the risk of impermanent loss, which occurs when the value ratio of the input tokens changes.
- **Market Volatility:** The highly volatile nature of cryptocurrencies can drastically affect the value of the assets staked and the returns generated.
- **Regulatory Risks:** Regulatory actions against certain DeFi protocols or tokens could impact the user's ability to participate or use earned tokens.

By understanding and managing these risks, participants can make informed decisions while exploring the profitable avenues offered by yield farming and liquidity mining. The dynamic interplay between liquidity providers, borrowers, and protocol developers continues to drive innovation within the DeFi landscape.

8.8 DeFi Insurance and Risk Management

In Decentralized Finance (DeFi), risk management holds paramount importance due to the inherent vulnerabilities and complexities involved in blockchain-based applications. As DeFi platforms facilitate substantial financial transactions and holdings, safeguarding assets against potential threats is critical. DeFi insurance emerges as a pivotal instrument in mitigating these risks, offering protection against various contingencies such as smart contract failures, exchange hacks, and protocol attacks.

DeFi Insurance Overview

DeFi insurance operates under decentralized protocols designed to provide coverage without reliance on traditional insurance entities. These digital insurance solutions leverage smart contracts to automate claims and payouts, ensuring transparency, efficiency, and reduced administrative overhead. Key participants in DeFi insurance include policyholders, underwriters, and claim assessors, all functioning within a blockchain ecosystem.

Smart Contracts and Coverage Automation

Smart contracts form the backbone of DeFi insurance systems, enabling autonomous insurance processes. These contracts execute predefined terms and conditions, systematically managing policy issuance, premium collection, and claim disbursement. For instance, consider the following simplified smart contract snippet to illustrate a basic insurance logic:

```
pragma solidity ^0.8.0;

contract Insurance {
    address payable public insurer;
    address payable public policyholder;
    uint public premium;
    uint public coverageAmount;
    bool public active;

    constructor(uint _premium, uint _coverageAmount) {
        insurer = payable(msg.sender);
        premium = _premium;
        coverageAmount = _coverageAmount;
        active = false;
    }

    function purchasePolicy() public payable {
        require(msg.value == premium, "Incorrect premium amount");
        policyholder = payable(msg.sender);
        active = true;
    }

    function claim(uint _claimAmount) public {
        require(msg.sender == policyholder, "Only policyholder can claim");
        require(active, "Policy not active");
        require(_claimAmount <= coverageAmount, "Claim exceeds coverage");

        active = false;
        policyholder.transfer(_claimAmount);
    }
}
```

In the above example, the contract outlines an insurance policy where a policyholder pays a premium and can later claim coverage up to a specified amount. The contract's state transitions and conditions ensure that only valid claims are processed, automating the insurer's role.

Types of Coverage

DeFi insurance addresses multiple risk categories.

- **Smart Contract Vulnerabilities**: Insurance can protect users from losses due to security breaches or bugs in a smart contract's code. Given the immutable nature of blockchain transactions, any exploitation can result in irreversible loss. Insurance solutions like Nexus Mutual provide such coverage, enabling users to insure their smart contract interactions.

- **Exchange Hacks**: Decentralized exchanges (DEXs) and centralized exchanges (CEXs) are susceptible to security breaches. Insurance protocols can safeguard traders against stolen funds from exchange hacks. Projects like Unslashed Finance offer comprehensive policies to mitigate these risks.

- **Stablecoin Depegging**: Stablecoins, which are fundamental to DeFi operations, are pegged to fiat currencies. If a stablecoin deviates significantly from its pegged value, it can lead to substantial financial loss. DeFi insurance can offer coverage against such depegging events, maintaining users' asset value.

- **Protocol Failures**: Comprehensive policies can also cover systemic risks such as operational failures within DeFi platforms, including governance hacks and erroneous code implementations. By insuring protocol-level risks, users gain protection from broader systemic vulnerabilities.

Risk Management Strategies

While DeFi insurance provides a safety net, it is also crucial to adopt robust risk management strategies to minimize exposure.

- **Code Audits and Formal Verification**: Employing third-party security audits and formal verification techniques can help identify and rectify vulnerabilities in smart contract code before deployment. Regular updates and rigorous testing are vital for maintaining code integrity.

- **Decentralized Oracles**: Reliable data feeds from decentralized oracles ensure that smart contracts operate on accurate and tamper-proof information. Oracles like Chainlink provide off-chain data integration that bolsters contract reliability.

- **Diversification**: Just as in traditional finance, portfolio diversification mitigates risk in DeFi. Users should spread their investments across multiple protocols and assets to minimize potential losses from any single failure point.

- **Governance Participation**: Active participation in protocol governance allows users to have a say in critical decisions affecting platform security and risk management. By being involved in DAOs, users contribute to collective oversight and strategic direction, enhancing the protocol's resilience.

As DeFi continues to evolve, the landscape of risks and the corresponding insurance solutions will also advance. Continuous innovation in smart contract security, oracle reliability, and decentralized governance mechanisms are essential to fortifying the DeFi ecosystem. By balancing innovative solutions with prudent risk management practices, stakeholders can harness the benefits of DeFi while safeguarding their financial assets.

8.9 Governance and Decentralized Autonomous Organizations (DAOs)

Governance within the context of Decentralized Finance (DeFi) refers to the mechanisms, processes, and institutions through which stakeholders influence and control the functions and evolution of DeFi protocols and platforms. Traditional governance relies heavily on centralized entities such as boards of directors and executive teams making key decisions. However, DeFi shifts this paradigm by utilizing decentralized governance frameworks designed to be transparent, distributed, and resistant to centralized control.

A Decentralized Autonomous Organization (DAO) embodies this principle of decentralized governance. A DAO is effectively a digital organization that operates through smart contracts on a blockchain. These smart contracts encode the organization's rules and facilitate transparent operation, ensuring that decisions are executed automatically based on pre-defined rules and consensus mechanisms.

The foundational aspect of a DAO is its decentralized nature. Unlike traditional organizations, DAOs have no centralized leadership. Instead, decision-making power is distributed among stakeholders, often represented by token holders who can propose and vote on governance decisions.

Consider the following core elements of DAOs:

- **Smart Contracts:** The backbone of a DAO is its smart contract, which is an automated and self-executing code that enforces the rules and decisions of the organization without needing human intervention. For example, a treasury management smart contract may automatically distribute funds based on the result of a voting process.

- **Governance Tokens:** DAOs typically issue governance tokens that grant stakeholders voting rights proportional to the number of tokens they hold. The voting power incentivizes token holders to participate actively in governance since their stake in the DAO is directly impacted by the outcomes of governance decisions.

- **Proposal and Voting System:** Stakeholders can submit proposals for changes or new initiatives within the DAO. A robust voting system is crucial for ensuring that all token holders can participate in the decision-making process. This system often employs various voting mechanisms, such as quadratic voting or delegated voting, to balance influence and mitigate centralization of power.

- **Transparency and Trust:** Since DAOs operate on public blockchains, their actions and finances are transparent and can be audited by any participant or external observer. This transparency is fundamental to building and maintaining trust among stakeholders.

To illustrate the practical operation of a DAO, consider the following pseudocode of a simple proposal and voting smart contract:

```
pragma solidity ^0.8.0;

contract SimpleDAO {
    struct Proposal {
        string description;
        uint256 voteCount;
        mapping(address => bool) voters;
    }

    Proposal[] public proposals;
    address public chairperson;
    mapping(address => uint256) public tokenBalance;

    constructor() {
        chairperson = msg.sender;
    }

    // Function to submit a proposal
    function submitProposal(string memory description) public {
        Proposal memory newProposal;
        newProposal.description = description;
        newProposal.voteCount = 0;
        proposals.push(newProposal);
```

```
    }

    // Function to vote on a proposal
    function vote(uint proposalIndex) public {
        Proposal storage proposal = proposals[proposalIndex];
        require(!proposal.voters[msg.sender], "Already voted.");

        proposal.voters[msg.sender] = true;
        proposal.voteCount += tokenBalance[msg.sender];
    }

    // Function to deposit governance tokens
    function depositTokens(uint256 amount) public {
        tokenBalance[msg.sender] += amount;
    }

    // Function to get the result of a vote
    function proposalResult(uint proposalIndex) public view returns (string memory
          description, uint voteCount) {
        Proposal storage proposal = proposals[proposalIndex];
        return (proposal.description, proposal.voteCount);
    }
}
```

The provided smart contract is a rudimentary DAO implementation written in Solidity, the programming language used for Ethereum smart contracts. The contract allows participants to submit proposals, vote on them, deposit governance tokens, and retrieve the results of votes.

Enhancing this basic framework to fully-fledged DAOs involves integrating more sophisticated mechanisms such as:

- **Incentive Systems:** Proper incentives can encourage participation in governance activities. For instance, staking rewards might be provided for those who vote or contribute to governance decisions.
- **Governance Models:** Advanced models like liquid democracy or holographic consensus can be used to refine the voting process, ensuring higher resilience and fairness.
- **Security Audits:** Regular independent audits to detect and correct vulnerabilities in the smart contracts are essential for maintaining security and trust.

The real-world impact of DAOs in the DeFi space is substantial. Several well-known DeFi projects have adopted DAO structures to manage protocol upgrades, fee structures, and other key decisions. Uniswap, Compound, and Yearn Finance, for example, leverage DAOs to guide their governance frameworks.

DAO-based governance democratizes control and aligns the interests of all stakeholders. However, it also brings challenges, such as ensuring broad participation and mitigating the risks of governance attacks, where malicious actors might acquire large amounts of governance tokens to influence decisions adversely.

Maintaining and evolving DAO governance requires continuous engagement from the community, addressing the nuances of decentralized participation, and embedding robustness into governance processes. As DAOs mature, the collective decision-making mechanism will likely play a pivotal role in shaping the future directions of DeFi projects, embodying the principles of decentralization and community-centric governance.

8.10 Security and Risks in DeFi

The distributed and permissionless nature of Decentralized Finance (DeFi) introduces substantial security challenges unique to this domain. Security and risk management in DeFi cannot be adequately discussed without understanding the underlying technological structure, primarily built on blockchain and smart contracts. This section will delve into various aspects of security and risks associated with DeFi, including smart contract vulnerabilities, oracle manipulation, governance risks, and systemic risks.

Smart contracts, the backbone of DeFi applications, automate transactions and operations based on pre-defined rules encoded within the blockchain. However, the immutable nature of blockchain makes it imperative that these contracts are free from errors or vulnerabilities. One prominent example of smart contract risk is the reentrancy attack. In a reentrancy attack, an attacker exploits the contract by repeatedly calling an external function before the initial execution is complete, thereby draining funds.

```
pragma solidity ^0.6.0;

contract Vulnerable {
    mapping(address => uint256) public balances;

    function withdraw(uint256 _amount) public {
        require(balances[msg.sender] >= _amount);
        (bool success, ) = msg.sender.call{value: _amount}("");
        require(success);
        balances[msg.sender] -= _amount;
    }
```

```
    function deposit() public payable {
        balances[msg.sender] += msg.value;
    }
}
```

The contract code above is vulnerable to reentrancy attacks. The call to msg.sender allows control to be transferred back to the sender before the state change (i.e., balances[msg.sender] -= _amount) occurs. To mitigate such risk, using a withdrawal pattern or reentrancy guard is recommended.

```
pragma solidity ^0.6.0;
import "@openzeppelin/contracts/security/ReentrancyGuard.sol";

contract Secure is ReentrancyGuard {
    mapping(address => uint256) public balances;

    function withdraw(uint256 _amount) public nonReentrant {
        require(balances[msg.sender] >= _amount);
        balances[msg.sender] -= _amount;
        (bool success, ) = msg.sender.call{value: _amount}("");
        require(success);
    }

    function deposit() public payable {
        balances[msg.sender] += msg.value;
    }
}
```

Insecure or malicious DeFi protocols can also result in oracle manipulation attacks. Oracles are third-party services providing external data to smart contracts. Since DeFi applications often rely on price feeds and other data from oracles, their reliability and security are crucial. When oracles are manipulated, attackers can exploit price discrepancies to execute arbitrage attacks, extracting value from the protocol.

For instance, during the bZx attack, the attacker manipulated the price feed to artificially inflate the value of a token used as collateral, enabling the borrowing of significant funds against collateral that wasn't actually worth what was represented.

Another critical risk in DeFi arises from governance mechanisms. Decentralized Autonomous Organizations (DAOs) typically govern DeFi protocols through voting by token holders. However, governance token distribution can become highly centralized, leading to governance attacks where those with significant voting power manipulate the protocol for personal gain. Security audits and thorough token distribution mechanisms can help mitigate such risks by ensuring a fairer and more decentralized governance process.

Systemic risks are another concern in DeFi. The interdependency of

DeFi protocols means that a vulnerability or failure in one protocol could have a cascading effect on the entire ecosystem. This interconnectedness is heightened through financial derivatives, composability of smart contracts (Lego-like ability to combine multiple smart contracts to form a more complex system), and liquidity shared across multiple platforms. An example of such systemic risk was evident in the "Black Thursday" event in March 2020, where a sudden drop in the value of Ether (ETH) led to a cascade of liquidations and insolvencies across several DeFi protocols.

Risk management in DeFi must incorporate diversified approaches, such as:

- Frequent and comprehensive code audits
- Employing formal verification methods
- Using multi-signature schemes for executing transactions
- Insurance mechanisms to reimburse users in case of losses
- Implementation of decentralized oracle frameworks like Chainlink to mitigate oracle risks

Organizations and developers must remain vigilant and proactive due to the evolving threat landscape in DeFi. Continuous improvement of security protocols and best practices is paramount to reducing vulnerabilities and ensuring the integrity and reliability of DeFi systems for users.

8.11 The Future of DeFi

The future of Decentralized Finance (DeFi) is poised for significant transformation and growth, driven by continuous advancements in blockchain technology, increased adoption, regulatory developments, and the integration of artificial intelligence (AI) and machine learning. Understanding these factors is crucial for grasping the potential directions and innovations that DeFi may follow.

- First, advancements in blockchain scalability and interoperability will play a pivotal role. Current blockchain platforms often struggle with scalability issues, leading to high transaction fees and slower processing times. Emerging technologies such as sharding, layer-2 solutions (like rollups), and more efficient consensus mechanisms (such as Proof of Stake) aim to address these challenges. As these technologies mature, DeFi platforms can expect to offer faster, more cost-effective, and highly scalable financial services.

- Interoperability between different blockchain networks is another critical factor. Protocols such as Polkadot, Cosmos, and cross-chain bridges enable different blockchains to communicate and transfer assets seamlessly. Improved interoperability will facilitate a more interconnected DeFi ecosystem, allowing users to leverage services across various platforms without friction.

- A noteworthy area of development is the integration of artificial intelligence and machine learning within DeFi. These technologies can enhance trading strategies, automate lending and borrowing processes, optimize yield farming, and predict market trends. For instance, AI-driven algorithms could analyze vast amounts of market data to provide insights for more effective liquidity provision and risk management. Furthermore, AI could facilitate more sophisticated security measures to detect and respond to fraudulent activities promptly.

- Another perspective involves the potential regulatory landscape evolution. Currently, DeFi exists in a relatively unregulated environment, but as it grows, regulatory scrutiny is inevitable. It is anticipated that regulators worldwide will establish frameworks to govern DeFi operations, ensuring consumer protection, reducing fraud, and maintaining financial stability. Compliance with Anti-Money Laundering (AML) and Know Your Customer (KYC) regulations could become standard practice within the DeFi ecosystem. Though regulatory measures may initially pose challenges, they can also provide legitimacy and encourage broader adoption by institutional investors.

- The rise of Central Bank Digital Currencies (CBDCs) could also intersect with the DeFi landscape. CBDCs represent a digital form of fiat currency, issued and regulated by central banks. Their introduction could revolutionize the DeFi space by providing stable and widely accepted digital currencies, reducing reliance on traditional stablecoins. Additionally, CBDCs could streamline cross-border transactions and integrate with DeFi platforms to enable more straightforward and secure financial operations.

- In terms of user experience, the development of more intuitive and user-friendly interfaces is essential to drive mainstream adoption. Currently, DeFi platforms can be complex and intimidating for non-technical users. Future enhancements might include seamless onboarding processes, educational resources, and interfaces that abstract away complexities while maintaining transparency.

- The tokenization of real-world assets also presents significant opportunities for DeFi. Tokenization involves converting physical or traditional assets, like real estate, stocks, or bonds, into digital tokens on a blockchain. This approach could unlock liquidity for otherwise illiquid assets and provide users with new opportunities for investment and financial management within the DeFi ecosystem. Additionally, the ability to fractionalize ownership of high-value assets could democratize investment opportunities and foster a more inclusive financial environment.

- Governance within DeFi is expected to evolve significantly as well. Decentralized Autonomous Organizations (DAOs) will likely gain prominence, providing a decentralized structure for decision-making and governance. Through DAO frameworks, stakeholders can propose, vote on, and implement changes to the platform, ensuring that the community retains control over the direction and policies of the DeFi ecosystem. Mechanisms for more effective and inclusive governance may emerge, balancing power among stakeholders and enhancing the resilience and adaptability of DeFi protocols.

The future of DeFi is multi-faceted, holding immense potential for innovation and disruption in the financial sector. By leveraging advancements in blockchain technology, AI, regulatory integration, CBDCs, user experience enhancements, asset tokenization, and decentralized governance, DeFi can continue to evolve and expand, potentially reshaping how financial services are accessed and utilized globally.

Chapter 9

Investing in Bitcoin and Cryptocurrency

Investing in Bitcoin and cryptocurrency requires understanding market dynamics, investment strategies, and associated risks. This chapter provides guidance on setting up investment accounts, purchasing cryptocurrencies, and employing strategies like HODLing, trading, and diversification. It covers fundamental and technical analysis, risk management, tax implications, and the importance of securely storing investments. Additionally, it offers insights into market sentiment and long-term investment outlook, equipping investors with the knowledge to navigate the volatile cryptocurrency market.

9.1 Introduction to Investing in Bitcoin

Investing in Bitcoin requires an understanding of its unique characteristics and the broader cryptocurrency ecosystem. Bitcoin, designed by the pseudonymous Satoshi Nakamoto in 2008, was introduced in the Bitcoin whitepaper, titled "Bitcoin: A Peer-to-Peer Electronic Cash System." It is a decentralized digital currency that operates without a central authority or intermediaries, relying on a combination of cryptographic principles and a public ledger, the blockchain, to secure transactions.

- **Decentralization and Peer-to-Peer Network:** Bitcoin's decentralized nature means that it does not rely on a central authority, such as a bank or government, to manage the currency or validate transactions. Instead, it uses a peer-to-peer (P2P) network where nodes, which are computers running the Bitcoin software, collectively maintain the blockchain by validating new transactions and adding them to the ledger through a process called mining.

- **Mining and the Blockchain:** Bitcoin mining is the process through which new bitcoins are created and transactions are verified. Miners solve complex mathematical problems to add new blocks to the blockchain, which is the chronological chain of all verified transactions. This process is computationally intensive and requires significant computational power, incentivized by rewards in the form of newly minted bitcoins and transaction fees.

- **Scarcity and Supply Cap:** Unlike traditional currencies, Bitcoin has a finite supply. The total number of bitcoins that can ever exist is capped at 21 million, a feature coded into the Bitcoin protocol. This scarcity is often compared to precious metals like gold, which contributes to Bitcoin being referred to as "digital gold."

- **Volatility and Market Dynamics:** Bitcoin is known for its price volatility. Its value can fluctuate significantly over short periods due to various factors, including market sentiment, macroeconomic trends, regulatory news, technological advancements, and changes in demand and supply. As an investor, understanding these dynamics is crucial for making informed investment decisions.

- **Digital Wallets and Security:** To own and use Bitcoin, individuals must have a digital wallet, which can be software-based (hot wallet) or hardware-based (cold wallet). These wallets store private keys, which are cryptographic keys required to access and manage your Bitcoin holdings. The security of these wallets is paramount, as losing access to your private keys means losing access to your bitcoins.

- **Investment Considerations:** Before investing, consider your financial goals, risk tolerance, and investment horizon. Bitcoin can be a valuable addition to an investment portfolio, offering potential for high returns, diversification, and hedging against traditional financial market risks. However, the cryptocurrency market is speculative and high-risk, necessitating thorough research and a strategic approach.

- **Regulatory Environment:** Bitcoin's regulatory landscape is complex and varies significantly across jurisdictions. Some governments are supportive, others are cautious, and some are outright hostile. Regulatory developments can impact the value and legality of Bitcoin, influencing market dynamics and investor sentiment. Keeping abreast of regulatory changes is critical for Bitcoin investors.

- **Market Participation and Exchanges:** To buy Bitcoin, investors typically use cryptocurrency exchanges, which act as intermediaries allowing users to trade fiat currency for Bitcoin and vice versa. Examples of popular exchanges include Coinbase, Binance, and Kraken. These platforms vary in terms of user experience, security features, available trading pairs, fees, and regulatory compliance. Selecting a reliable and secure exchange is essential for a safe investing experience.

```
import requests

# Example function to get Bitcoin price from an exchange
def get_bitcoin_price(api_url):
    response = requests.get(api_url)
    data = response.json()
    return data['bitcoin']['usd']

api_url = 'https://api.coingecko.com/api/v3/simple/price?ids=bitcoin&vs_currencies=
    usd'
print(f"Current Bitcoin Price: ${get_bitcoin_price(api_url)}")
```

- **Storage and Protection of Assets:** Once you acquire Bitcoin, securely storing your investment is crucial. Many investors use a combination of hot and cold wallets to balance convenience and security. Hardware wallets are recommended for long-term storage due to their robustness against online threats. Additionally, using multi-signature wallets can enhance security by requiring multiple approvals before transactions can be made.

Thus, investing in Bitcoin involves comprehending its innovative technology, market behavior, security mechanisms, regulatory environment, and strategic management of assets. By being well-informed, investors can navigate the complexities of the cryptocurrency market and make prudent investment choices.

9.2 Setting Up an Investment Account

Before one can invest in Bitcoin or other cryptocurrencies, setting up a proper investment account is an essential prerequisite. This section outlines the steps required to set up an investment account, ranging from choosing the right platform to completing necessary verification procedures. Adhering to these steps ensures that investors are compliant with regulations and have access to secure systems for managing their investments.

To begin, selecting a reputable cryptocurrency exchange is paramount. Exchanges act as intermediaries that facilitate the buying, selling, and holding of cryptocurrencies. Prominent examples include Coinbase, Binance, Kraken, and Gemini. When choosing an exchange, consider factors such as security features, fees, user-friendliness, available cryptocurrencies, and regulatory compliance.

Once an exchange is selected, the next step is to create an account.

```
1. Visit the exchange's website, e.g., www.coinbase.com.
2. Click on the "Sign Up" or "Get Started" button.
3. Enter the required personal information (name, email, password).
4. Agree to the terms and conditions.
5. Click "Create Account".
```

A verification email is usually sent to the provided email address, which requires action to verify the account. Follow the instructions in the email to complete this step.

Subsequent to email verification, the user must undergo a KYC (Know Your Customer) process. KYC is a regulatory requirement aimed at preventing illegal activities like money laundering. This process involves providing additional personal information and documentation. Typically required documents include a government-issued ID (e.g., passport, driver's license) and, in some cases, a proof of address document (e.g., utility bill, bank statement). The steps to complete the KYC process are:

```
1. Log in to the exchange account.
2. Navigate to the account settings or verification section.
3. Upload a clear image of the required identification documents.
4. Fill in any additional necessary personal information.
5. Submit the documents for verification.
```

Verification may take several hours to a few days, depending on the exchange. During this period, it is crucial to ensure the provided documents are clear and not expired to avoid delays.

After successful verification, the investor must secure their account using two-factor authentication (2FA). 2FA adds an additional layer of security by requiring not only a password but also a second factor, which is usually a temporary code received via an authenticator app (e.g., Google Authenticator) or SMS. The process to enable 2FA is as follows:

1. Log in to the exchange account.
2. Go to the security settings or 2FA section.
3. Select the preferred 2FA method (authenticator app is recommended).
4. Follow the instructions to link the authenticator app (e.g., scan a QR code).
5. Enter the code generated by the authenticator app to verify the setup.

With the account verified and secured, the next step is funding the account. Exchanges typically support various funding methods, including bank transfers, credit/debit cards, and, in some cases, PayPal. The steps to deposit funds are:

1. Log in to the exchange account.
2. Go to the "Deposit" or "Funding" section.
3. Choose the preferred funding method.
4. Follow the provided instructions to link your bank account or card.
5. Enter the amount to deposit and confirm the transaction.

Deposits may take some time to reflect in the account, depending on the method chosen. Bank transfers can take a few days, while card deposits are generally quicker.

Finally, once the funds are available, the investor is ready to purchase Bitcoin or other cryptocurrencies.

1. Log in to the exchange account.
2. Navigate to the trading or buy/sell section.
3. Select the cryptocurrency to purchase (e.g., Bitcoin).
4. Choose the desired amount or quantity.
5. Review the transaction details, including fees.
6. Confirm the purchase.

The purchased cryptocurrency will be credited to the exchange wallet, from where it can be managed, traded, or transferred to an external wallet for added security.

By meticulously following these steps, investors can ensure that their investment accounts are robust, compliant, and secure, thus laying a solid foundation for engaging in cryptocurrency investments.

9.3 How to Buy Bitcoin and Other Cryptocurrencies

Acquiring Bitcoin and other cryptocurrencies involves a series of precise steps that ensure a secure and efficient transaction process. This section delineates the crucial stages, from choosing a reliable cryptocurrency exchange to executing the purchase and securing your new assets.

The initial step is selecting a cryptocurrency exchange platform. The exchange acts as a marketplace where buyers and sellers interact to trade digital currencies. Key factors to consider when selecting an exchange include security measures, fees, liquidity, and supported cryptocurrencies. Prominent exchanges like Coinbase, Binance, Kraken, and Bitstamp are renowned for their robust security protocols and user-friendly interfaces.

Once an exchange is selected, the next step is to create an account. During this process, providing accurate personal information is vital for identity verification. This step is crucial to comply with Know Your Customer (KYC) and Anti-Money Laundering (AML) regulations, which help prevent illegal activities. Verification typically involves uploading identification documents such as a passport or driver's license.

After account creation and verification, the next task is funding the account. Exchanges offer various methods to deposit funds, including bank transfers, credit card payments, and cryptocurrency deposits. It's important to understand the associated fees and processing times for each method. Bank transfers generally incur lower fees but take longer to process, whereas credit card payments process quickly but may involve higher fees.

With a funded account, you are ready to buy Bitcoin or other cryptocurrencies. The buying process on most exchanges is straightforward. Here is a simple example using Python and the 'ccxt' library to illustrate a typical API call for purchasing Bitcoin on Binance:

```
import ccxt

binance = ccxt.binance({
    'apiKey': 'YOUR_API_KEY',
    'secret': 'YOUR_SECRET_KEY',
})

# Assuming deposit in USD, buying Bitcoin (BTC) with USD
ticker = binance.fetch_ticker('BTC/USD')
price = ticker['last'] # Get the latest price
```

```
order = binance.create_market_buy_order('BTC/USD', amount_in_usd / price)
print(order)
```

In this example, the code initiates a market buy order for Bitcoin using the specified amount in USD, converting the quantity to the equivalent in Bitcoin based on the current price.

Upon purchasing the cryptocurrency, it is critical to withdraw the assets to a secure wallet. Trusting funds with an exchange can be risky due to potential hacks or bankruptcies. Wallet options include hardware wallets, software wallets, and paper wallets. Hardware wallets like Ledger Nano S and Trezor offer high levels of security by storing private keys offline. Software wallets, such as Electrum and Mycelium, provide a balance of convenience and security, while paper wallets involve printing the private keys on a physical medium, ensuring they're not exposed to digital threats.

To ensure a comprehensive understanding, here are the steps in a summarizing format using a tabular representation:

- **Select an Exchange:** Choose a platform with strong security, low fees, and good liquidity. Examples include Coinbase, Binance, and Kraken.

- **Create an Account:** Sign up for an account and complete the KYC verification process by providing personal identification documents.

- **Fund the Account:** Deposit funds using methods such as bank transfer, credit card, or cryptocurrency. Be mindful of associated fees and processing times.

- **Purchase Cryptocurrency:** Use the exchange interface to buy Bitcoin or other cryptocurrencies. Market orders execute immediately at the current price, while limit orders execute at a specified price.

- **Transfer to a Secure Wallet:** Withdraw your purchased assets to a secure wallet. Hardware wallets are highly recommended for long-term security; options like Ledger or Trezor are industry standards.

This process might seem intricate initially but becomes routine with practice. Engaging in small transactions initially is advisable before scaling up your investments to ensure comfort and familiarity with the platform's interface and processes. Security should always be prioritized, as maintaining control over your private keys is essential for safeguarding your investments.

Acquiring cryptocurrencies successfully inherently relies on meticulous attention to detail and a comprehensive understanding of each step involved. This structured approach ensures investors are well-equipped to navigate the complexities of buying and securing digital assets.

9.4 Investment Strategies: HODLing, Trading, and Diversification

Investors approach the Bitcoin and cryptocurrency market utilizing diverse strategies aimed at maximizing returns while managing risks. Three prominent strategies in the realm of cryptocurrency investment are HODLing, trading, and diversification. Each of these strategies has distinct characteristics, advantages, and drawbacks, making it crucial for investors to understand their nuances and applications.

HODLing refers to the practice of buying and holding onto cryptocurrencies over an extended period, disregarding short-term market fluctuations. The term "HODL" originated from a misspelling of "hold" in a Bitcoin forum post and has since become synonymous with a long-term investment mindset. The rationale behind HODLing is grounded in the belief that, despite periods of volatility, the value of Bitcoin and other cryptocurrencies will appreciate over time due to increasing adoption and limited supply.

The primary advantage of HODLing lies in its simplicity and the potential for significant long-term gains. By maintaining a long-term perspective, HODLers can avoid the panic selling often triggered by market corrections and downturns. This strategy requires a strong conviction in the future potential of the cryptocurrencies held and the discipline to withstand market volatility.

To illustrate the HODLing approach, consider the following code, which simulates the accumulation of Bitcoin over a period of time:

```
import numpy as np
import matplotlib.pyplot as plt

# Simulating Bitcoin price over 10 years with volatility
np.random.seed(0)
years = 10
```

```
days = years * 365
btc_price = 10000 * np.exp(np.cumsum(np.random.randn(days) * 0.02))

# Plotting the simulated Bitcoin price
plt.figure(figsize=(10, 5))
plt.plot(btc_price, label='Simulated Bitcoin Price')
plt.title('Bitcoin Price Simulation Over 10 Years')
plt.xlabel('Days')
plt.ylabel('Price in USD')
plt.legend()
plt.show()
```

The above code generates a simulated Bitcoin price over a 10-year period, reflecting the inherent volatility of the market. Investors who adopt a HODLing strategy would buy and hold Bitcoin throughout this period, potentially reaping substantial gains by riding out the volatility.

In contrast to HODLing, **trading** involves actively buying and selling cryptocurrencies to capitalize on short-term price movements. Traders utilize various techniques, including technical analysis, chart patterns, and market indicators, to predict price direction and timing their trades. Trading can be highly lucrative but also demands a deep understanding of market dynamics, quick decision-making, and the ability to manage emotions.

There are various trading strategies, such as day trading, swing trading, and scalp trading, each with its own time horizon and risk profile. Day traders, for instance, open and close positions within a single day, aiming to profit from intraday price movements. Swing traders hold positions for several days or weeks to capture medium-term trends. Scalpers engage in very short-term trades, often lasting just minutes, to exploit small price changes.

The following code snippet demonstrates a simple moving average crossover strategy, a popular technical analysis technique used by traders:

```
import pandas as pd

# Generating a sample DataFrame with Bitcoin prices
prices = pd.DataFrame(btc_price, columns=['Close'])

# Calculating the short-term and long-term moving averages
short_window = 40
long_window = 100
prices['Short_MA'] = prices['Close'].rolling(window=short_window).mean()
prices['Long_MA'] = prices['Close'].rolling(window=long_window).mean()

# Creating signals based on moving average crossover
prices['Signal'] = 0
prices['Signal'][short_window:] = np.where(
    prices['Short_MA'][short_window:] > prices['Long_MA'][short_window:], 1, -1
)
```

```
# Plotting the price and moving averages
plt.figure(figsize=(10, 5))
plt.plot(prices['Close'], label='Close Price')
plt.plot(prices['Short_MA'], label='40-Day Moving Average')
plt.plot(prices['Long_MA'], label='100-Day Moving Average')
plt.title('Moving Average Crossover Strategy')
plt.xlabel('Days')
plt.ylabel('Price in USD')
plt.legend()
plt.show()
```

In this example, signals are generated when the short-term (40-day) moving average crosses above or below the long-term (100-day) moving average, indicating potential buy or sell opportunities.

Diversification refers to the strategy of spreading investments across different assets to reduce risk. In the context of cryptocurrency, diversification involves investing in a variety of cryptocurrencies rather than concentrating funds in a single asset. By doing so, investors can mitigate the impact of a poor-performing asset on their overall portfolio.

Diversification can be achieved by creating a balanced portfolio composed of various types of cryptocurrencies, such as Bitcoin, Ethereum, and other altcoins, each with unique characteristics and use cases. Investors might also consider including assets with different risk profiles, from high-growth potential tokens to stablecoins that offer lower risk and volatility.

To visualize portfolio allocation, the following Python code demonstrates a simple portfolio diversification strategy:

```
import matplotlib.pyplot as plt

# Defining portfolio allocation
portfolio = {
    'Bitcoin (BTC)': 0.5,
    'Ethereum (ETH)': 0.3,
    'Cardano (ADA)': 0.1,
    'Stablecoins (USDT/USDC)': 0.1
}

# Plotting the portfolio allocation
labels = portfolio.keys()
sizes = portfolio.values()

plt.figure(figsize=(8, 8))
plt.pie(sizes, labels=labels, autopct='%1.1f%%', startangle=140)
plt.title('Cryptocurrency Portfolio Diversification')
plt.axis('equal')
plt.show()
```

This pie chart visually represents a diversified cryptocurrency portfolio, with allocations to Bitcoin, Ethereum, Cardano, and stablecoins. By spreading investments across various assets, investors can reduce the overall volatility and risk of their portfolio.

9.5 Fundamental Analysis and Valuation

Fundamental analysis in the context of Bitcoin and cryptocurrencies involves evaluating various intrinsic factors to determine the potential future value of the asset. Unlike traditional stocks, cryptocurrencies do not have earnings reports, dividends, or tangible products. Therefore, fundamental analysis focuses on unique metrics and indicators pertinent to the cryptocurrency realm.

Network Value to Transactions (NVT) Ratio:

The Network Value to Transactions (NVT) ratio is often referred to as the Bitcoin equivalent of the Price to Earnings (P/E) ratio for stocks. It is calculated by dividing the market capitalization (network value) by the daily transaction volume. A high NVT ratio may suggest that the network is overvalued or that transaction volumes are low. Conversely, a low NVT ratio could indicate that the market is undervaluing the network given its transaction volume.

$$\text{NVT Ratio} = \frac{\text{Market Capitalization}}{\text{Daily Transaction Volume}}$$

Active Addresses:

The number of active addresses, which refers to unique addresses that participate in transactions within a given period, is another critical fundamental metric. This metric provides insights into the level of activity and interest in the network.

```
# Example Python code to count active addresses from blockchain data
from bitcoinrpc.authproxy import AuthServiceProxy, JSONRPCException

def count_active_addresses(block_hash):
    addresses = set()
    try:
        block = rpc_connection.getblock(block_hash)
        for tx in block['tx']:
            raw_tx = rpc_connection.getrawtransaction(tx, True)
            for vout in raw_tx['vout']:
                addresses.add(vout['scriptPubKey']['addresses'][0])
    except JSONRPCException as e:
        print(f"Error: {e}")
    return len(addresses)

# Example usage with a specified block hash
```

```
rpc_user = 'user'
rpc_password = 'password'
rpc_host = 'localhost'
rpc_port = '8332'

rpc_connection = AuthServiceProxy(f"http://{rpc_user}:{rpc_password}@{rpc_host
    }:{rpc_port}")
block_hash = '0000000000000000000cac33e258b6fb40fef5bbb41e811b2b96995c1fb7d5e4'
number_of_active_addresses = count_active_addresses(block_hash)
print(f"Active Addresses: {number_of_active_addresses}")
```

```
Active Addresses: 1273
```

Hash Rate:

The hash rate, which reflects the computational power dedicated to mining Bitcoin, is another fundamental indicator. A higher hash rate suggests a more secure network, as it becomes more resistant to attacks. Additionally, a rising hash rate indicates growing interest and investment in Bitcoin mining operations, often correlating with a bullish market sentiment.

$$\text{Hash Rate (TH/s)} = \frac{\text{Number of Hashes}}{\text{Time(seconds)} \times 10^{12}}$$

Market Capitalization:

Market capitalization, or market cap, is calculated by multiplying the current price of the cryptocurrency by its circulating supply. For Bitcoin, this metric is crucial as it indicates the scale and size of the network.

$$\text{Market Capitalization} = \text{Current Price} \times \text{Circulating Supply}$$

Supply Metrics:

Analyzing the total supply (maximum supply), circulating supply, and inflation rate (rate at which new coins are created) are essential for understanding the scarcity and long-term value proposition of a cryptocurrency like Bitcoin.

```
# Example Python code to calculate market capitalization
current_price = 60000 # Assume current price of Bitcoin in USD
circulating_supply = 18800000 # Example circulating supply of Bitcoin

market_cap = current_price * circulating_supply
print(f"Market Capitalization: ${market_cap} USD")
```

```
Market Capitalization: $1128000000000 USD
```

Development Activity:

Tracking the development activity, such as the frequency of updates or commits to the cryptocurrency's codebase, can provide insights into the ongoing support and innovation behind the project. Platforms like GitHub are often used to monitor this activity.

Partnership and Adoption:

Strategic partnerships with established brands and real-world adoption can significantly impact the valuation of a cryptocurrency. For instance, large-scale partnerships that enable Bitcoin for payment methods or its use in various applications signal confidence in the technology's viability and future use.

Regulatory Environment:

The regulatory landscape can greatly influence Bitcoin's valuation. Positive regulatory developments, such as endorsements or clarifications from financial authorities, can enhance investor confidence. Conversely, restrictive regulations can dampen market sentiment and inhibit growth.

Market Sentiment:

Analyzing market sentiment through social media trends, news articles, and public discussions can offer a gauge of the collective mood of investors. Sentiment analysis tools and platforms provide quantitative insights into how positive or negative the sentiment is towards Bitcoin at any given moment.

By synthesizing these metrics and diligently monitoring the evolution of the Bitcoin ecosystem, investors are equipped to make informed investment decisions. The holistic appraisal resulting from fundamental analysis enables a deeper understanding of the underlying factors affecting Bitcoin's long-term value.

9.6 Technical Analysis Basics

Technical analysis is a methodology for forecasting the direction of prices through the study of past market data, primarily price and volume. It is predicated on the notion that all known information about a security is already factored into its price, and that prices generally move in trends that are discernible through historical data patterns.

A foundational concept in technical analysis is the *price chart*. Several types of price charts are employed in the analysis, each providing a different perspective on market behavior. The most common price charts include:

- **Line Chart**: Connects closing prices over a specified time period.
- **Bar Chart**: Displays the open, high, low, and close (OHLC) of each period within the chart.
- **Candlestick Chart**: Similar to bar charts but with bodies (candlesticks), visually distinguishing opening and closing prices.

Candlestick Charts are particularly popular in cryptocurrency analysis due to their visually intuitive format. Each candlestick represents one period (e.g., one day) and includes the opening, highest, lowest, and closing prices. The body of the candlestick is filled if the closing price is lower than the opening price, and hollow if the closing price is higher.

Example of a **Candlestick Chart**:

```
import matplotlib.pyplot as plt
import matplotlib.dates as mdates
import pandas as pd
from mplfinance.original_flavor import candlestick_ohlc
from matplotlib.dates import DateFormatter, date2num

# Sample data
data = pd.DataFrame({
    'Date': pd.date_range('2021-01-01', periods=10, freq='D'),
    'Open': [1, 2, 3, 4, 5, 6, 7, 8, 9, 10],
    'High': [2, 3, 4, 5, 6, 7, 8, 9, 10, 11],
    'Low': [1, 1, 2, 3, 4, 5, 6, 7, 8, 9],
    'Close': [2, 2, 3, 4, 5, 6, 7, 8, 9, 10]
})

data['Date'] = data['Date'].apply(mdates.date2num)
fig, ax = plt.subplots()
candlestick_ohlc(ax, data.values, width=0.6, colorup='g', colordown='r')
ax.xaxis.set_major_formatter(mdates.DateFormatter('%Y-%m-%d'))
plt.show()
```

Trendlines are another essential component, used to identify the general direction of price movements. Uptrends are characterized by a series of higher highs and higher lows, whereas downtrends feature lower highs and lower lows. Correctly drawing trendlines enhances the predictive accuracy of market trends.

Support and Resistance Levels indicate the price points where a security tends to stop and reverse. Support levels are where the price tends to find support as it falls, and resistance levels are where the price tends to find resistance as it rises.

- **Support**: Typically identified by previous lows.
- **Resistance**: Typically identified by previous highs.

Example of Support and Resistance Levels:

```
import matplotlib.pyplot as plt

data = [1, 2, 3, 4, 5, 6, 5, 4, 3, 2, 1]
dates = pd.date_range('2021-01-01', periods=len(data))

plt.plot(dates, data, marker='o')
plt.axhline(y=1, color='green', linestyle='--', label='Support')
plt.axhline(y=6, color='red', linestyle='--', label='Resistance')
plt.legend()
plt.show()
```

Technical Indicators are formula-based, providing statistical analysis of price movements and allowing the identification of market entry and exit points. Notable indicators include:

- **Moving Averages**: Smooth out price data to identify trends easier.
- **Relative Strength Index (RSI)**: Measures the speed and change of price movements over a specified period.
- **Moving Average Convergence Divergence (MACD)**: Shows the relationship between two moving averages of a security's price.

Example of Moving Averages:

```
# Sample data
data = pd.DataFrame({
    'Date': pd.date_range('2021-01-01', periods=100, freq='D'),
    'Close': pd.Series([i + (i * 0.01 * pd.np.sin(i / 10)) for i in range(100)]),
})

data.set_index('Date', inplace=True)
data['30_MA'] = data['Close'].rolling(window=30).mean()
data['50_MA'] = data['Close'].rolling(window=50).mean()

plt.plot(data['Close'], label='Closing Price')
plt.plot(data['30_MA'], label='30-Day MA')
plt.plot(data['50_MA'], label='50-Day MA')
plt.legend()
plt.show()
```

To gain proficiency in technical analysis, it is critical to practice interpreting charts and indicators in diverse market conditions. Developing a deep understanding of these tools enables investors to make more informed decisions, potentially improving their market strategies.

9.7 Understanding Market Sentiment and Trends

Understanding market sentiment and trends is crucial for any investor in Bitcoin and other cryptocurrencies. Market sentiment refers to the overall attitude of investors towards a particular market or asset. It is a combination of opinions, feelings, and moods that can drive the price movements of cryptocurrencies. Two primary types of sentiment influence the market: bullish and bearish sentiments. Bullish sentiment indicates a positive outlook where investors expect prices to rise, while bearish sentiment reflects a negative outlook with expectations of price declines.

Market sentiment can be influenced by various factors including news events, social media activity, regulatory announcements, market trends, and macroeconomic indicators. To effectively analyze market sentiment, investors must consider both qualitative and quantitative data sources.

Quantitative analysis involves the use of numerical data and statistical methods. Various tools and platforms provide metrics to gauge market sentiment quantitatively. One prominent tool is the Fear and Greed Index, which aggregates various data points such as volatility, market volume, social media trends, and other elements to provide a numerical value representing the sentiment. The index ranges from 0 (extreme fear) to 100 (extreme greed).

Efficient analysis of sentiment data can be achieved through the use of software and programming languages. Python, for instance, offers libraries such as sentiment-analysis and APIs that can be used to extract sentiment metrics. Below is an example of Python code that utilizes an API to analyze cryptocurrency-related tweets for sentiment:

```
import requests
from textblob import TextBlob

api_url = "https://api.twitter.com/2/tweets/search/recent"
query = {"query": "Bitcoin", "max_results": "100"}
headers = {"Authorization": "Bearer YOUR_ACCESS_TOKEN"}
```

```
response = requests.get(api_url, params=query, headers=headers)
tweets = response.json()

sentiments = [TextBlob(tweet['text']).sentiment.polarity for tweet in tweets['data']]
average_sentiment = sum(sentiments) / len(sentiments)

if average_sentiment > 0:
    print("Overall sentiment is positive")
elif average_sentiment < 0:
    print("Overall sentiment is negative")
else:
    print("Overall sentiment is neutral")
```

Qualitative analysis, on the other hand, involves assessing text-based data through observation. This can include analyzing news articles, blog posts, and social media comments to gauge investor sentiment. One of the significant challenges in qualitative analysis is distinguishing between noise and valuable information. Investors can leverage news aggregator platforms and sentiment analysis tools to streamline this process.

Trends in the cryptocurrency market often follow cyclical patterns. A widely observed cycle is the "market cycle," consisting of four key phases: accumulation, uptrend, distribution, and downtrend. During the accumulation phase, the market exhibits low volatility, and investors begin to buy gradually. The uptrend phase is characterized by a significant increase in prices as market confidence builds up. In the distribution phase, the market sees high volatility with prices peaking, where early investors start taking profits. The downtrend phase follows with falling prices, leading to panic selling and eventual stabilization.

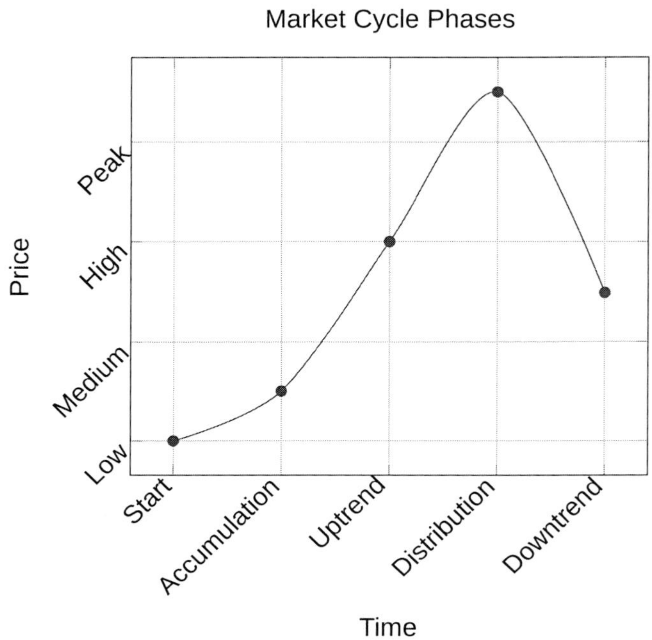

Another important concept to grasp is the trend within the market itself. Trends can be categorized as uptrends, downtrends, and sideways trends. Uptrends are characterized by higher highs and higher lows, downtrends by lower highs and lower lows, and sideways trends by horizontal price movement typically within a range.

Several technical indicators help in identifying and confirming these trends. Moving averages are among the most popular indicators, which smooth out price data to identify the direction of the trend. A simple moving average (SMA) is calculated by averaging a set number of past prices, providing insight into the overall direction. For instance, a commonly used metric is the 50-day SMA:

$$SMA_{50} = \frac{P_1 + P_2 + \cdots + P_{50}}{50}$$

When the current price is above the 50-day SMA, it generally indicates a bullish trend, and conversely, a price below the SMA suggests a bearish trend.

The relative strength index (RSI) is another crucial indicator, which measures the magnitude of recent price changes to evaluate overbought or oversold conditions in the market. RSI values range from 0 to 100. An RSI above 70 is typically considered overbought, while an RSI below 30 indicates oversold conditions.

$$RSI = 100 - \frac{100}{1 + \frac{\text{average gain}}{\text{average loss}}}$$

Analyzing market sentiment and trends provides valuable insights that can inform investment decisions. Combining this analysis with fundamental analysis and technical analysis offers a comprehensive approach to navigating the complexities of the cryptocurrency market.

9.8 Managing Risks and Avoiding Scams

Managing risks and avoiding scams is a crucial aspect of investing in Bitcoin and other cryptocurrencies. Given the decentralized and digital nature of these assets, investors are exposed to a range of risks including market volatility, security threats, and fraudulent schemes. This section delves into practical strategies and best practices to mitigate these risks and protect investments.

Cryptocurrencies are inherently volatile, with their prices often subject to rapid and unpredictable changes. Historical data suggests that this volatility arises from a multitude of factors such as market speculation, regulatory news, technological advancements, and macroeconomic conditions. To manage this risk, it is prudent for investors to diversify their portfolios. Diversification can be achieved by spreading investments across different cryptocurrencies, assets, and sectors to minimize the impact of a decline in any single asset.

The volatility can be further managed using techniques such as dollar-cost averaging (DCA). This involves investing a fixed amount of money at regular intervals regardless of the cryptocurrency's price. This strategy smoothens out the purchase price over time and reduces the impact of market volatility. For instance, if an investor decides to invest $100 every week in Bitcoin, they might buy more Bitcoin during periods of low prices and less when the prices are high, resulting in a more favourable average purchase price over time.

Security risks are another significant concern. Investors must ensure that they are using reputable platforms and wallets for their transactions and storage. Two-factor authentication (2FA), strong passwords, and secure storage solutions such as hardware wallets are essential measures to protect digital assets. Hardware wallets store private keys offline, which significantly reduces the risk of hacking and online theft. It is also vital to back up wallet recovery phrases in a secure and offline location to prevent loss of access to the funds.

An additional layer of security can be achieved by using multi-signature (multi-sig) wallets. Multi-sig wallets require multiple private keys to authorize a transaction, which adds complexity for attackers trying to gain unauthorized access. The use of multi-sig can be particularly beneficial for institutional investors or those holding significant amounts of cryptocurrency.

Phishing attacks are common in the cryptocurrency space, where malicious actors attempt to steal sensitive information such as private keys and passwords through deceptive emails, fake websites, or social engineering tactics. Investors should always verify the authenticity of websites and links before entering any sensitive information and be wary of unsolicited communications claiming to be from legitimate cryptocurrency platforms.

Avoiding scams requires a thorough understanding of the types and signs of fraudulent schemes. Ponzi schemes and fake initial coin offerings (ICOs) are prevalent in the cryptocurrency space. A Ponzi scheme typically promises high returns with little risk and relies on funds from new investors to pay returns to earlier investors, eventually collapsing when the influx of new investors tapers off. Before investing, it is essential to research the credibility of the investment opportunity, the team behind the project, and the underlying technology.

Another scam to be aware of is the pump and dump scheme. In this scheme, fraudsters artificially inflate the price of a cryptocurrency through false or misleading statements, only to sell their holdings at the peak, leaving other investors with significant losses. Indicators of such schemes include sudden and unexplained spikes in price and volume, often followed by sharp declines. Investors should be cautious of assets displaying these patterns and should rely on fundamental and technical analysis to inform their investment decisions.

Regulatory risks also pose a threat to cryptocurrency investments. Regulatory environments vary significantly across different regions and can change rapidly, affecting the legality and usability of certain cryptocurrencies. Staying informed about the regulatory landscape and considering the geopolitical implications of investments can help manage this risk. For example, an investor might choose to focus on cryptocurrencies that have been expressly endorsed or regulated by reputable financial authorities.

A comprehensive risk management strategy includes setting stop-loss orders. Stop-loss orders automatically sell an asset when its price falls to a predetermined level, thereby limiting potential losses. For traders, this can be an effective way to manage the downside risk in highly volatile markets.

Engaging with the cryptocurrency community and participating in forums and discussions can also provide valuable insights into potential risks and prevailing scams. Reputable sources of information include official project websites, whitepapers, recognized financial news outlets, and established cryptocurrency forums such as BitcoinTalk or Reddit.

Ultimately, staying educated and vigilant is key to managing risks and avoiding scams in the cryptocurrency market. Regularly reviewing and updating security practices, diversifying investments, understanding regulatory developments, and conducting thorough due diligence can significantly enhance the safety and success of cryptocurrency investments.

9.9 Tax Implications of Cryptocurrency Investment

Understanding the tax implications of cryptocurrency investments is crucial for compliance and financial planning. Cryptocurrency transactions are subject to taxation in many jurisdictions, affecting both individual investors and institutions. This section delves into the intricacies of tax regulations surrounding cryptocurrency investments, providing detailed guidance on record-keeping, reporting requirements, and potential deductions.

Cryptocurrency is often treated as property for tax purposes. This classification has significant consequences for how transactions are reported and taxed. Each jurisdiction may have specific regulations, but common themes include capital gains and losses, taxable events, and special considerations for mining and staking activities.

Capital Gains and Losses:

When cryptocurrencies are sold, traded, or otherwise disposed of, capital gains or losses are realized. The difference between the acquisition cost (basis) and the selling price determines the gain or loss.

- *Short-term capital gains:* If the cryptocurrency is held for one year or less, the gains are classified as short-term and are typically taxed at ordinary income tax rates.
- *Long-term capital gains:* If the cryptocurrency is held for more than one year, the gains are long-term and usually benefit from lower tax rates.
- *Capital losses:* Losses can offset gains and reduce taxable income. Unused losses might be carried forward to future tax years, depending on the jurisdiction.

Taxable Events:

Several events can trigger tax obligations:

- *Selling cryptocurrency for fiat currency:* When cryptocurrency is converted to a government-issued currency, the transaction must be reported.
- *Trading one cryptocurrency for another:* Exchanging Bitcoin for Ethereum, for example, is a taxable event.
- *Using cryptocurrency for purchases:* Spending cryptocurrency to buy goods or services also results in a taxable event equivalent to selling the cryptocurrency.
- *Receiving cryptocurrency as income:* This includes mining rewards, staking benefits, and payments for services rendered. The fair market value of the cryptocurrency at the time of receipt must be reported as ordinary income.

Record-Keeping:

Accurate record-keeping is essential for tracking the basis of each cryptocurrency transaction. Important details to record include:

- Date and time of acquisition.
- Fair market value at acquisition.

- Date and time of disposal.
- Fair market value at disposal.
- Associated transaction fees, which can be included in the basis.

Deductible Expenses:

Certain expenses can potentially be deducted to reduce taxable income:

- *Transaction fees:* Fees paid during the acquisition or sale of cryptocurrency can be added to the cost basis or deducted from the proceeds.
- *Mining expenses:* Costs associated with mining operations, such as equipment and electricity, may be deductible for those operating as businesses.

Special Considerations:

In addition to basic taxable events, other significant considerations include:

- *Hard forks and airdrops:* When a blockchain splits and creates a new cryptocurrency (hard fork), the new coins received could be considered income. Similarly, airdrops, where free tokens are distributed, also generally count as income.
- *Staking rewards:* Earnings from staking can be classified as income at the fair market value when received.

Reporting Requirements:

Cryptocurrency transactions must be accurately reported on tax returns. The specifics vary by country:

In the United States, for example:

```
Form 8949: Details individual transactions and calculates capital gains and losses.
Schedule D: Summarizes capital gains and losses.
Form 1040: Reports total income, including from cryptocurrencies.
```

In other jurisdictions, similar forms and schedules may apply. It's essential to consult tax regulations specific to the investor's country of residence and potentially engage a tax professional specializing in cryptocurrency.

Penalties for Non-Compliance:

Failing to report cryptocurrency transactions can result in severe penalties, including fines and interest charges. It's imperative to remain compliant with tax regulations to avoid legal repercussions. The complexities of cryptocurrency taxation necessitate diligent record-keeping and possibly professional assistance to ensure accurate reporting and maximization of potential deductions.

```
Sample output of taxable calculation report:
Cryptocurrency Transaction Report
Date of Acquisition: 01/01/2022
Date of Disposal: 06/01/2022
Cost Basis: $2,000
Selling Price: $2,500
Capital Gain: $500 (short-term)
```

9.10 Storing and Protecting Your Investment

When investing in Bitcoin and other cryptocurrencies, the security and integrity of your holdings should be a paramount consideration. Cryptocurrencies, being digital assets, require specific storage solutions distinct from traditional asset storage methods. This section delves into various storage options and best practices to safeguard your investments against potential threats.

Types of Cryptocurrency Wallets

Cryptocurrency wallets can be broadly categorized into two types: hot wallets and cold wallets. Understanding the difference between these wallet types is essential for making informed decisions about the security of your investments.

Hot Wallets: Hot wallets are internet-connected devices or software applications that facilitate quick and easy access to cryptocurrencies. They are typically used for everyday transactions and frequent trading due to their convenience. However, the internet connectivity exposes them to potential cyber threats such as hacking, malware, and phishing attacks.

- **Software Wallets**: These are applications that you download and install on your computer or mobile device. Common examples include Exodus, Electrum, and Mycelium.
- **Web Wallets**: These wallets are browser-based and can be accessed from any device with an internet connection. Examples

include Coinbase and Blockchain.info.

- **Mobile Wallets**: Optimized for mobile usage, these wallets provide ease of access and mobility. Examples include Trust Wallet and BRD.

Cold Wallets: Cold wallets are offline storage options that reduce the attack vectors available to malicious actors. They are considered the most secure form of cryptocurrency storage as they are not connected to the internet.

- **Hardware Wallets**: Dedicated physical devices designed to securely store cryptocurrencies. Examples include Ledger Nano S, Ledger Nano X, and Trezor.
- **Paper Wallets**: Physical printouts containing your public and private keys. They can be generated using services like BitAddress or WalletGenerator.
- **Air-Gapped Computers**: Computers that have never been connected to the internet, used to generate and store keys securely.

Best Practices for Securing Your Wallets

Use Strong Passwords and Two-Factor Authentication: Always use strong, unique passwords for your cryptocurrency wallets and associated accounts. Implement two-factor authentication (2FA) to add an additional layer of security by requiring a second form of verification beyond your password.

```
Sample Password: Qg7$29sK!x@3BfTl
```

Regularly Update Software: Ensure that all your wallet applications and devices are running the latest versions of their software. Updates often include vital security patches to protect against newly discovered vulnerabilities.

```
$ sudo apt-get update && sudo apt-get upgrade
```

Backup Your Wallet Data: Periodically create backups of your wallet data. Store these backups in multiple secure locations to prevent loss from device failure or other unforeseen circumstances. For software and mobile wallets, this may involve securely storing recovery seeds (mnemonics).

```
Example of a Recovery Seed:
"witch collapse practice feed shame open despair creek road again ice least"
```

Cold Storage for Long-Term Holdings: Consider using cold wallets for long-term holdings you're not planning to trade frequently. Hardware wallets, paper wallets, and other cold storage methods are less susceptible to cyber-attacks.

Protecting Against Physical Threats

Ensure the physical security of your cold storage devices and backup materials. Place them in secure locations such as safes or safety deposit boxes. Avoid disclosing the whereabouts of your wallets and private keys to unauthorized individuals.

Avoiding Scams and Phishing Attacks

Be vigilant against phishing attempts and scams. Always verify the authenticity of websites before entering sensitive information. Be wary of unsolicited communications via email, social media, or messaging platforms, particularly those requesting private keys or personal information.

Legal and Regulatory Compliance

Stay informed about the legal and regulatory frameworks surrounding cryptocurrency storage and transactions in your jurisdiction. Compliance with relevant laws can protect you from legal issues and ensure that your investments are secure within the bounds of current regulations.

By implementing these strategies and maintaining a proactive approach to security, you can significantly reduce the risks associated with storing and protecting your cryptocurrency investments. Proper security measures are crucial for safeguarding your digital assets against threats in the evolving landscape of cryptocurrency markets.

9.11 Long-Term Investment Outlook

The longevity and potential of Bitcoin and other cryptocurrencies as investment vehicles rely on several key factors: technological advancements, market adoption, regulatory frameworks, and economic trends. Understanding these elements can guide investors toward making more informed long-term investment decisions.

Bitcoin and several major cryptocurrencies have demonstrated resilience and significant growth since their inception. Bitcoin, for example, has transitioned from a niche technology to a globally recognized digital asset. This progression is largely attributed to its underlying blockchain technology, a decentralized and secure ledger system that ensures transparency and immutability of transactions.

Technological advancements continue to shape the landscape of cryptocurrency investment. Innovations such as the Lightning Network aim to address Bitcoin's scalability issues by enabling faster transactions with lower fees. Ethereum's transition from Proof of Work (PoW) to Proof of Stake (PoS) with the Ethereum 2.0 upgrade promises enhanced security, energy efficiency, and transaction throughput. These developments suggest the potential for increased adoption and value appreciation of cryptocurrencies over the long term.

Market adoption is another crucial factor. Institutional investors, including hedge funds, pension funds, and publicly traded companies, have started to recognize Bitcoin as a store of value akin to digital gold. This shift is highlighted by significant investments from entities like MicroStrategy and Tesla. The entry of institutional players introduces greater liquidity and stability into the cryptocurrency market and can act as a catalyst for further adoption by retail investors.

Regulatory frameworks play a pivotal role in the cryptocurrency ecosystem. Governments and regulators have varied approaches, ranging from outright bans to supportive legislation. In jurisdictions with favorable regulations, cryptocurrencies have generally performed better due to increased investor confidence and market participation. Understanding the regulatory environment in one's country and globally is essential for anticipating potential risks and opportunities.

The broader economic context influences the long-term outlook for cryptocurrency investments. Factors such as inflation, monetary policy, and financial crises can impact investor sentiment and drive interest toward decentralized assets like Bitcoin. For instance, during periods of high inflation, Bitcoin is often perceived as a hedge against currency devaluation.

Economic crises can lead to an erosion of trust in traditional financial systems, prompting individuals and institutions to seek alternatives that offer a higher degree of sovereignty and security. This was evident following the 2008 financial crisis, which precipitated the creation of Bitcoin.

Considering these perspectives, investors should evaluate diverse scenarios and adopt a proactive approach to their long-term cryptocurrency investment strategy. One technique is Dollar-Cost Averaging (DCA), which involves investing a fixed amount of money at regular intervals, regardless of the asset's price. This can help mitigate the volatility inherent in cryptocurrency markets by spreading the investment over time.

Another consideration is the potential for new cryptocurrencies or blockchain technologies to disrupt the market. While Bitcoin and Ethereum dominate the market capitalization, emerging projects with novel use cases and technological breakthroughs could offer substantial returns. Evaluating whitepapers, development team credibility, technological uniqueness, and community support are critical when exploring new investments.

The long-term investment outlook for cryptocurrencies also hinges on infrastructural developments such as robust exchanges, secure custody solutions, and efficient payment systems. Centralized exchanges like Coinbase and Binance offer ease of access and liquidity, while decentralized exchanges (DEXs) emphasize security and user control. The growth of financial products such as Bitcoin ETFs (Exchange-Traded Funds) and futures contracts also indicate maturation and acceptance within traditional financial systems.

Evaluating the long-term investment outlook in Bitcoin and cryptocurrencies involves a multidimensional assessment of technological progress, market dynamics, regulatory landscape, and macroeconomic trends. While promising, these investments also come with inherent risks and uncertainties that necessitate careful analysis and strategic planning. Investors should remain informed, adaptive, and vigilant to navigate the evolving cryptocurrency landscape effectively.

Chapter 10

Future of Bitcoin and Cryptocurrency

The future of Bitcoin and cryptocurrency involves ongoing advancements in technology, scalability solutions like the Lightning Network, and increased interoperability between blockchains. This chapter examines potential mainstream adoption, institutional investment, and evolving regulatory frameworks. It discusses the challenges and threats facing the ecosystem, including security concerns and market volatility, and explores the broader impact on the global financial system. The chapter also considers expert predictions and the long-term vision for Bitcoin and decentralized finance.

10.1 Introduction to the Future of Bitcoin and Cryptocurrency

The landscape of Bitcoin and cryptocurrency, a subset of digital currencies, is evolving rapidly, influenced by advances in technology, economic trends, and regulatory policies. The future, though not easily predictable, can be charted by analyzing current trajectories and understanding the underlying principles and potential developments within the ecosystem.

Bitcoin, introduced by an anonymous entity known as Satoshi

Nakamoto in 2008, has grown from a novel concept into a significant player in the financial world. As a decentralized digital currency, Bitcoin leverages blockchain technology to provide a secure, immutable ledger of transactions. The decentralized nature of Bitcoin means that it is not controlled by any single entity or government, promoting a transparent and globally accessible financial system.

The potential future of Bitcoin and cryptocurrency must be viewed through several lenses, including technological advancements, scalability, interoperability, adoption, investment, regulation, challenges, and broader societal impacts.

- Technological advancements consist of enhancements to the underlying blockchain technology, the development of new consensus algorithms, and the implementation of layer-two solutions such as the Lightning Network. These advancements aim to increase transaction throughput, improve security, and reduce latency, thereby fostering a more efficient and robust infrastructure.
- Scalability is a critical issue for Bitcoin, which currently has a lower transaction processing capacity compared to traditional payment systems like Visa. The Lightning Network, a second-layer protocol, is one such solution seeking to address this by enabling off-chain transactions. By allowing users to transact without recording each transaction on the blockchain, the Lightning Network significantly reduces the load on the Bitcoin network, thereby increasing its scalability.
- Interoperability between different blockchains is another area of focus for the future. The ability to transfer assets and information between various blockchain networks seamlessly can lead to a more integrated and versatile cryptocurrency ecosystem. Cross-chain solutions and protocols such as atomic swaps and decentralized exchanges (DEXs) are paving the way for this interoperability.
- Mainstream adoption of Bitcoin and cryptocurrency is gradually increasing, with various use cases emerging beyond just an investment vehicle. Cryptocurrencies can facilitate remittances, provide financial services to the unbanked, and enable peer-to-peer transactions with lower fees than traditional banking systems. Additionally, as more merchants accept cryptocurrencies as payment, the infrastructure for everyday usage will continue to develop and mature.

- Institutional investment in Bitcoin and cryptocurrencies is growing, showcasing a shift in perception from speculative assets to legitimate financial instruments. This trend is evidenced by the entry of well-established financial institutions, hedge funds, and corporations into the cryptocurrency market. These entities bring legitimacy and potentially stabilize the market by providing liquidity and long-term investment perspectives.

- Regulatory developments play a crucial role in shaping the future of Bitcoin and cryptocurrencies. Governments and regulatory bodies worldwide are grappling with how to best integrate and regulate cryptocurrencies within existing financial systems. The development of clear, supportive regulatory frameworks can promote innovation while protecting consumers and maintaining financial stability.

- Despite the promising future, several challenges and threats need to be addressed. These include technological vulnerabilities, market volatility, and the environmental impact of cryptocurrency mining. Security concerns, such as the potential for hacking and fraudulent activities, must also be continually mitigated.

- The broader impact on the global financial system is profound, with cryptocurrencies challenging traditional banking and monetary policies. The decentralized finance (DeFi) movement exemplifies this, enabling financial activities such as lending, borrowing, and trading without intermediaries. This burgeoning sector highlights the potential of blockchain technology to revolutionize the financial landscape.

- Predictions about the future of Bitcoin and cryptocurrency vary widely. Experts offer diverse viewpoints ranging from cautious optimism to visionary expectations. These expert opinions provide insight into possible future trajectories and help stakeholders prepare for various scenarios.

- The long-term vision for decentralized finance includes greater financial inclusion, democratized financial services, and a more resilient global financial system. As technological innovations continue to advance, and as adoption grows, Bitcoin and cryptocurrency are likely to become integral components of the future financial infrastructure.

The subsequent sections of this chapter delve deeper into each of these aspects, providing a comprehensive view of the dynamic and evolving world of Bitcoin and cryptocurrency.

10.2 Technological Advancements and Innovation

Technological advancements and innovations constitute essential forces driving the evolution and future trajectory of Bitcoin and the broader cryptocurrency ecosystem. Focusing on key technological developments provides critical insights into the enhancements in security, efficiency, and functionality that underpin this burgeoning field.

One significant technological advancement in Bitcoin is the implementation of the Segregated Witness (SegWit) protocol. SegWit was introduced to address Bitcoin's transaction malleability problem and improve its scalability. By separating the digital signatures (witness data) from the transaction data, SegWit reduces the space required per transaction, effectively increasing the block size limit without necessitating a hard fork. This development not only enhances transaction throughput but also lays the groundwork for further innovations such as the Lightning Network.

```
// Sample pseudo-code representing SegWit implementation
class Transaction {
    public:
        string txID;
        int segData; // Segregated witness data
        int txData; // Transaction data
};
```

The Lightning Network is another groundbreaking innovation aimed at addressing Bitcoin's scalability issues. This off-chain solution facilitates instant, low-cost transactions by enabling payment channels between parties. These channels allow multiple transactions to take place off the main blockchain, reducing congestion and fees. When a dispute arises or a channel is closed, the final state is broadcast to the Bitcoin blockchain, ensuring security and trustless operation.

```
# Example code snippet for opening a payment channel
class LightningNetwork:
    def open_channel(self, partner, deposit):
        self.channel = PaymentChannel(partner, deposit)

    def close_channel(self):
```

```
        self.channel.settle()
        self.broadcast_channel()
```

Smart contracts, though initially introduced by platforms like Ethereum, are increasingly relevant in Bitcoin's evolution thanks to projects like RSK (Rootstock). RSK aims to bring Turing-complete smart contracts to the Bitcoin network through a sidechain architecture. This innovation enables complex financial agreements, automated transactions, and decentralized applications (dApps) to leverage Bitcoin's security and liquidity.

```
// Simple RSK smart contract example
pragma solidity ^0.5.0;

contract SimpleContract {
    uint public count = 0;

    function increment() public {
        count += 1;
    }
}
```

Another area witnessing rapid technological progress is privacy enhancement. Privacy coins like Monero and Zcash have pioneered techniques such as ring signatures, stealth addresses, and zero-knowledge proofs to ensure transaction confidentiality. Inspired by these advancements, Bitcoin developers have proposed and implemented solutions like Taproot and Schnorr signatures. Taproot allows complex transactions to appear indistinguishable from simple transactions, thereby enhancing privacy. Schnorr signatures improve both privacy and efficiency by aggregating multiple signatures into a single one.

```
# Simplified Schnorr signature verification
def verify_signature(public_key, message, signature):
    # Schnorr signature verification logic
    return schnorr_verify(public_key, message, signature)
```

Quantum computing presents a potential threat to classical cryptographic systems. To safeguard against this, research is ongoing in developing quantum-resistant cryptographic algorithms. Bitcoin's community is actively investigating and preparing for post-quantum cryptographic methods like lattice-based cryptography, which can withstand quantum attacks.

```
# Pseudo-code for quantum-resistant signature
def quantum_resistant_signature(message):
    # lattice-based signature logic
    return lattice_sign(message)
```

Blockchain interoperability is another area of innovation. Projects like Polkadot and Cosmos aim to create ecosystems where diverse blockchains can interact seamlessly. Cross-chain communication protocols enable the exchange of assets and data across different blockchain networks, fostering collaboration and enhancing the utility of decentralized technologies.

```
# Example code for cross-chain asset transfer using Polkadot
class CrossChainTransfer:
    def transfer_assets(self, from_chain, to_chain, asset):
        bridge = find_bridge(from_chain, to_chain)
        bridge.transfer(asset)
```

Furthermore, advancements in the field of decentralized finance (DeFi) are pushing the boundaries of what is possible with Bitcoin and cryptocurrency. DeFi platforms leverage blockchain technology to deliver financial services like lending, borrowing, and trading without intermediaries. Integrating these services with Bitcoin enhances its usability and positions it as a central player in a decentralized financial ecosystem.

DeFi Platform Overview
Lending
Borrowing
Decentralized Trading

Continual technological progress is imperative for the sustained growth and mainstream adoption of Bitcoin and cryptocurrencies. By addressing existing limitations and introducing novel functionalities, these innovations enhance the robustness, security, and capability of the Bitcoin network.

10.3 Scalability Solutions and Lightning Network

Scalability is one of the critical issues in the evolution of Bitcoin and other cryptocurrencies. As the number of users and transactions increases, the demand for efficient and scalable solutions becomes paramount. Bitcoin's original design, while robust and secure, faces limitations regarding transaction throughput and latency. To address these challenges, several scalability solutions have been proposed and implemented. One of the most prominent of these is the Lightning Network.

The Lightning Network is a second-layer protocol designed to enhance Bitcoin's scalability by enabling off-chain transactions. It operates on top of the Bitcoin blockchain, allowing transactions to be conducted securely without recording every individual transaction on the blockchain itself. This method significantly reduces the load on the Bitcoin network, enabling faster and cheaper transactions.

The Lightning Network relies on a system of payment channels established between participants. These channels allow participants to transact freely with each other without broadcasting each transaction to the blockchain. This is achieved through a series of complex cryptographic operations to ensure security and transparency.

```
# Example pseudocode for establishing a payment channel
def create_payment_channel(participant_A, participant_B, initial_amount):
    # Generate multisig address
    multisig_address = generate_multisig_address(participant_A, participant_B)

    # Funding transaction
    funding_tx = create_funding_transaction(participant_A, multisig_address,
          initial_amount)
    broadcast_transaction(funding_tx)

    # Payment channel established
    return "Payment channel successfully created between {} and {}".format(
          participant_A, participant_B)
```

Upon establishing a payment channel, any number of transactions can occur between the participants without creating a new entry in the blockchain for each transaction. Instead, the transactions are recorded locally within the payment channel. When participants decide to settle their balances, they can close the channel, and the final state is broadcast to the blockchain, ensuring the correct balance for each participant.

```
# Output from establishing a payment channel
Payment channel successfully created between Participant A and Participant B
```

One of the crucial benefits of the Lightning Network is its ability to perform microtransactions efficiently. These microtransactions, sometimes referred to as "micropayments," allow for very small amounts of Bitcoin to be transferred between participants quickly and with minimal fees. This capability is particularly useful for applications such as tipping, pay-per-use services, and other scenarios where small-value transactions are frequent.

The protocol uses a series of smart contracts known as Hash Time-Locked Contracts (HTLCs) to ensure the security of off-chain transactions. HTLCs require certain conditions to be met before funds can be transferred, providing a secure and trustless environment for participants. Here, hashed secrets and time-locks are employed to ensure that neither party can cheat, creating a robust system for off-chain transactions.

Another innovative aspect of the Lightning Network is the concept of routing. Participants can transact with others even if they do not have a direct payment channel by routing payments through a network of participants. The network's topology ensures that payments can find a path from sender to receiver, leveraging the interconnected channels.

```
# Example pseudocode for routing a payment
def route_payment(sender, receiver, amount):
    # Find a route from sender to receiver
    route = find_route(sender, receiver)

    # Create HTLC for the route
    htlc = create_htlc(sender, receiver, amount, route)

    # Execute payment through the route
    execute_payment(htlc)

    return "Payment of {} BTC successfully routed from {} to {}".format(amount,
        sender, receiver)
```

```
# Output from routing a payment
Payment of 0.01 BTC successfully routed from Sender A to Receiver B
```

Despite its potential, the Lightning Network is not without challenges. Network liquidity, the requirement for active management of payment channels, and the complexity of the technology can hinder widespread adoption. Additionally, off-chain transactions introduce new attack vectors and vulnerabilities that must be carefully managed. Ongoing research and development are dedicated to addressing these issues, improving the robustness and usability of the network.

The Lightning Network represents a significant stride towards enhancing Bitcoin's scalability, offering a practical solution for increasing transaction throughput and reducing fees. As the Lightning Network continues to evolve, it holds the promise of enabling Bitcoin to support a broader range of applications and use cases, thereby advancing its role in the global financial ecosystem.

10.4 Interoperability Between Blockchains

Blockchains inherently operate as isolated systems, which can lead to issues such as fragmentation and lack of synergy between different platforms. The concept of interoperability addresses these challenges by enabling diverse blockchains to communicate, transfer data, and perform transactions with each other seamlessly. This interconnectivity aims to enhance the utility, efficiency, and scalability of blockchain technology.

Interoperability mechanisms can generally be categorized into three primary types:

- Centralized or federated interoperability
- Decentralized or trustless interoperability
- Hybrid models

Centralized or federated interoperability relies on a trusted third party to facilitate communication between blockchains. For instance, an intermediary node or service that has access to multiple blockchains can consolidate and coordinate data transfer. This approach, while effective, introduces a single point of failure and potential security risks associated with the centralization of trust. Therefore, it necessitates the implementation of rigorous security protocols and trust measures.

Decentralized or trustless interoperability models eliminate the need for a centralized intermediary by enabling direct interactions between blockchains through cryptographic protocols and algorithms. Examples include sidechains, atomic swaps, and hash time-locked contracts (HTLCs).

A sidechain is a separate blockchain that is linked to a main chain through a two-way peg. This connection allows assets to be transferred from the main chain to the sidechain and vice versa. A notable implementation of sidechains is the Liquid Network, developed by Blockstream, which facilitates faster and more confidential transactions between Bitcoin and other assets. The primary advantage of sidechains is their ability to offload transactions from the main blockchain, thereby enhancing scalability and reducing congestion.

Atomic swaps enable the direct exchange of cryptocurrencies from two different blockchains without the need for an intermediary. The swaps are executed through HTLCs, which ensure that either both parties complete the transaction within a specified time frame, or the transaction is cancelled, and funds are returned to the respective parties. The process is initiated through a cryptographic hash function that locks the transaction until both parties provide the required cryptographic proofs.

The Interledger Protocol (ILP) is another significant advancement in the realm of interoperable blockchain technologies. ILP is designed to facilitate payments across different ledgers, including blockchains and traditional financial systems. It operates by creating connectors that can process transactions across different ledgers, encapsulating the details of each ledger's protocol. This standardized method of communication helps reduce complexity and friction between divergent financial systems.

Hybrid models, combining elements of both centralized and decentralized approaches, are also being explored. These systems aim to leverage the security and trustless nature of decentralized models while incorporating the practicality and efficiency of centralized systems. Polkadot and Cosmos are key examples of such hybrid frameworks.

Polkadot is an interoperability protocol developed by the Web3 Foundation. It enables multiple blockchains to share information and assets through a system of parachains (parallel blockchains) and a central relay chain. The relay chain maintains the consensus and security of the network, allowing parachains to interoperate while benefiting from a shared security model.

Cosmos, on the other hand, uses the Inter-Blockchain Communication (IBC) protocol to connect independent blockchains. Each blockchain, referred to as a "zone" within the Cosmos ecosystem, communicates with other zones through a central blockchain known as the "hub." This hub-and-spoke model allows seamless asset transfers and data sharing while preserving the autonomy of each individual blockchain.

These technologies are foundational to the development of a more interconnected and efficient blockchain ecosystem, enabling the creation of decentralized applications (dApps) that can interact across different platforms, thereby enhancing their functionality and reach.

The progress in achieving effective interoperability between blockchains holds substantial implications for the future of decentralized finance (DeFi) and cryptocurrency markets. It paves the way for innovative financial products and services that leverage the strengths of multiple blockchains, potentially reducing reliance on any single blockchain and spreading risk. Additionally, it can enhance liquidity and unlock new market opportunities by allowing assets to flow more freely between different blockchain networks.

As the technology matures, regulatory considerations will play a critical role in shaping the direction and adoption of interoperability solutions. Regulators may need to develop frameworks that address the complexities of cross-chain transactions and ensure compliance with existing financial regulations while fostering innovation.

The implementation of robust, secure, and efficient interoperability mechanisms between blockchains is essential for the continued evolution and maturation of the cryptocurrency ecosystem. By enabling diverse blockchains to collaborate and share resources, we can move towards a more unified and versatile decentralized financial system.

10.5 Mainstream Adoption and Use Cases

Mainstream adoption of Bitcoin involves the widespread acceptance and utilization of Bitcoin and other cryptocurrencies by the general public, financial institutions, businesses, and governments. This section explores the current state, potential, and implications of mainstream adoption, as well as various use cases that demonstrate the versatility and impact of Bitcoin in different sectors.

Bitcoin's adoption can be attributed to several critical factors, including its capability to enable peer-to-peer transactions without intermediary oversight, enhanced security through blockchain technology, and the promise of financial inclusivity. Businesses and consumers alike are increasingly recognizing the benefits of using Bitcoin for various purposes beyond speculative investment.

- **Payment Systems and E-commerce:** Bitcoin functions as a medium of exchange and a store of value, leading to its integration into payment systems and e-commerce platforms. Merchants accepting Bitcoin can offer more payment options, thus attracting more customers. The use of Bitcoin as a payment method can reduce transaction fees compared to traditional payment systems like credit cards. Companies like Overstock, Microsoft, and Amazon (via Purse.io) permit customers to make purchases using Bitcoin. Online payment processors like BitPay and Coinbase Commerce further facilitate Bitcoin transactions by converting Bitcoin payments to local currencies in real-time, minimizing the risk of volatility for merchants.
- **Remittances and Cross-Border Transactions:** Traditional remittance services often involve substantial fees and delays. Bitcoin eliminates intermediaries, reducing costs and transfer times. Services like BitPesa and Abra leverage Bitcoin to provide faster, cheaper cross-border payments. These platforms allow users to send money internationally with lower fees than traditional remittance services, benefiting migrant workers and their families.

- **Decentralized Finance (DeFi):** Bitcoin is a foundational element of the DeFi ecosystem, where financial services are provided in a decentralized manner using blockchain technology. DeFi platforms like BlockFi and Celsius Network offer lending and borrowing services with Bitcoin as collateral. These platforms enable users to earn interest on their Bitcoin holdings or obtain loans without traditional financial institutions' involvement. Smart contracts on networks such as Ethereum expand Bitcoin's functionality through tokenized representations like Wrapped Bitcoin (WBTC), which can be used in various DeFi protocols.

- **Investment and Store of Value:** Bitcoin is increasingly viewed as ”digital gold” due to its deflationary nature and limited supply. Institutional investors and asset management firms are adding Bitcoin to their portfolios as a hedge against inflation and economic instability. The inclusion of Bitcoin in exchange-traded funds (ETFs) and mutual funds, as seen with products like Grayscale Bitcoin Trust (GBTC), provides traditional investors with exposure to Bitcoin. The increasing interest from institutional investors signifies broader acceptance and can drive further mainstream adoption.

- **Smart Contracts and Programmable Money:** Bitcoin's scripting language, though limited compared to Ethereum's, enables the creation of simple smart contracts. Projects like RSK (Rootstock) aim to enhance Bitcoin's capabilities by facilitating Ethereum-compatible smart contracts on the Bitcoin network. This interoperability could open new possibilities for programmable money and complex financial instruments on the Bitcoin blockchain.

- **Charitable Donations and Crowdfunding:** Bitcoin presents an innovative way to facilitate charitable donations and crowdfunding. Its transparency and ease of transfer make it an attractive option for non-profit organizations and donors. Platforms like BitGive and The Water Project accept Bitcoin donations, ensuring faster and more secure fund transfers. Crowdfunding campaigns, such as those on Tallycoin, allow projects to raise funds directly in Bitcoin, circumventing traditional financial gatekeepers and expanding the donor base globally.

- **Corporate Treasury and Payroll:** Some companies are incorporating Bitcoin into their corporate treasury strategies or offering employee salaries in Bitcoin. Firms like MicroStrategy, Square, and Tesla have allocated part of their treasuries to Bitcoin, citing its potential for high returns and as a hedge against inflation. Crypto payroll services, including Bitwage and CoinCorner, facilitate employees to receive part or all of their wages in Bitcoin, providing financial flexibility and currency diversification.

```
from bitcoinrpc.authproxy import AuthServiceProxy, JSONRPCException

# Configuration for connecting to the Bitcoin Core RPC
rpc_user = "your_rpc_user"
rpc_password = "your_rpc_password"
rpc_port = 8332
rpc_host = "127.0.0.1"

# Establish connection to Bitcoin Core
rpc_connection = AuthServiceProxy(f"http://{rpc_user}:{rpc_password}@{rpc_host
    }:{rpc_port}")

# Example parameters for sending Bitcoin
recipient_address = "1ExampleAddress1ExampleAddress1ExampleA"
amount_to_send = 0.001 # Amount in BTC

# Send Bitcoin transaction
try:
    txid = rpc_connection.sendtoaddress(recipient_address, amount_to_send)
    print(f"Transaction sent with TXID: {txid}")
except JSONRPCException as e:
    print(f"An error occurred: {e}")
```

- **Gaming and Virtual Goods:** The gaming industry is integrating Bitcoin for purchasing virtual goods, in-game assets, and other digital content. Game developers and platforms like Steam (until 2017) and various online casinos have adopted Bitcoin to facilitate microtransactions and payments. Bitcoin's support for microtransactions allows gamers to buy in-game items or currency more efficiently and securely.

Bitcoin adoption and use cases are continuously evolving, driven by technological advancements, regulatory changes, and market dynamics. Understanding these use cases provides insight into Bitcoin's potential to revolutionize traditional finance and other industries, fostering a more inclusive and efficient financial system.

10.6 Institutional Investment and Market Maturity

The involvement of institutional investors in the cryptocurrency market signifies a pivotal moment in the maturation and acceptance of digital assets. Historically, the cryptocurrency market was dominated by retail investors, but the entry of institutional players has brought significant changes in terms of liquidity, market stability, and credibility.

Institutional investment refers to the investment activities conducted by organizations such as hedge funds, pension funds, insurance companies, mutual funds, and other large financial entities. Their involvement typically introduces substantial capital inflows, rigorous due diligence processes, and advanced trading strategies.

One key factor driving institutional investment in Bitcoin and other cryptocurrencies is the potential for high returns. Cryptocurrencies have exhibited substantial price appreciation over the past decade, making them attractive to institutions seeking higher yields relative to traditional assets. Moreover, the low correlation of Bitcoin with conventional asset classes such as stocks and bonds provides a compelling case for portfolio diversification. This characteristic allows investors to hedge against market volatility and systemic risks present in traditional financial markets.

The maturation of the cryptocurrency market is also evidenced by the development and regulation of infrastructure supporting institutional participation. Below are several critical elements contributing to market maturity:

- **Custody Solutions**

  Institutional investors require secure and compliant custody solutions to safeguard their digital assets. Traditional methods of storing cryptocurrencies, such as private wallets, are often deemed inadequate for large-scale operations due to security and operational risks. Therefore, numerous custodial services have emerged, providing insurance-backed, high-security storage solutions. Examples include Fidelity Digital Assets, Coinbase Custody, and BitGo Trust, which adhere to regulatory standards and offer robust security features.

- **Regulatory Clarity**

Regulatory clarity is paramount in promoting institutional adoption of cryptocurrencies. Uncertainty regarding the legal status and regulatory requirements for trading, holding, and reporting digital assets can deter institutional engagement. Governments and regulatory bodies across the globe are progressively establishing frameworks to address these obstacles. For instance, the U.S. Securities and Exchange Commission (SEC), the Commodity Futures Trading Commission (CFTC), and the Financial Crimes Enforcement Network (FinCEN) have issued guidance and regulations specific to cryptocurrency operations. Clear regulatory guidelines help mitigate compliance risks and foster confidence among institutional investors.

- **Financial Instruments and Derivatives**

  The introduction of sophisticated financial instruments, such as futures, options, and exchange-traded funds (ETFs), allows institutions to gain exposure to cryptocurrencies without the complexities of direct ownership. Products like Bitcoin futures, offered by CME Group and Bakkt, provide a regulated environment for hedging and speculating. Furthermore, ETFs, like the Grayscale Bitcoin Trust and other potential cryptocurrency ETFs, facilitate easier access to the market, adhering to traditional investment structures familiar to institutional investors.

- **Market Transparency and Data Availability**

  Transparent and reliable market data are crucial for institutional investors. The availability of extensive historical data, real-time price feeds, order books, and transaction records supports informed decision-making. Market data providers such as CoinMarketCap, CryptoCompare, and Glassnode offer comprehensive datasets and analytical tools that enable institutions to perform in-depth market analyses and develop quantitative trading strategies.

- **Institutional-Grade Exchanges and Trading Platforms**

  The emergence of institutional-grade exchanges and trading platforms has also facilitated market maturity. These platforms provide high liquidity, advanced trading features, and regulatory compliance, catering to the sophisticated requirements of institutional traders. Examples include platforms like Binance Institutional, Kraken OTC, and Gemini Exchange, which offer deep liquidity pools, high-frequency trading capabilities, and compliance with anti-money laundering (AML) and know your customer (KYC) regulations.

```
import pandas as pd
import numpy as np

# Load historical Bitcoin price data
data = pd.read_csv('bitcoin_price.csv')
prices = data['Close']

# Define the window for the simple moving average (SMA)
window = 50

# Calculate the SMA
sma = prices.rolling(window=window).mean()

# Generate signals based on SMA strategy
data['Signal'] = 0
data['Signal'][window:] = np.where(prices[window:] > sma[window:], 1, 0)
data['Position'] = data['Signal'].shift(1) # Lag by one day

# Calculate daily returns
data['Daily Return'] = prices.pct_change()
data['Strategy Return'] = data['Daily Return'] * data['Position']

# Output the strategy performance
total_return = (data['Strategy Return'] + 1).cumprod()[-1] - 1
print(f'Total Return from SMA Strategy: {total_return:.2f}%')
```

```
Output Example for SMA Strategy
--------------------------------
Total Return from SMA Strategy: 45.67%
```

Overall, the influx of institutional investment has elevated the cryptocurrency market, driving advancements in infrastructure and fostering a more stable, credible environment. The alignment of technological innovation, regulatory frameworks, and sophisticated financial instruments will likely continue to pave the way for greater institutional adoption, contributing to the ongoing evolution and maturity of the cryptocurrency ecosystem.

10.7 Regulatory Developments and Impact

The regulatory landscape surrounding Bitcoin and other cryptocurrencies is rapidly evolving, influenced by various national and international bodies aiming to establish frameworks that ensure security, prevent fraud, and promote financial stability. This section explores the scope and implications of regulatory measures, shedding light on how these regulations might shape the future of cryptocurrency.

Governments and regulatory agencies across the globe have taken diverse approaches to cryptocurrency regulation, ranging from strict bans to open acceptance and integration into the broader financial system. Notably, the principal objectives of these regulations include anti-money laundering (AML), combatting the financing of terrorism (CFT), consumer protection, and maintaining the integrity of financial markets.

Anti-Money Laundering (AML) and Combatting the Financing of Terrorism (CFT)

A major concern for regulators has been the use of cryptocurrencies for illicit activities. To address these issues, regulatory bodies have introduced AML and CFT regulations to ensure that cryptocurrency transactions are monitored and reported. For instance, the Financial Action Task Force (FATF) has issued guidelines requiring cryptocurrency exchanges and wallet providers to comply with standard AML/CFT measures. These guidelines emphasize the need for "Know Your Customer" (KYC) procedures, transaction monitoring, and reporting of suspicious activities.

```
# Sample KYC Compliance Check
import re

def validate_kyc(details):
    # Validate customer details for KYC compliance
    if re.match(r'^[a-zA-Z0-9]+$', details['customer_id']) and \
       re.match(r'^\d{10}$', details['phone_number']) and \
       re.match(r'^[a-zA-Z\s]+$', details['name']):
        return True
    return False

customer_details = {
    'customer_id': 'ABC1234567',
    'phone_number': '0123456789',
    'name': 'John Doe'
}

if validate_kyc(customer_details):
    print("KYC Compliance Verified")
else:
    print("KYC Compliance Failed")
```

The adoption of AML and CFT regulations has significant implications for the cryptocurrency industry. While promoting transparency and reducing the risk of fraud and crime, these regulations also impose operational burdens on crypto enterprises, requiring sophisticated infrastructure for compliance.

Consumer Protection

Regulatory frameworks also focus on safeguarding consumer interests. This encompasses ensuring the security of digital assets, preventing market manipulation, and protecting consumers from fraudulent activities. For example, the European Union's Markets in Crypto-Assets Regulation (MiCA) aims to establish a consistent regulatory framework across member states, providing greater legal certainty and enhancing consumer protection.

The consumer protection regulations enforce requirements for secure custody of crypto assets, transparency in business operations and communications, and mandatory insurance against certain risks. This involves not only technological measures to secure assets but also organizational measures to prevent conflicts of interest and protect consumer funds.

Market Integrity

Ensuring the integrity of cryptocurrency markets is a key regulatory objective. Regulators aim to prevent market manipulation, insider trading, and other practices that could disrupt market stability. The U.S. Securities and Exchange Commission (SEC), for instance, oversees the trading of digital assets considered as securities, enforcing rules and regulations to safeguard against unethical trading practices.

To protect market integrity, regulatory bodies may impose various requirements on trading platforms, including real-time reporting, audit trails, and compliance with standardized trading practices. Crypto exchanges are often required to implement mechanisms for surveillance and control to detect and mitigate market abuses.

International Coordination and Harmonization

Given the borderless and decentralized nature of cryptocurrencies, international coordination is critical. Governments and regulatory agencies are increasingly recognizing the need to harmonize regulations to prevent regulatory arbitrage and ensure coherent policy implementation globally.

Organizations such as the International Organization of Securities Commissions (IOSCO) and the Bank for International Settlements (BIS) have been instrumental in fostering international dialogue and cooperation. Their efforts are complemented by initiatives like the G20's Financial Stability Board (FSB), which works towards developing consistent regulatory approaches and monitoring the potential impacts of cryptocurrencies on global financial stability.

Impact of Regulatory Developments

The aforementioned regulatory developments carry profound impacts on the cryptocurrency ecosystem. While robust regulation can enhance the legitimacy and adoption of cryptocurrencies by mitigating risks and fostering trust, it poses challenges to innovation and operational flexibility within the industry. Compliance costs can be substantial, particularly for smaller entities, potentially stifling innovation and limiting market entry.

On the other hand, clear regulatory frameworks can provide legal certainty and encourage institutional investment in cryptocurrency markets. Institutional investors often require adherence to strict regulatory standards and the presence of a stable, compliant environment. Hence, well-crafted regulations can act as catalysts for market maturation and mainstream adoption.

Moreover, regulatory clarity can stimulate technological advancements as crypto enterprises develop compliance solutions and security protocols. For example, the rise of RegTech, or regulatory technology, showcases how technological innovation can support regulatory compliance, offering automated and scalable solutions for AML, KYC, and reporting requirements.

Regulatory developments play a critical role in shaping the future trajectory of Bitcoin and cryptocurrencies. Balancing regulation and innovation remains a dynamic and ongoing process, with stakeholders across the ecosystem striving to achieve a harmonious integration of digital currencies into the global financial framework.

10.8 Potential Challenges and Threats

Bitcoin and cryptocurrencies contend with numerous challenges and threats as they evolve. These issues encompass technological limitations, regulatory scrutiny, security vulnerabilities, market volatility, and environmental concerns. A comprehensive understanding of these threats is crucial for proponents, investors, and developers who seek to navigate the complex landscape of digital finance.

One significant challenge lies in the technological limitations inherent in the current Bitcoin infrastructure. Bitcoin's blockchain, while groundbreaking, faces issues such as limited transaction throughput and high latency. The average block time of approximately ten minutes combined with the one-megabyte block size limit constrains the number of transactions processed per second (TPS). Compared to traditional payment systems like Visa, which can handle thousands of TPS, Bitcoin's capacity to manage just 3-7 TPS is starkly insufficient for global-scale adoption. Efforts to enhance scalability, such as the implementation of the Lightning Network, aim to mitigate these limitations, but widespread and seamless integration remains an ongoing endeavor.

Regulatory scrutiny presents another formidable challenge. Governments and regulatory bodies worldwide grapple with how to treat and govern cryptocurrencies. The diversity of regulatory approaches—from outright bans in certain jurisdictions to favorable treatment in crypto-friendly regions—creates an inconsistent global regulatory environment. This inconsistency introduces considerable uncertainty for businesses and users operating across borders. Moreover, regulations aimed at preventing money laundering and other illicit activities can impose significant compliance costs and operational burdens on cryptocurrency exchanges and custodians.

Security vulnerabilities within the Bitcoin ecosystem underscore another critical threat. Despite the robustness of Bitcoin's underlying cryptographic protocols, the surrounding infrastructure, including exchanges, wallets, and smart contracts, remain susceptible to breaches and exploits. High-profile hacks, such as the Mt. Gox and Bitfinex incidents, have resulted in significant financial losses and have eroded trust in the ecosystem. The continuous arms race between cyber attackers and security professionals necessitates ongoing advancements in cybersecurity measures and best practices.

Market volatility is a well-documented characteristic of Bitcoin and other cryptocurrencies. Extreme price fluctuations, driven by factors ranging from speculative trading to global economic events, create an unpredictable investment environment. The lack of intrinsic value and the reliance on market sentiment can result in dramatic booms and busts, deterring potential investors and users who seek stability. For example, Bitcoin's price soared to nearly $20,000 in December 2017, only to plummet below $4,000 within a year. Such volatility poses substantial risks for everyday transactions, long-term investment strategies, and the broader financial system.

Environmental concerns, particularly those arising from Bitcoin's proof-of-work (PoW) consensus mechanism, present an increasingly pressing challenge. The energy-intensive nature of PoW mining has drawn criticism for its substantial carbon footprint. With a significant proportion of Bitcoin mining operations powered by non-renewable energy sources, the environmental impact has become a focal point for critics. Efforts to transition to more sustainable and energy-efficient consensus mechanisms, such as proof-of-stake (PoS), are underway in other blockchain platforms, but Bitcoin's adherence to PoW remains an ongoing subject of debate within the community.

Scalability, regulation, security, volatility, and environmental impact constitute a complex and interrelated web of challenges that Bitcoin and other cryptocurrencies must navigate. Addressing these threats requires a multifaceted approach that includes technological innovation, regulatory collaboration, enhanced security protocols, market stabilization mechanisms, and environmental sustainability initiatives. The continued evolution of the cryptocurrency space will undoubtedly hinge on the ability to effectively mitigate these challenges while harnessing the transformative potential of decentralized digital finance.

10.9 Impact on the Global Financial System

The global financial system is a vast network of interconnected institutions and markets facilitating the flow of capital and liquidity across borders. As Bitcoin and other cryptocurrencies gain traction, their impact on traditional financial structures becomes increasingly significant. This section examines various dimensions of such impact, from the potential disruption of existing financial intermediaries to the broader socio-economic implications.

Bitcoin's primary innovation—decentralization—eliminates the need for financial intermediaries such as banks and payment processors. By leveraging blockchain technology, Bitcoin allows peer-to-peer transactions without any centralized oversight. This could reduce the cost of financial transactions and increase access to financial services, particularly in regions with underdeveloped banking infrastructure. For instance, remittances—a critical financial service for many developing countries—can be streamlined with lower fees compared to traditional money transfer services.

```
# Example Bitcoin transaction using a library such as bitcoinlib in Python

from bitcoinlib.wallets import Wallet

wallet = Wallet.create("MyWallet")
address = wallet.get_key().address
output = "Destination Bitcoin Address"
amount = 0.01 # Amount in BTC
txn = wallet.send_to(output, amount)

print(f"Transaction ID: {txn}")
```

The above Python snippet exemplifies how programmatically streamlined Bitcoin transactions can be, minimizing reliance on legacy financial systems.

Another significant aspect is the possibility of Bitcoin acting as a "digital gold." Owing to its finite supply capped at 21 million coins, Bitcoin is often compared to precious metals, providing a hedge against inflation and currency devaluation. Central banks and institutional investors are increasingly considering Bitcoin as a part of their asset allocations. The inclusion of Bitcoin in investment portfolios introduces new dynamics in global financial markets, affecting asset diversification strategies and risk management practices.

```
Output example of a Bitcoin transaction execution:
Transaction ID: tb1q4eyyjkdv4kesyfr8nmsmzp6v9dasxypkuz6y9t
```

Policy implications and regulatory responses are also critical factors shaping Bitcoin's impact on the global financial system. Governments and regulatory bodies around the world are striving to develop frameworks that balance innovation with risk mitigation. These regulations vary widely, ranging from outright bans to the implementation of comprehensive legal structures supporting cryptocurrency operations. The development and enforcement of such regulations will determine the extent to which cryptocurrencies can be integrated into the global financial system.

The volatility intrinsic to Bitcoin presents a unique set of challenges and opportunities. High volatility might impede its use as a stable medium of exchange, yet it attracts speculators and traders looking for significant returns. Over time, as market liquidity deepens and broader adoption occurs, it is conceivable that such volatility may stabilize, thus enhancing Bitcoin's functionality as a transactional currency.

Moreover, Bitcoin's transparency and security features have substantial ramifications. Blockchain's immutable ledger provides a high level of transaction transparency, reducing fraud and enhancing accountability. This could transform aspects of the financial industry, from auditing practices to supply chain verification.

The environmental footprint of Bitcoin mining is another pressing issue with global financial implications. Bitcoin mining consumes substantial computational power and energy, prompting concerns about its sustainability. However, advancements in mining efficiency and a potential shift to renewable energy sources could mitigate some of these adverse effects.

Bitcoin's influence on monetary policy is a topic of ongoing debate. Traditional monetary policy tools—interest rates, reserve requirements, and open market operations—are designed for centralized fiat currencies. The decentralized nature of Bitcoin poses challenges to these conventional mechanisms, potentially limiting the ability of central banks to control money supply and respond to economic crises effectively.

Finally, the role of Bitcoin in fostering financial inclusion cannot be understated. Cryptocurrencies have the potential to offer banking services to the unbanked and underbanked populations, providing access to capital and financial instruments unavailable through traditional means. This democratization of finance could drive significant socio-economic changes, reducing poverty and enhancing economic opportunities globally.

10.10 Predictions and Expert Opinions

The future trajectory of Bitcoin and cryptocurrency is an area of significant speculation and analysis by financial experts, technologists, and institutional investors. Examining these predictions and expert opinions provides insight into possible future developments in the ecosystem, as well as fuel for further academic and practical exploration.

One of the primary predictions revolves around the adoption rate of Bitcoin as a digital store of value. Experts like Caitlin Long, founder of Avanti Financial Group, suggest that Bitcoin's attributes as "digital gold" will solidify over time. This prediction is driven by Bitcoin's finite supply of 21 million coins, its decentralized nature, and increasing public awareness and trust in the technology. Long posits that institutional investors will increasingly view Bitcoin as a hedge against inflation and economic instability, similar to traditional precious metals.

Another interesting prediction comes from economist Saifedean Ammous, who argues in his book "The Bitcoin Standard" that Bitcoin could challenge traditional reserve currencies. According to Ammous, the inherent qualities of Bitcoin, such as its predictable monetary policy and resistance to censorship, make it a viable alternative to fiat currencies, particularly in countries experiencing severe financial instability or hyperinflation.

In addition to Bitcoin-specific forecasts, broader predictions about the cryptocurrency market emphasize the evolution and maturity of decentralized finance (DeFi). DeFi protocols, which leverage blockchain technology to create open and permissionless financial systems, are expected to revolutionize traditional banking and financial services. Charles Hoskinson, the co-founder of Cardano, envisions a future where DeFi platforms provide banking services to the unbanked populations globally, bypassing the need for traditional banking infrastructure. Hoskinson anticipates that increasing smart contract functionality and interoperability between blockchains will facilitate this transformation.

Venture capitalist and Bitcoin advocate Tim Draper has made bold predictions concerning the market capitalization of Bitcoin. Draper famously forecasted that Bitcoin would reach a price of $250,000 by 2023, citing increasing mainstream adoption and a wave of innovation in Bitcoin-related technologies. Draper's optimism is rooted in the belief that Bitcoin's superior technology and advantages over traditional currencies will eventually be recognized on a global scale.

Some opinions reflect cautious optimism, recognizing significant potential growth coupled with necessary developments and improvements in the ecosystem. Alyse Killeen, founder of Stillmark, highlights the importance of Bitcoin's Layer 2 solutions, such as the Lightning Network. Killeen believes that these scalability solutions will be pivotal in making Bitcoin more efficient for everyday transactions, promoting wider adoption.

Additionally, analysts like Meltem Demirors, Chief Strategy Officer at CoinShares, emphasize the importance of diversification within the cryptocurrency market. Demirors argues that while Bitcoin will remain a dominant force, the proliferation of various altcoins and their respective technologies will enrich the ecosystem, creating a more robust and versatile financial landscape. These altcoins, each designed with unique features to address specific use cases, could complement Bitcoin and fill niches that Bitcoin alone cannot address.

On the regulatory front, experts such as Andreas M. Antonopoulos predict that regulatory clarity and acceptance will play a critical role in the mainstream adoption of Bitcoin and other cryptocurrencies. Antonopoulos envisions a future where proactive regulatory frameworks balance the need for consumer protection with the innovative potential of blockchain technology. Clear regulations may reduce uncertainties and promote a safer environment for investors and users, potentially accelerating adoption rates.

Finally, a recurring theme among expert opinions is the impact of technological advancements on the future of Bitcoin and cryptocurrency. Continued innovation in blockchain technology, cryptographic security, and decentralized infrastructures is expected to drive the evolution of the entire cryptocurrency market. Experts anticipate these advancements will address current limitations, such as scalability issues, energy consumption concerns, and transaction speeds, thereby enhancing the attractiveness and functionality of Bitcoin and other digital assets.

10.11 Long-Term Vision for Decentralized Finance

Decentralized Finance (DeFi) represents a paradigm shift from traditional financial systems, leveraging blockchain technology to create an open, trustless, and automated landscape for financial transactions. As we explore the long-term vision for DeFi, several components play crucial roles in shaping its evolution, including technological advancements, regulatory frameworks, user adoption, and economic models.

The DeFi ecosystem envisions a world where financial services are universally accessible without the need for intermediaries. Smart contracts, which are self-executing contracts with the terms directly written into code, form the backbone of this vision. By utilizing blockchain, these contracts eliminate the need for trusted third parties, reducing costs and execution times while enhancing transparency and security.

DeFi's long-term goals are underpinned by several core principles:

- **Accessibility and Inclusivity:** The ultimate vision for DeFi is to provide financial services to unbanked and underbanked populations globally. By leveraging blockchain, DeFi platforms can offer services without the constraints of geographical boundaries or traditional banking infrastructures. This financial inclusion empowers individuals in developing regions, enabling access to loans, insurance, savings, and payment systems.
- **Interoperability and Standardization:** The future of DeFi hinges on the ability of various platforms to interoperate seamlessly. Achieving interoperability requires adherence to standardized protocols and development of cross-chain technologies. Projects like Polkadot, Cosmos, and others are focused on creating ecosystems where distinct blockchains can communicate efficiently, facilitating a more cohesive financial network.
- **Security and Risk Management:** As DeFi grows, so does the

sophistication of threats. The long-term vision includes robust security measures, including formal verification of smart contracts, decentralized insurance mechanisms, and improved audit practices. Enhancing the resilience of DeFi platforms is paramount to gaining user trust and ensuring the stability of the ecosystem.

- **Decentralization and Governance:** A key tenet of DeFi is governance by the community. Various models, such as Decentralized Autonomous Organizations (DAOs), enable stakeholders to participate in decision-making processes. Effective governance mechanisms ensure that the platform evolves in line with the community's best interests, promoting sustainability and accountability.

- **Innovation and Ecosystem Growth:** Continuous innovation drives the DeFi space forward. The development of novel financial instruments, such as decentralized derivatives and synthetic assets, expands the utility of DeFi platforms. Encouraging an ecosystem where developers can create and deploy innovative solutions ensures the competitive edge and broadens the applicability of DeFi.

Consider the technological innovations required to sustain and scale DeFi. Layer 2 solutions, such as Plasma and state channels, enhance scalability by offloading transactions from the main blockchain. The integration of zero-knowledge proofs (ZKPs) further improves privacy and efficiency. For example:

```
from py_ecc import bn128
from zksnark import generate_proof, verify_proof

# Example parameters for zk-SNARK
def generate_keys():
    proving_key, verification_key = bn128.setup()
    return proving_key, verification_key

def prove_transaction(transaction, proving_key):
    proof = generate_proof(proving_key, transaction)
    return proof

def verify_transaction(proof, verification_key):
    return verify_proof(verification_key, proof)

# Usage within a smart contract
transaction = {"from": "Alice", "to": "Bob", "amount": 10}
proving_key, verification_key = generate_keys()
proof = prove_transaction(transaction, proving_key)
is_valid = verify_transaction(proof, verification_key)
```

Advancements like these contribute to the reliability and efficiency of DeFi platforms, enabling them to handle mass adoption while preserving system integrity.

Economic models within DeFi also play a critical role in shaping its trajectory. Decentralized finance must navigate issues like liquidity, inflation, and market stability. Automated Market Makers (AMMs), such as those employed by Uniswap, represent a shift from traditional order book models. These systems rely on liquidity pools and provide continuous market-making services, enhancing market efficiency.

```
class AutomatedMarketMaker:
    def __init__(self, token_reserve, eth_reserve):
        self.token_reserve = token_reserve
        self.eth_reserve = eth_reserve

    def get_price(self, eth_amount):
        token_amount = self.token_reserve * eth_amount / (self.eth_reserve +
              eth_amount)
        return token_amount

    def swap(self, eth_amount):
        token_amount = self.get_price(eth_amount)
        self.token_reserve -= token_amount
        self.eth_reserve += eth_amount
        return token_amount

# Example usage
amm = AutomatedMarketMaker(token_reserve=10000, eth_reserve=100)
price = amm.get_price(eth_amount=1)
tokens_out = amm.swap(eth_amount=1)
```

Such models ensure liquidity and dynamic pricing mechanisms, fostering a more resilient and adaptable financial ecosystem.

Regulatory landscapes will inevitably evolve to accommodate DeFi. Clear, consistent, and fair regulations are pivotal to fostering innovation while protecting consumers. Regulatory frameworks need to strike a balance between oversight and autonomy, ensuring that DeFi remains secure and inclusive without stifling its decentralizing ethos.

Public perception and trust in DeFi will shape its future. Transparent communication, education, and addressing misinformation are essential for user adoption and retention. The success of DeFi rests not only on technological robustness but also on its ability to cultivate a knowledgeable and engaged user base.

As decentralized finance continues to mature, its vision encompasses a robust, secure, and inclusive global financial system. DeFi aims to democratize access to financial services, innovate with new economic models, and build resilient, self-governing communities poised to redefine the fabric of modern finance.